ADVANCE PRAISE

"This book uses the interesting biographical details of well-known successful people to make practical observations about how others can also succeed. Zitelmann's background, being a highly successful entrepreneur himself in addition to having a PhD in sociology, gives him unique credibility, and the result is a very satisfying read."
Dr. Richard Smith, Professor of Psychology, University of Kentucky

"Zitelmann shines the light of inquiry on the success of well-known people. It is not another self-improvement book full of platitudes without any application. On the contrary, Zitelmann's insights are based on extensive research and a firm understanding of the psychology of ultra-successful people. A solid foundation combined with an accessible writing style makes the book a gem for people that have the courage to be different."
Dr. Wolf von Laer, CEO, Students For Liberty

"There are plenty of books that purport to tell you how to succeed. Many of them are full of platitudes. But Rainer Zitelmann approaches the topic methodically, logically and consistently. The result is completely convincing. And he is a man who knows what he is talking about when it comes to commercial success."
Daniel Hannan, Member of the European Parliament,
Journalist and President, The Initiative for Free Trade

"*Dare to Be Different and Grow Rich* is an illuminating book which has brought me to the conclusion that entrepreneurs do not exist to create jobs, but to supply products and services with as little effort and cost as possible. The substance and purpose of a company is to provide a profitable product or service that benefits customers. Zitelmann's book examines how high-profile entrepreneurs have achieved just that in the past, and the methodology and the mindset behind their success."
Theo Müller, Founder, Müller Milch, successful entrepreneur
and multibillionaire businessman

"Rainer Zitelmann is a rare talent – a combination of analytical, scientific, creative and contrarian forces. His voice is an important one and his work tackles some of the most fascinating and misunderstood issues of our time."
Christian May, Editor in Chief, *City A.M.*

Published by
LID Publishing Limited
The Record Hall, Studio 204,
16-16a Baldwins Gardens,
London EC1N 7RJ, UK

info@lidpublishing.com
www.lidpublishing.com

A member of:

Business Publishers Roundtable
www.businesspublishersroundtable.com

© Rainer Zitelmann, 2020
© LID Publishing Limited, 2020

Printed in Latvia by Jelgavas Tipogrāfija
ISBN: 978-1-912555-63-5

Translation: Silke Lührmann and Sebastian Taylor
Cover and page design: Matthew Renaudin

RAINER ZITELMANN

Dare
to Be
Different
and Grow Rich

THE SECRETS OF SELF-MADE PEOPLE

MADRID | MEXICO CITY | LONDON
NEW YORK | BUENOS AIRES
BOGOTA | SHANGHAI | NEW DELHI

CONTENTS

INTRODUCTION

Howard Schultz was born the son of an unskilled laborer in Brooklyn in 1953 and grew up in a deprived neighborhood. This book tells the story of how he went on to turn his company Starbucks into a leading brand with more than 27,000 branches worldwide. He prefaced his 1997 autobiography by advising readers: "Dream more than others think practical. Expect more than others think possible."[1] Larry Page, who created Google, is a strong proponent of what he calls "a healthy disregard for the impossible." He lived by the maxim: "You should try to do things that most people would not."[2] Sam Walton, the founder of Walmart, which was at one time the largest corporation in the world, explained the secret of his success by saying: "I've always held the bar pretty high for myself: I've set extremely high personal goals."[3]

Another legendary entrepreneur and billionaire, Richard Branson, stated pithily: "The lesson I have learned throughout all this is that no goal is beyond our reach and even the impossible can become possible for those with vision and belief in themselves."[4]

That's the topic of this book. I have studied the careers of a number of extraordinarily successful men and women – most of them entrepreneurs, but I have also included top managers, athletes and others who were successful in various areas. By analyzing their life stories, I have found that what distinguishes them above all is their courage to be different from the majority of those around them and to question traditional ways of thinking. They also set their goals and ambitions considerably higher than most people. This book looks at the examples of men and women like Arnold Schwarzenegger and Madonna, Steve Jobs and Bill Gates, Jack Ma and Warren Buffett in order to elicit the crucial secrets of their success. Their stories serve as guidelines which can teach you how to aim far higher and achieve much more than you would ever have thought possible.

Rarely have I met anybody who set his or her goals too high. Most people either live their lives without any real goals at all, or they set their goals far too low. I consider this to be the main reason why they fail to achieve more and fall short of their potential.

Why is it that some people are so much more successful than others? Education or social privilege can hardly account for the difference between winners and losers. Many of the successful personalities featured in this book had difficult childhoods. And among self-made billionaires, the quota of high school or college drop-outs may be even higher than in society at large.

A well-known legend, which for obvious reasons is especially popular with people who have failed in life, has it that success is simply a question of 'luck'. According to this theory, large corporations might as well hold raffles to fill management positions. The lucky winner would be promoted to CEO, while losers would have to work in the mail room.

Of course, there may well be an element of luck involved, though overestimating its significance would be a mistake. Nobody is always lucky or always unlucky. Over the course of several years or even decades, the balance between fortunate and unfortunate incidents tends to even itself out. A majority of those who become millionaires by pure chance lose their fortunes later on. Within the space of just a few years, many major lottery winners are worse off financially than they were before they hit the jackpot. Why? Because they lack the necessary mental resilience to build and retain wealth. On the other hand, there are countless examples of people who lost their entire fortune – which they had worked hard for – and were able to rebuild it after only a few years.

Being successful means achieving far better results than the average contender in a certain area, and it means reaching your goals. This book is about certain attitudes and ways of thinking which all successful people share. In our culture, imitating others and copying what they do is frowned upon, although even children learn mainly by copying those around them. And children usually learn faster and more successfully than adults. In his autobiography, Walmart founder Sam Walton confesses: "Most everything I've done I've copied from somebody else."[5]

In order to aim high in life, avoid taking advice from those who have not achieved any overwhelming success themselves. Make sure to take guidance only from the winners and to study the attitudes and actions which helped them to achieve their goals.

This book is based on a systematic study of the autobiographies and biographies written by and about more than 50 successful men and women, all of whom have shown the willpower and fortitude to achieve successes beyond what others considered possible. It also contains some of my own experiences – not because I would ever consider myself the equal of these great personalities. Rather, as a reader of self-help guides to success, I have frequently asked myself whether the authors of such books have successfully tried and tested their own recipes. In my opinion, those who have achieved success in various areas are in a far better position to give credible advice than others who have never achieved anything of note themselves.

From the outside, successful careers often appear to be an unstoppable progression from one phenomenal success to the next. This view fails to take into account the huge problems and seemingly insurmountable hurdles many successful people have had to overcome. It also ignores the failures and setbacks they have often suffered along the way and which, far from discouraging them, have spurred them on to set their goals even higher. The successful men and women featured in this book have all had the courage to approach and solve problems in unconventional ways and to take unpopular positions in opposition to the majority. What is more, they frequently took great pleasure in distinguishing themselves from their competitors by doing things differently, rather than following the conventions of what was considered the 'proper' way. If you are faced with problems and setbacks yourself, these stories will encourage you in your own endeavor. And they will help you to understand the mental strength which is the secret of their success, allowing them to solve seemingly impossible problems.

This book tells the stories of successful entrepreneurs, investors, athletes and artists. The majority of them have also been able to build huge fortunes. But whether your goal is to get rich or to become a successful musician, athlete or writer is really immaterial. In any case, the road to personal success starts by setting your goals higher than you yourself and those around you would consider 'sensible'. This book is intended to encourage you to aim higher and to start fulfilling your dreams. "If you play without long-term goals, your decisions will become purely reactive and you'll be playing your opponent's game, not your own," Garry Kasparov warns. "As you jump from one thing to the next, you will be pulled off course, caught up in what's right in front of you instead of dealing with what you need to achieve."[6]

If you follow the ground rules laid down in this book and apply the laws of success established on the basis of analysis, you will definitely have success. Did you know that most extremely successful people are insatiable readers? Warren Buffett, the most successful investor in the history of finance, has often been asked for the secret of his success. This is his answer: "Read everything you can."[7] At the legendary meetings of his Omaha-based company, Berkshire Hathaway, he has been dispensing this very advice for many years. Buffett is convinced that it was the reading he did in his formative years that shaped his approach to investing and prepared the groundwork for the next 50 unprecedented successful years.[8] He himself says: "By the age of ten, I'd read every book in the Omaha Public Library with the word finance in the title, some twice."[9] At a book signing, he once casually mentioned having 50 books at home which were waiting to be read.[10]

Buffett's reading was not restricted to books on finance – he also read self-help manuals such as Dale Carnegie's *How to Make Friends and Influence People*, and he developed his own system for implementing the advice he gleaned from that book. Many people have read books like the one written by Carnegie – in fact, you might well be among those readers. But reading alone does not guarantee anybody's success. After studying Carnegie's methods, Buffett decided to perform a statistical analysis in order to test what would happen if he applied them in his own life. "People around him did not know he was performing an experiment on them in the silence of his own head, but he watched how they responded. He kept track of his results. Filled with a rising joy, he saw what the numbers proved: The rules worked."[11]

Buffett's closest business associate, Charlie Munger, with whom he has spent decades building a billion-dollar empire, was nicknamed "book with legs" by his children because he was always reading books about the achievements of other successful personalities.[12] Munger reportedly read a book a day.

This book is about outstanding personalities and the secrets of their success. Exemplary episodes from their lives serve to expose and illustrate those secrets. The episodes frequently deal with difficulties confronting these men and women on their way up, and with the ways in which they mastered them.

The secret of their success will reveal itself to you as soon as – following Buffett's example – you move on from merely studying the rules and patterns inherent in these stories and start applying them to your own life. The right moment to start acting on this advice is – now.

CHAPTER 1

Aiming Higher

In 1966, when Arnold Schwarzenegger was only 19 years old, he had a conversation with Rick Wayne during the Mr. Universe championship in London. The journalist, a bodybuilder himself, later recalled that Schwarzenegger had asked him: "Do you think a man can get whatever he wants?" The question had puzzled Wayne, who replied: "A man's got to know his limitations." Schwarzenegger did not agree with him: "You're wrong." Wayne, who was older and more experienced and had traveled widely, found himself growing increasingly annoyed by the cocky young upstart from Austria: "What do you mean, I am wrong?" To which Schwarzenegger responded: "A man can get anything he wants – provided he's willing to pay the price for it."[13]

This episode is taken from Laurence Leamer's biography *Fantastic: The Life of Arnold Schwarzenegger*. When Leamer's book was published in 2005, Schwarzenegger was governor of California. Before embarking on a political career, he had been a Hollywood star earning $20 million and more for each of his films – one of the best-paid actors in the world. Schwarzenegger, who had moved to the United States at the age of 21, had become a multimillionaire by investing in real estate, and up to now has earned several hundred million dollars.

Schwarzenegger himself attributes his success largely to the determination and commitment with which he pursues his goals. "I set a goal, visualize it very clearly, and create the drive, the hunger, for turning it into reality."[14] He did not say: "Well, it would be nice if I could make this work, maybe I should give it a go." That kind of attitude will not get you anywhere. Most people, he observes, "do it in a conditional way ... Wouldn't it be nice if that happened. That's not enough. You have to make a big emotional commitment into it, that you want it very much, that you love the process and will take all the steps to achieve your goal."[15]

Schwarzenegger, his muscles, his films, or his politics may not be to everybody's liking. But that's beside the point. The point is: how was it possible for the son of a policeman from a small town in Austria, whose childhood was far from easy, to achieve so much in so many different areas – in sports, in business, in show business and in politics?

Let's take a closer look at Schwarzenegger's amazing career. There are lessons to be learned from his rise about the ways in which successful people think and act – above all, these are lessons about the importance of ambitious and unambiguous goals.

Even as a teenager back in Austria, young Arnold had been a fervent believer in the rags-to-riches promise of the American Dream. "My friends wanted to work for the government so they'd get a pension. I was always impressed by stories about greatness and power," says Schwarzenegger.[16] He spent his money on magazines, devouring any feature or article on the United States he could find. Former classmates remember him constantly talking about America. His biographer Marc Hujer writes: "He has always taken his career one step further, from bodybuilder to Hollywood star to politician, there was always a new goal, a new surprise. He was always thinking ahead, he only ever moved backwards in order to take a good run-up for the next leap forward."[17]

Schwarzenegger himself describes his recipe for success as follows: "I set a goal, visualized it very clearly and created the drive, the hunger for turning it into reality. There's a kind of joy in that kind of ambition, in having a vision in front of you. With that kind of joy, discipline isn't that difficult, or negative, or grim. You love doing what you have to do – going to the gym, working hard on the set. Even when pain is part of reaching your goal – and it usually is – you can accept that, too."[18] He even developed a high tolerance for pain, which, he says, is par for the course if you want to succeed.

At the age of 30, he explained his successes by saying: "What I am most happy about is that I can zero in on a vision of where I want to be in the future. I can see it so clearly in front of me, when I daydream, that it's almost a reality. Then I get this easy feeling, and I don't have to be uptight to get there because I already feel like I'm there, that it's just a matter of time."[19]

In his youth, Schwarzenegger had already set himself the goal to become the best bodybuilder in the world. "The first day Arnold trained," his former coach recalls, "he said, 'I will be Mr. Universe.' He trained six, sometimes seven days a week, about three hours a day. Within three or four years he had put on twenty kilos of pure muscle."[20]

Arnold trained like a man obsessed. There were times when his arms hurt so much he could not even comb his hair properly. On weekends, when his training gym was locked, he would force open a window like a burglar to get in. Whenever his friends asked him to play soccer with them after school, he would refuse because running fast would have interfered with the development of his muscles.

His hero was Reg Park, one of the most successful bodybuilders of the time. Some years later, Schwarzenegger would beat him in competition, but as a teenager he looked up to Park, who played Hercules in a number of movies. "If he could do it, so could I. I would become Mr. Universe. I would be a movie star. I would be rich. I had found my passion. I had a goal," Schwarzenegger remembered later.[21]

At the time, bodybuilding was not taken seriously as a sport. There were no large fitness studios in every city in the world. Instead, there were dusty back rooms populated by dubious characters. Schwarzenegger did not care that most people thought bodybuilding was a strange pastime. He was determined to excel in his chosen sport.

His parents disapproved of Arnold's hobby. His mother asked: "Why Arnold, why do you want to do it to yourself?" His father challenged him: "What will you do with all these muscles once you've got them?" Arnold was unfazed by their objections: "I want to be the best-built man in the world. Then I want to go to America and be in the movies." His father thought him simply crazy: "I think we better go to the doctor with his one, he's sick in the head."[22]

When Schwarzenegger traveled to the United States in September 1968 for a bodybuilding competition, he was full of confidence. After all, he had just won his second Mr. Universe title in London. But although Schwarzenegger's muscles were far bigger than those of his opponent Frank Zane and he outweighed him by over 50 pounds, he still lost. Zane's body was better proportioned and his muscles showed more definition. For Schwarzenegger, it was a devastating defeat. Desperately unhappy, he cried all night long. He could not shake the terrible feeling: "I'm far away from home, in this strange city, in America, and I'm a loser."[23]

After that, he did not want to return to Europe. He learned his lesson and came to understand the reasons why he had lost. He began to tackle his weaknesses systematically. Because he saw his calf muscles as his greatest weakness, he started wearing a tracksuit to cover up all his 'good' muscles, cutting the bottoms of his pants off so that only his weak calf muscles were visible to other athletes in his gym. The looks he got from them motivated him to work on those muscles until they could no longer be considered weak.

Schwarzenegger went on to win every major bodybuilding title. A 13-time world champion and seven-time winner of the most prestigious accolade in the world of bodybuilding, the 'Mr. Olympia' competition, which is open only to world champions, he achieved phenomenal success even by his own high standards.

But his ambitions went beyond bodybuilding. He also wanted to grow rich. When he arrived in the United States, he spoke hardly any English. He took lessons and later took a degree in economics, which he hoped would provide him with the necessary skills to make his fortune. Making money became another obsession with him. Even when he had very little money, he started saving in order to invest. He bought up real estate in Santa Monica for redevelopment and invested in office buildings and shopping malls. By the time he turned 30, he had already made his first million. An article published in *California Business* in 1986 said: "Schwarzenegger has acquired a reputation in the last two decades as a razor-sharp entrepreneur and as one of the most prosperous real estate developers in Southern California."[24]

Schwarzenegger still was not satisfied. He stated his intention to become one of the best-paid actors in Hollywood. People laughed at him. They thought he would never get further than playing small parts in action movies that did not require a lot of talking. His first films seemed to prove them right.

"Forget it," Schwarzenegger was told again and again. "You've got a weird-looking body and you've got a weird-sounding accent and you'll never make it."[25] People informed him that he did not stand a chance – after all, no male actor from Europe had ever made it in Hollywood, let alone a musclebound bodybuilder.

Schwarzenegger started taking acting lessons. At first, it was not easy for him. His teacher, who could read him like a book, told him in front of the whole class: "Get up there, Arnold." Schwarzenegger stood slowly. "Okay, it's obvious you're upset. What's the matter?" the teacher asked. "I'm pissed off! It's bullshit! They don't like my name, they don't like my accent, they don't like my body, but fuck them! I'm going to be a superstar!" Later he said: "I know how to become a star. Maybe I don't have the talent to become an actor, but I'll become a star."[26]

Explaining the secret of his success, he comments: "You have to think positive and program yourself to be a winner. I am simply not programmed to think bad thoughts. Successful people have the ability to take a risk and make a tough decision, no matter what everyone around them says."[27]

His first major roles were in action movies like *Conan* and *Terminator*, which did very well at the box office, but which type-cast him as a muscle man. But Schwarzenegger wanted to be taken seriously as a 'real' actor, as well as making millions of dollars – he certainly didn't want to be reduced to playing action heroes.

In 1988, he starred in *Twins*, a comedy which became a surprise success and propelled him to superstardom. The film grossed $112 million in the United States and Canada alone, and another $105 million in the overseas market. Altogether, it earned Schwarzenegger over $20 million. His biographer Marc Hujer comments: "Schwarzenegger gains a lot by distancing himself from his previous, rather one-dimensional parts. Now audiences can see his funny, his likeable side. He has transformed himself from machine to man."[28] To phrase it in political terms, Schwarzenegger now had majority appeal.

Having now achieved everything he had aimed to achieve in the movie industry, Schwarzenegger started looking for a new goal to inspire him. Early on in his career, he had already considered entering politics. As he told the German magazine *Stern* in 1977: "After you've become the best in the movies as well, what else is there that might be interesting? Maybe power. So you turn to politics and become governor or president or something."[29]

But his popularity and success as a bodybuilder and as a Hollywood actor proved to be a burden as much as a benefit. Some people felt provoked by his macho image and women accused him of sexual harassment. When he announced his intention to run for governor of California in August 2003, all the mainstream papers in the United States focused on these stories. He was also alleged to have been a Nazi in his youth. Remarks he had made in his youth were taken out of context and *The New York Times* quoted some comments of his to allege that he was a great admirer of Adolf Hitler. The leftist media joined forces against the Republican candidate – but to no avail. Despite their hostility, Schwarzenegger scored an easy victory, winning 48.6% of the vote while his opponents only got 31.5% and 13.5%.

Schwarzenegger took on an extremely difficult task because California's debt was – and today remains – substantial. Reforms that might have helped to balance the budget were blocked by numerous special interest groups and by the unions. After a few initial successes, Schwarzenegger started losing his fight against those groups. In November 2005, he lost an important referendum. His budget reform was rejected by a huge margin of 38% to 62%, his proposal to reform the tenure system for teachers by 45% to 55%. Political failure seemed imminent and his chances of reelection looked very slim.

Once again, Schwarzenegger proved to be a very fast learner. Ever the pragmatist, he discovered ecology and environmental concerns, topics which won him support even among Democrats. The fact that his wife Maria, whom he married in 1986 and separated from in 2011, is a member of the extended Kennedy clan certainly helped. During his second term in office, Schwarzenegger gained a reputation as an enlightened conservative able to bridge the gap between the two parties, who did more for the environment than any other governor.

But even Schwarzenegger was unable to balance the hugely overextended budget. His friend Warren Buffett commented: "He hasn't got a lot of room to maneuver. In Washington, they can print money, in California they can't. Plus the budget has to be passed with a two-thirds majority. Some of the people he has to deal with are completely against taxes of any kind, some are against new taxes, and some are against cuts of any kind. Obtaining a two-thirds majority is extremely difficult."[30] In January 2011, Schwarzenegger left office after having served the maximum two terms and passed the governorship on to a Democrat successor. Today, Schwarzenegger is a global champion in the war against climate change; he has also played the leading role in six films since he retired from politics.

So what can we learn from Schwarzenegger? In his autobiography, published in 2012, he emphasizes that he would never have prospered the way he did if he had not always put his goals into writing. "I always wrote down my goals, like I'd learned to do in the weight-lifting club back in Graz. It wasn't sufficient just to tell myself something like 'My New Year's resolution is to lose 20 pounds and learn better English and read a little bit more.' No. That was only a start. Now I had to make it very specific so that all those fine intentions were not just floating around. I would take out index cards and write that I was going to:
- get 12 more units in college;
- earn enough money to save 5,000 dollars;
- work out five hours a day;

- gain seven pounds of solid muscle weight; and
- find an apartment building to buy and move into.

It might seem like I was handcuffing myself by setting such specific goals, but it was actually just the opposite: I found it liberating. Knowing exactly where I wanted to end up freed me totally to improvise how to get there."

Schwarzenegger also stressed how important it is to set very big goals for yourself: "People were always talking about how few performers there are at the top of the ladder, but I was always convinced there was room for one more. I felt that, because there was so little room, people got intimidated and felt more comfortable staying on the bottom of the ladder. But, in fact, the more people that think that, the more crowded the bottom of the ladder becomes! Don't go where it's crowded. Go where it's empty. Even though it's harder to get there, that's where you belong and where there's less competition."

He was uncompromising when it came to achieving his goals and he ignored some seemingly sound and lucrative opportunities whenever he felt they did not help him achieve his fixed objectives: "Nothing was going to distract me from my goal. No offer, no relationship, nothing."[31]

How much success you achieve in life largely depends on how high you set your goals. Arnold Schwarzenegger's career bears witness to the truth of this observation. Other examples can be found in the histories of many large international corporations.

In many cases, the founder and creator of a company is not the person that company owes its success and expansion to. More usually, the driving force behind phenomenal business success turns out to be somebody else who thought in larger dimensions than the company founders did.

Chapter 3 tells the story of the Starbucks chain, whose founders were quite happy with the five shops they owned in Seattle. It took the entrepreneurial genius of Howard Schultz to recognize the potential of their business idea and to envisage its expansion on a national scale. Today, he is rightly credited as the creator of Starbucks, while the original founders have long been forgotten.

A similar thing happened with McDonald's. The company was founded by two brothers who achieved a number of groundbreaking innovations in the fast-food industry. Although the restaurant they opened in San Bernardino in 1948 did very well, the honor of being the real founding father of McDonald's has to go to Ray Kroc, who saw the potential of this new type of restaurant long before anybody else did and who was willing to do whatever it took to turn this new idea into a growth industry.

But let's start at the beginning. In 1937, the McDonald brothers opened a tiny drive-in restaurant in eastern Pasadena, followed by a larger one in San Bernardino a few years later. Built in an octagonal shape, their restaurant did such good business that the two brothers soon entered the upper echelon of San Bernardino society. They moved into one of the most spectacular houses in town – a 25-bedroom villa – and took great pride in being the first to own the latest model Cadillac. By 1948, they were rich beyond their wildest dreams.

But there were difficult times ahead for their restaurant as for many other drive-in places. Their customers were mainly teenagers, which meant a lot of breakage and high staff turnover. The brothers were loath to spend so much money on replacing stolen or broken dishes and cutlery. Above all, they were keen on attracting a different kind of clientele – at the time, drive-ins had a bad reputation as favorite spots for teenagers to meet and cause trouble.

They closed their restaurant for three months in order to rethink their concept. What they came up with was the prototype of the McDonald's restaurant as we know it. The kitchens were geared towards mass production and fast service. The brothers embraced any technical innovation which might help to speed up processes in their restaurants. No longer did the quality of the dishes on the menu depend on the expertise of individual chefs. Instead, they pioneered a completely new way of producing a strictly limited selection of items. Just as Henry Ford had revolutionized the automobile industry by dividing the production process into a succession of automated steps, the brothers devised a new approach to food preparation by splitting the process into a number of small routine tasks that required no previous kitchen experience. They developed a whole range of kitchen appliances that were created specifically for their purposes.

In order to serve customers' orders within 30 seconds or less, dishes were prepared and packaged in advance. A new kind of restaurant was born. It boasted self-service, disposable dishes and cutlery, super-fast service and 'assembly-line' food production, and crucially, it attracted a new kind of clientele: instead of teenagers, families with children started frequenting McDonald's.

However, change was gradual and did not happen overnight. At first it looked as though the brothers had miscalculated. They had to wait a full six months until the restaurant's takings were back to what they had been before the restructuring. But the brothers refused to give up – and eventually, their gamble paid off. In 1955, they made $277,000, around 40% up from their annual turnover before the relaunch. By the mid-1950s, with increasing automation, their turnover went up to $300,000, earning them a profit of $100,000, a considerable sum at the time.

News of the restaurant's success spread like wildfire. Owners and would-be-owners of other restaurants came from everywhere in the country to find out the secret of the McDonald brothers' success. Full of pride in what they had achieved, the brothers were only too happy to give visitors a guided tour of their restaurant and to explain in detail their innovative concept. They thought it amusing that their visitors would draw sketches of the restaurant's interior and ask about every detail of the work routine. Of course, their success attracted a fair share of imitators, who copied the McDonald's concept as best they could – in many cases, their best was not very good.

The McDonald brothers started selling a few licenses, and soon there were about a dozen restaurants operating under the McDonald name. But when the powerful Carnation Corporation offered to invest in a national franchise system, the brothers refused. "We are going to be on the road all the time, in motels, looking for locations, finding managers ... I can see just one hell of a headache if we go into that type of chain."[32] John F. Love, author of the impressive 500-page volume *McDonald's: Behind the Arches*, concludes that "their only 'problem' in expanding beyond San Bernardino was that they were content with the way things were. "We couldn't spend all the money we were making," McDonald recalls. "We were taking it easier and having a lot of fun doing what we wanted to do. I had always wanted financial independence, and now I had it."[33] If they started making even larger profits, they reasoned, the next tax return would become one big headache.

Modesty and frugality have their place, but building a business empire requires a different kind of attitude. The honor of having built the McDonald's empire goes to Ray Kroc, who is today regarded as the founder of McDonald's and is still venerated within the company.

Kroc was then working as a salesmen of milkshake mixers with diminishing returns. He started wondering why his best customers, the McDonald brothers, kept buying more milkshake mixers than anybody else. By the way, this is one of the many interesting parallels between the histories of McDonald's and Starbucks. The latter, too, was discovered by a salesman – Howard Schultz, who was wondering why a small retailer in Seattle kept ordering such large quantities of a particular type of coffee maker. He started investigating and thus discovered Starbucks, which he would turn into the leading coffeehouse chain worldwide. We will return to his story later.

Back to Ray Kroc: He went to San Bernardino and, like so many other visitors, was immediately taken by this new kind of fast-food restaurant. He recognized its huge potential for growth much better than the McDonald brothers did. As a salesman for restaurant products, he had traveled far and wide and had developed an excellent instinct for market trends and changes in consumer demands. "Kroc," John F. Love writes, "immediately saw the potential for expanding McDonald's nationwide. Unlike the homebound McDonalds, he had traveled extensively, and he could envision hundreds of large and small markets where a McDonald's could be located. He knew the existing food service businesses and understood how a McDonald's unit could be a formidable competitor."[34]

A few days after his trip to San Bernardino, Kroc picked up the phone to ask Dick McDonald whether he had found a franchising agent yet. "No, Ray, not yet," McDonald answered. "Well then, what about me?" Kroc retorted.[35]

The very next day, Kroc drove back to San Bernardino to negotiate a contract with the two brothers that gave him the exclusive right to franchise the restaurant all over the United States. The contract put Kroc in charge of the chain's expansion, while the brothers retained control over production and were entitled to a percentage of the profits. In the early 1960s, the brothers sold their rights to the McDonald's brand to Kroc for $2.7 million. He had found investors to put up the money.

Kroc devised an ingenious system that allowed franchisees to have a say in important strategic decisions such as planning promotional actions and campaigns in individual restaurants. His system was very different from the usual franchising practices. In order to turn a fast profit, most franchisers either asked for horrendous licensing fees, or forced franchisees to buy expensive appliances and products. Kroc, on the other hand, was in for the long haul and aiming higher. He regarded franchisees as his customers and did everything he could to ensure their success. After all, the success of the McDonald's brand depended on them.

Kroc retained more supervisory control than other franchisers because he realized how easily variations in quality between different outlets could destroy a brand. Franchisees who did not take food hygiene seriously, or who decided to dispense with tried and tested procedures, might do real damage to the brand's image.

A very gifted salesman, Kroc was able to convince more and more people of the virtues of his concept. He won franchisees over by his obvious honesty, by refusing to make impossible promises, as was common practice at the time. Instead, he provided prospective franchisees with relevant and accurate information. "When you sell something like that, anyone can say you are a con man. But if they figure you are honest, then that's something different," Kroc observed.[36]

Today, McDonald's runs more than 36,000 restaurants in over 100 countries. The turnover for 2018 was just over $21 billion. Even Kroc could not have foreseen the huge international success the company would enjoy in decades to come. But the difference between him and the company's original founders, the McDonald brothers, was in the scale of his goals and ambitions. Our actions are determined by the goals we set for ourselves. Ray Kroc's career bears witness to this simple truth, as does the story of the comparatively modest McDonald brothers.

"Simply put, Kroc charmed people into McDonald's," Love comments in *Behind the Arches*, "and the ultimate source of that charm was Kroc's unshakeable belief in the future of the fast-food concept he had discovered on the fringe of the Mojave Desert ... What was motivating Ray Kroc more than anything else was the belief that he had at last found the idea that could be the foundation of the major enterprise he had been hoping to build since ... the late 1930s. This was now 1954, and at age 52 Ray Kroc was still looking for the magic – something that would allow him to capitalize on his three decades of sales experience."[37]

Yes, Kroc had already turned 52 by the time he created the McDonald's franchising system. At an age when others start contemplating retirement, or at least consider themselves too old to start something new, he was willing to work 70 hours or more a week. Most importantly, he enjoyed what he was doing. He was not in it for the quick buck. For a long time, he had to live on his savings and on the money he made selling milkshake mixers. In fact, he did not earn a single dollar from the company until 1961, seven years after signing the contract with the brothers. In Chapter 10, we will return to the story of how Ray Kroc made McDonald's such an exceptional success.

In 1984, 18-year-old Michael Dell set himself a goal that most people would have considered completely 'unrealistic'. Still a student and with a capital of only $1,000, he formed PCs Limited (today, the company is called Dell) and announced his intention to become the U.S. market leader in the IT industry, a position IBM had held for many years since its creation in 1924. In April 2001, Dell Computer did even better than that by taking global leadership in the PC market with a market share of 12.8%, beating their closest rival Compaq by 0.7 of a point, while IBM was only in fourth position with a market share of 6.2%. Michael Dell always stressed the importance of aiming high: "Set your sights high and achieve your dreams and do it with integrity, character, and love. And each day you're moving toward your dreams without compromising who you are, you're winning."[38]

Dell stood out even when he was at school. Like some of his classmates, he collected stamps – but unlike them, he turned it into a business by publishing an auction catalog. He made $2,000 when he was only 12 – peanuts compared with the $18,000 profit he turned a few years later by identifying specific target groups to sell newspaper subscriptions to.

Aged 15, Dell became interested in computers. Having bought his first machine – an Apple 2, a popular model at the time – he proceeded to take it apart completely, explaining to his dismayed parents that he wanted to understand its inner workings. Tinkering with the computer, he figured out how to upgrade and improve it, then helped his friends and neighbors to upgrade their machines.

In 1983, he enrolled at the University of Texas to appease his parents. He did not pay much attention to his studies, though, spending his time upgrading IBM computers instead and selling them on for a higher price. As a freshman, he was already earning between $50,000 and $80,000 a month – far more than his professors.

Next, he started building his own computer, the Turbo PC, as he called it. While other computer manufacturers used retailers to distribute their products, Dell marketed his directly over the phone in order to save on commissions. Doing this, he was able to offer his Turbo PC at 40% less than IBM were charging for their models.

His business took off instantly. Every few months he had to move the company to larger premises and hire more staff to satisfy the huge demand for his products. He was convinced that end customers wishing to buy a computer had nothing to gain from dealing with a retailer. Retailers added to the expense, but lacked the knowledge and expertise to be able to advise customers, who were much better off talking to a competent IT specialist on the phone.

Because some customers were hesitant to buy computers over the phone, Dell offered them the opportunity to return a purchased item within 30 days of delivery if they were not satisfied. He also offered a one-year warranty and launched a 24-hour hotline to answer questions and give trouble-shooting advice.

Dell did not consider his youth and inexperience a drawback – on the contrary, in many ways they proved to be an advantage to him. "I didn't know all kinds of things, but that turned out to be a strength ... Not being bound up by conventional wisdom can be extremely helpful," he affirms.[39] For business matters that he felt unable to handle, he poached experienced executives from other large corporations.

Michael Dell did not only sell directly to end customers. It didn't take him long to discover the benefits of a business-to-business model. Large companies such as Boeing, Arthur Andersen or Dow Chemical appreciated the low prices and good customer service as much as individual consumers did. With an incredible annual growth rate of 250% in the first years, Dell became one of the fastest-growing businesses in American history – beating even world-famous companies like Walmart, Microsoft or General Electric. In June 1988, only four years after forming the company in his dorm room, Dell took it public, accumulating another $30 million, which he then invested in expanding even further. He himself only retained a 35% share.

Quite suddenly, however, Dell was confronted with unexpected trouble. He had just stocked up on 256-kilobyte chips when a chip with a much larger capacity of one megabyte came on the market. His 256-kilobyte chips being as good as worthless, Dell incurred a huge loss. To make matters worse, his latest product range flopped on the market.

In the new laptop market, Dell's products didn't perform very well, either. They turned out to be uncompetitive. Purely by chance, he discovered that Sony's laptop computers came with a new kind of extremely long-lasting battery. Once he had integrated them into his own models, he had a huge advantage over other competitors. Since laptops were mainly used for travel, the longer operating times proved a definite selling point.

Furthermore, Dell soon recognized the opportunities the internet offered for his direct-business model. "If you could order a T-shirt online, you could order anything – including a computer. And the great thing was, you needed a computer to do this! I couldn't imagine a more powerful creation for extending our business."[40]

Adding online sales to phone orders enabled Dell to expand even faster. In 1996, the company sold computers worth a billion dollars to customers in over 170 countries. A year later, Dell's own share of the company, now a mere 16%, was worth over $4.3 billion, making him one of the richest men in the United States.

Even Dell was not immune to crises. In 1996, fires caused by faulty laptop batteries forced the company to issue a large-scale call-back. The company's image suffered considerable damage. In 2006, Dell was put under investigation by the financial watchdog authority SEC on suspicion of fraud. Michael Dell, who had already stepped down as CEO to join the supervisory board, returned to the helm in 2007 to steer his company safely through these troubled waters. Then, in 2013, Michael Dell joined forces with the private equity firm Silver Lake Partners to buy Dell for $25 billion.

Today, Dell is the third-largest computer manufacturer in the world, and with a personal fortune of $37.6 billion, Michael Dell is among the planet's 20 richest people. One of the crucial lessons his successes have taught him is to ignore the negative comments of others. "Believe in what you're doing. If you've got an idea that's really powerful, you've just got to ignore the people who tell you it won't work," he emphasizes.[41] Who would have taken seriously the ambitions of an 18-year-old would-be entrepreneur to beat the IT giant IBM at their own game? Over and over, the people around him would tell him to aim for something more realistic. He upset his parents by dropping out of college, instead of following in his father's footsteps and studying medicine. They wanted their son to be sensible and apply himself to his studies rather than tinkering with computers. When he first came up with the idea of selling directly to consumers, this plan too was met with skepticism. Would people really be willing to buy expensive machines over the phone?

Like Arnold Schwarzenegger and Ray Kroc, Dell set himself higher and more challenging goals than other people. His success finally proved him right.

If he had set himself less ambitious goals, he probably would not have been as successful.

How about yourself? Have you spent your whole life aiming for what appears to be 'possible', 'attainable' or 'realistic'? Have you allowed others to persuade you to 'keep your feet on the ground', preferring the bird in the hand over the two in the bush? Have you always been told that "dreams are but shadows"? If so, now is the time to change your outlook on life: Dare to dream big and to aim high, as Schwarzenegger, Kroc and Dell did. This book will show you how to make those dreams come true – but the first step is up to you. You have to allow yourself the courage to dream, to set yourself goals instead of limits. Don't listen to the advice of those who want you to aim for what they consider 'realistic', and who laugh at your 'unreasonable' and 'impossible' goals. But remember: in order to achieve your goals, you have to win the support of others. You will not succeed on your own. And to win the support of others, first of all you have to win something else – their trust.

CHAPTER 2

How to Win Trust

For proof of the crucial role trust plays in achieving ambitious goals, look no further than the amazing life story of the richest man in history, John D. Rockefeller. For the young Rockefeller, realizing that "old men had confidence in me right away,"[42] soon after he had started his very first business, was a key to future success. Throughout his phenomenal career in business, he said his biggest problem was always "to obtain enough capital to do all the business I wanted to do and could do, given the necessary amount of money."[43] His ability to win the trust of banks and other investors was among his most valuable assets. "It is chiefly to my confidence in men and my ability to inspire their confidence in me that I owe my success in life," Rockefeller acknowledges.[44]

Rockefeller's biographer stresses: "In his business career, John D. Rockefeller was accused of many sins, but he took pride in paying his debts promptly and abiding strictly by contracts."[45] By treating each and every contract – whether sealed by gentlemen's agreement or in writing – as a sacred pact, you will win the trust of others. If, on the other hand, you like to reinterpret the spirit and the letter of contracts you have entered into, you will become known as an untrustworthy business partner and lose your most important capital – the trust of others.

So, how do you win the trust of others? By acting, and – even more crucially – by thinking in a way that inspires trust. Never underestimate the importance of your thinking and of the value system behind it. Other people can usually sense whether you are being sincere with them, or not.

Of course, business history has had its share of ingenious liars and fraudsters, geniuses at concealing their real intentions and winning trust they don't deserve. Bernard Madoff, who over many years managed to steal $65 billion from wealthy investors, corporations and foundations by lying and cheating, is a prime example.

Fortunately, Madoff's gift for dissembling is the exception rather than the rule. There will always be people who succeed in winning the trust of others at least for a time, even though they do not deserve it. But they are in a minority, while for the vast majority the simple truth is: the more trustworthy you are as a person and in your inner attitude to others, the more those others will trust you. Most people have good 'antennas' for sensing whether somebody is being sincere or not. We all emit a variety of different signals – most of them non-verbal – for our fellow human beings to read and interpret. Subconsciously, in business as in our personal lives, we are constantly assessing others and asking ourselves: how far can I trust this person?

Before sealing an important deal, businessmen frequently spend hours and hours talking about subjects that have nothing to do with the matter at hand, including details about their private lives. These conversations are a way of figuring out how far they can trust each other. There is no trust without honesty, and a person's honesty is not usually obvious until it is put to the test. You prove your honesty and win trust by telling the truth when it is hard or inconvenient to do so: by volunteering information that might prove damaging to yourself or your company at the earliest stage possible. Stephen M.R. Covey tells of an impressive display of exactly this kind of honesty: At the Masters tennis tournament in Rome in 2005, after Fernando Verdasco's second serve in a match against Andy Roddick, the line judge called the ball "out." The audience was already applauding Roddick's victory when he pointed to an impression in the sand which proved that Verdasco's serve had landed on the line rather than beyond it. Many in the audience were surprised to see that Roddick voluntarily revealed information which led to his opponent winning the match.[46] But by doing so, he showed himself to be the kind of man who will always win the trust of others, simply by thinking and acting in a way which inspires trust.

In the Formula One final at Jerez in 1997, definitely the lowest point in an otherwise extraordinary and fascinating career, Michael Schumacher did just the opposite. He rammed the Canadian Jacques Villeneuve, a maneuver which was to cost him the Formula One title as well as a lot of support worldwide. It took several days until Schumacher gave in to pressure from Ferrari and admitted that he had done something wrong. "Up to then, he seriously tried to blame the incident on his opponent, making many insiders wonder whether

Schumacher's Formula One victory in 1994 after crashing into Damon Hill had been the result of another intentional unfair attack."[47]

Schumacher lost the fans' trust, not so much because of his unfair conduct on the racetrack, but because he tried to cover it up instead of admitting to it. Even his most loyal German fans withdrew their trust and support, and in the winter of 1997, Schumacher merchandise could not be shifted. The decision to strip him of his silver title and of all points he had won during the season was "only the icing on the cake."[48]

The contrast between the two men's conduct – Roddick, who voluntarily disclosed information that lost him the match, and Schumacher, who denied his own wrongdoing and tried to put the blame on his opponent – and the public's reaction to it shows how trust is won through honesty and lost through dishonesty. Let me say it again: you will win the trust of others by volunteering information that may prove damaging to yourself or your company as early as possible.

David Ogilvy, one of the most successful advertising experts of all times, confirms this simple truth: "I always tell prospective clients about the chinks in our armor. I have noticed that when an antiques dealer draws my attention to flaws in a piece of furniture, he wins my confidence."[49]

Frank Bettger, once the most successful insurance salesman in the United States, tells the story of a colleague who taught him a lot about the business. Karl Collings, Bettger said, had a rare gift for winning other people's trust. "As soon as he began to talk, you felt: 'Here is a man I can trust; he knows his business, and he's dependable.'"[50]

The following incident made Bettger understand why: the two men had gone together to see a client who wanted to sign a life insurance policy. Bettger was happy about the size of the commission he was about to receive. A few days later, however, he was informed by the insurance company that a medical check-up had revealed a pre-existing condition and the client's policy would only be approved subject to restrictions.

"Must we tell the man it isn't standard?" Bettger asked his mentor. "He won't know it unless you tell him, will he?" Collings simply replied: "No, but I'll know it. And you'll know it."

He then told the client: "I could tell you this policy is standard and you probably would never know the difference, but it's not ... I believe this contract gives you the protection you need and I would like you to give it very serious consideration."[51] Without hesitating for a moment, the client signed the policy. Bettger was ashamed of himself for even considering concealing important information from the client. He would never forget Collings' simple words: "No, but I'll know it." They had taught him that to win the trust of others, he had to tell the unadorned truth about his product – however inconvenient that truth might be. Are these rules hard to stick to? They are if you lack basic values and principles; if, whenever you are confronted with the question of whether to tell the whole truth or only a part of it, the answer is not immediately obvious to you. If, on the other hand, you do have a clearly defined set of principles to live by, it isn't hard at all. Even better, you will quickly win the trust of others. The truth is the cleverest trick!

I was extremely impressed by the leading executive of a foreign real estate company, whose introduction to large German banks and distribution agencies I was facilitating. The banks were unfamiliar with his company and the aim of these talks was to create mutual trust. Although the company had been performing very well and the numbers looked impressive, there were a few issues which were likely to raise concerns. The foreign executive impressed me by drawing attention to those issues in the very first talk and without prompting. The other party's representatives were equally impressed and I sensed that his honesty made them trust him very quickly. Quite obviously, this was somebody who was not trying to dazzle them with hype and half-truths, as happens far too often.

For 15 years, I ran a consultancy that advised other businesses on communication and media relations. When it comes to unpleasant truths, many companies we dealt with were inclined to make molehills out of mountains, or to resort to euphemisms. I remember a heated discussion I had about a press release with a managing director who was determined to downplay or conceal certain aspects that might reflect negatively on his company. "If the journalists discover that you haven't told them the truth, they won't take kindly to it. You are bound to lose their trust." His reply was: "It's not like we're lying. We are simply omitting this one issue, which isn't all that crucial after all." I objected: "Whether it's crucial or not is a question you should leave to the journalist to decide. You know very well that he would probably come to a different conclusion if this additional bit of information had been made available to him.

What is he going to say later when he finds out? What are you planning to tell him when he asks you why you kept this from him?"

I once saw a company lose the media's trust completely. It started with a few fairly minor and insignificant lies the owner told to a single journalist, who took offense and started digging deeper. He found many more details that did not seem to add up. Like a dog with a bone, he would not let go – instead, he went on to write a whole series of damaging articles. He told fellow journalists working for other media that he had been lied to by the company's owner. The news spread quickly. Soon other media started targeting that company and eventually the negative coverage destroyed the company's reputation and operational basis. Apparently, the journalist had abided by Albert Einstein's dictum: "Whoever is careless with the truth in small matters cannot be trusted with important matters."[52]

Journalists are not the only people to feel deceived by others who harp on about the positive aspects (however slight and insignificant they may be) while trying to conceal anything negative, in the hope that they will never be found out. Of course, you may be lucky – just as you might be lucky if you were trying to cross the road blindfolded. But you'd be better off acting on the assumption that sooner or later you will always be found out. And you'd be better off asking yourself what that will do to your image.

Trust is most commonly linked to concepts such as honesty, integrity, truthfulness or sincerity. But in his remarkable book on *The Speed of Trust*, Stephen M.R. Covey points out that trust is not just a question of character, but rather a function of two vital factors, character and competence. If you believe that somebody is honest and sincere without being competent, you are unlikely to trust him or her. Covey uses a nice image to illustrate his assertion: "My wife, Jeri, recently had to have some surgery. We have a great relationship – she trusts me and I trust her. But when it came time to perform the surgery, she didn't ask me to do it."[53] His wife did trust him – but she knew better than to entrust her health to him.

In order to win the trust of others, it's not enough to convince them of your honesty and sincerity. That's what mathematicians would call a necessary, but not a sufficient, condition. In addition, you have to inspire trust in your ability to achieve the results others expect of you.

So, how do you go about winning this kind of trust? You need facts and you need references. That may sound banal, but it's a simple truth that companies all too often ignore at their peril. Instead of quoting facts and references as evidence of past achievements and potential for future performance, they get their marketing department to generate fluff pieces and speech bubbles. Companies use advertising brochures and websites to sing their own praises, protesting rather than proving the exceptional quality of their products and services, the excellence of their customer service, their competence, etc.

What would you think of a prospective candidate for a position in your company who is full of praise for his or her own performance and achievements, without producing any references or facts to support their application? Would you believe somebody who grandiloquently promises "highest standards," "impressive results" and "excellent customer service"? Personally, I would not hire that person. I rely on my intuition and my 'gut instinct' as far as judging somebody else's integrity and honesty is concerned. But when it comes to judging their competence, I rely on facts and references. So do most other people.

Covey has shown that far from being a 'soft' skill, as many people assume, trustworthiness is definitely a 'hard' factor in business life. If your clients and business partners lack complete trust in you, you will be charged a 'confidence tax.' If they do trust you, on the other hand, you will benefit from a 'confidence dividend.' In my work as the owner of a public relations agency, I often saw this principle in action: companies willing to disclose potentially damaging information voluntarily and completely at an early stage create 'credibility accounts,' as a journalist of my acquaintance succinctly put it. "Every time a company voluntarily shares information on negative aspects," he explained, "they are making a deposit in their credibility account." You should remember this term and remember to make regular sizeable deposits in your own credibility account.

There is something else you need to do to build trust – actively create networks. It is human nature to trust somebody we have been introduced to by a mutual acquaintance who has already won our trust far more than we would ever trust a stranger. Think about it: imagine being contacted by a complete stranger who would like to meet you – wouldn't you be far more likely to meet with somebody who has been recommended to you by a mutual friend? The trust you have in your friend means that you are willing to extend a certain amount of trust to their friend or acquaintance.

By all means, don't be afraid to approach strangers with whom you have never had any contact or mutual acquaintances. But building connections is a lot quicker and easier if you can get a mutual friend or acquaintance to 'introduce' or to recommend you. That way, some of the trust which exists between your friend and his or her friend will be transferred to you before you have even spoken to that other person. That's why building networks is of vital importance in the business world. Networks multiply trust.

Most people know how important connections are for achieving success. Asked what they thought was the most important factor in growing rich, the vast majority (82%) out of a total of 5,000 respondents in a representative poll said: "Knowing the right people, having connections."[54] But what most people don't realize is that "knowing the right people" isn't something we are born into. You can, and you have to, work at building connections.

In order to achieve high goals, you have to build and maintain networks and connections. You have to act and to think in such a way as to inspire trust in others. Set some time aside each week and each month to examine your own life. Ask yourself: what have I done to build new connections and to expand my existing network? Also: have I acted in such a way as to earn the trust of others? If the answer to both questions is yes, you are off to a good start towards achieving your goals.

Along the way, there will be huge obstacles to overcome. The more you succeed, the larger the problems you will be confronted with. But that's a good thing. Practice makes perfect: only by practicing on problems will you be able to develop the strength you will need to achieve whatever goals you have set yourself.

CHAPTER 3

Learn to Embrace Problems

To the superficial observer, the life stories of successful men and women will often appear as a steady succession of triumphs. However, this perspective often ignores the huge problems all high achievers have had to contend with – problems which at first sight seemed insurmountable and which might easily have caused a lesser personality to stumble and fail.

In fact, a lot of successful people owe their success to the problems they experienced along the way. Take the oil tycoon John D. Rockefeller, whose various enterprises made him the richest man in history. In today's currency, his fortune is estimated at between $200 billion and $300 billion, larger by far than those of contemporary billionaires such as Jeff Bezos or Bill Gates. Rockefeller grew rich by ingeniously exploiting the massive difficulties confronting the oil industry in its early years.

After working in the food trade, Rockefeller entered the energy sector as a kind of sideline. At 24, he formed an oil company to make some extra money. At the time, nobody could have guessed just how important oil was to become. Nobody knew how long the boom would last – would it prove to be as short-lived a trend as the gold rush had been? Or would the oil industry be able to establish itself as a profitable business? Oil prices were subject to extreme fluctuations. In 1861, a barrel was worth anything between 10 cents and $10. Three years later in 1864, prices still fluctuated between $4 and $12. Every time a new oil well was discovered, prices hit rock bottom – until fears that oil might soon become scarce would cause them to rise sky-high again.

Speculators saw the new industry as an opportunity to get rich quickly and effortlessly. Refineries sprung up everywhere, and by 1870, they already had the capacity to process three times as much oil as was being extracted from the earth at the time. Three-quarters of all refineries were running at a loss –

one of Rockefeller's main competitors offered him shares in his company at a tenth of their book value.

In the midst of this crisis, Rockefeller himself stood to lose his entire fortune. "As someone who tended toward optimism, 'seeing opportunities in every disaster,' he studied the situation exhaustively instead of bemoaning his bad luck. He saw that his individual success as a refiner was now menaced by industrywide failure and that it therefore demanded a systemic solution," Rockefeller's biographer writes.[55]

Rockefeller formed Standard Oil Company as a joint-stock firm, setting himself a huge goal: "The Standard Oil Company will someday refine all the oil and make all the barrels."[56] His aim was to gain control over the entire oil industry. He put seed capital of $1 million into his new company, at the time an unprecedented amount of money, which he soon raised to $3.5 million. He recruited exceptionally gifted managers and started expanding aggressively – in a time of severe economic crisis. "It was a sign of Rockefeller's exceptional self-confidence that he gathered strong executives and investors at this abysmal time, as if the depressed atmosphere only strengthened his resolve."[57]

That's the crucial difference between winners and losers: losers allow the general mood to affect them. When others around them are depressed, they become depressed, too. Winners have a different perspective on reality. They see opportunities where everybody else sees problems and they are able to focus exclusively on exploiting those opportunities. They know that an economically unstable situation is the perfect time to go shopping: to buy up other companies, shares or even human talent.

In the midst of the crisis, Rockefeller was able to negotiate favorable contracts with the railroad companies, which granted him discounts for transporting his company's oil, giving him an important advantage over his competitors. However, rumors of these deals were met with massive protests and boycotts against his company, which forced him to let go of 90% of his work force temporarily. Speculation about a secret pact between Rockefeller and the railroad companies increased the general feeling of fear and uncertainty, which in turn allowed Rockefeller to take over 22 of his 26 competitors in Cleveland in the space of a few weeks. In early March 1872, he took over six rival companies within two days. Since most other refineries were operating at a loss, he bought them up at bargain prices, frequently paying no more than scrap value for the companies' assets.

In 1873, the U.S. economy was in severe crisis. Several banks and railroad companies went bankrupt, and the stock market was forced to close down temporarily. This was only the beginning of a recession which would last six years. Who needed oil in a situation like that? The oil price fell to 48 cents – even water cost more than that in some places. Once again, Rockefeller saw the crisis as an opportunity. He continued to buy up rival companies at even lower prices, and raised capital for future takeovers by cutting dividends. He had not even hit 40 yet and already controlled the entire refinery industry. Even the railroad companies were dependent on him, because he had started investing in the construction of tank cars and would soon own the entire fleet.

But there was more trouble ahead. The Pennsylvanian oil fields had been almost exhausted and nobody knew whether more oil would ever be found anywhere else. At the same time, the largest oil reserves to date were discovered near Baku on the Caspian Sea. Yielding 280 barrels each a day, the Baku oil wells were many times more productive than the ones in America, which only yielded four to five barrels. The American share of the global refinery market – which effectively meant Standard Oil's share, since the company controlled 90% of the U.S. market – fell dramatically.

Rockefeller responded by drastically cutting expenses and by investing large sums of money into research. When new oil wells were discovered in Lima, Ohio, which proved to be too high in sulphur, Standard Oil developed a process to extract the sulphur, thus making the Lima wells exploitable. In the early 1890s, Rockefeller's company controlled two-thirds of the global oil market.

But Rockefeller's problems had only just begun. Soon he was confronted with accusations and lawsuits charging him with violating antitrust regulations and attempting to build a monopoly, just as Microsoft would be a hundred years later. On May 5, 1911, after two decades of legal wrangling, the Supreme Court ordered the divestiture of Rockefeller's Standard Oil Company. The business was given six months to sell its subsidiaries. Even in the midst of this crisis, which destroyed the company he had spent 41 years building, Rockefeller did not panic. The news of the Supreme Court's decision was brought to him while he was playing golf with a Catholic priest. "Father Lennon, have you some money?" Rockefeller asked him. The priest shook his head and inquired why Rockefeller had asked. "Buy Standard Oil," the 72-year-old entrepreneur advised him.[58]

"Precisely because he lost the antitrust suit, Rockefeller was converted from a mere millionaire, with an estimated net worth of $300 million in 1911, into something just short of history's first billionaire. In December 1911, he was finally able to jettison the presidency of Standard Oil, but he continued to hold on to his immense shareholdings. As the owner of about one-quarter of the shares of the old trust, Rockefeller now got a one-quarter share of the new Standard Oil of New Jersey, plus one-quarter of the 33 independent subsidiary companies created by that decision."[59]

Rockefeller's life shows in exemplary fashion how successful people thrive on problems. Every problem constitutes a challenge, and by solving it, they grow even stronger. Problems are tests you have to pass in order to move to the next, higher level. If you are confronted with a real problem, embrace it as John D. Rockefeller did and look for the opportunity that comes with it!

Swedish-born Ingvar Feodor Kamprad mastered that art early on. A farmer's son of German descent, he was only 17 years old when he founded IKEA in 1943. When he died in 2018 at the age of 91, his personal assets (including a charitable foundation) were estimated at €45 billion, making him one of the richest people in the world.

Kamprad had always been fixated on making money. Even as a child, he didn't go fishing for pleasure, but in the hope of catching something he could sell. "Selling became a kind of obsession," he would later remember. As an 11-year-old, he bought seeds by mail order and sold them on to small farmers in his neighborhood. "That was my first genuine business which I really earned money with." With the profits he made, young Ingvar bought a bicycle and a typewriter. "Both purchases," Rüdiger Jungbluth writes in his study on *Die 11 Geheimnisse des IKEA-Erfolges (The 11 Secrets of IKEA's Success)*, "were in fact investments, which would allow the youth to expand his business activities."[60]

Kamprad was severely dyslexic, which another man might have used as a convenient excuse for his lack of success. Instead, Kamprad focused on his strengths: business and commerce. At boarding school, he would trade anything and everything. He kept a big box full of belts, wallets, watches and pens under his bed. His business was doing so well that, fresh out of school, he decided to start his own company. He called it IKEA – the capital letters stand for his initials I.K., and the first letters of Elmtaryd, which was the name of his parents' farm, and Agunnaryd, the village in the municipality of Ljungby where he grew up.

Like many other successful men before and after him, fellow entrepreneurs Richard Branson and Michael Dell among them, Kamprad based his business on the principle of undercutting the competition with high-quality products. It did not take him long to discover that quality furniture could be manufactured and distributed at far lower prices than other companies were charging. His competitors did not take kindly to the young upstart. One of them, Dux, took him to court several times, accusing him of plagiarism. However, the charges did not stick. The national association of furniture makers wrote to IKEA's suppliers, threatening them with boycotts by established companies if they continued to do business with IKEA. Kamprad was able to circumvent the boycott by founding numerous subsidiaries under different names. But he created more trouble for himself by selling directly to end customers at trade fairs. Sometimes organizers would even ban his company.

IKEA's products were so popular that the company soon had trouble meeting customer demand. The problem was aggravated by the fact that many manufacturers refused to sell to IKEA for fear of offending established furniture dealers. Kamprad's reaction was unexpected. He wrote a letter to a Polish government minister, introducing his company and stating his interest in collaborating with Polish furniture sellers. He received an invitation to Poland, where negotiations got off to a bad start when he was refused permission to travel outside of Warsaw in order to inspect factories. Kamprad came close to leaving, but finally the Poles gave in.

In the long run, being boycotted by the Swedish furniture industry proved a stroke of luck for Kamprad. It taught him that every problem is an opportunity waiting to be exploited. After some initial hiccups, his collaboration with the Polish furniture makers proved to be a huge success. There was a time when half the products on offer in the IKEA catalog were made in the Socialist People's Republic of Poland. "It was a crisis which became an impetus because we were always forced to find new solutions," Kamprad says. "Who knows whether we would have been as successful if they had fought fair and square?"[61] The attitude to hardships and problems which this statement bears witness to is an attitude that all successful personalities share. Kamprad's first conclusion was: every problem is an opportunity. Secondly, he concluded: "There's never any point in negative actions." In the business world, wasting your energy on trying to put obstacles in the way of your competitors, rather than fighting them by offering constructive and convincing alternatives, will not get you anywhere.[62]

His competitors did not share his outlook, but did whatever they could to make life as difficult as possible for Kamprad. After a well-known magazine had published a test report proving that IKEA's more cost-efficient products were equal in quality to those of their competitors, the furniture industry retaliated with an advertising boycott. However, the magazine's editor refused to budge. In a counterattack, he read out the furniture association's newsletter calling for a boycott on public television. In the long run, the story worked in IKEA's favor because people started rooting for Kamprad as a David figure taking on the Goliath of the furniture industry.

The furniture makers were not Kamprad's only adversaries. At the time, Sweden was governed by a peculiar version of socialism, which in its attempt to suppress market forces almost crushed entrepreneurs like him. Those in the highest tax bracket had to pay a whopping 85% of their earnings to the state. Add to that the capital gains tax levied on his private fortune, and the government's demands almost suffocated him. To pay off the debt he owed to IKEA as a private citizen, he attempted to sell one of the smaller companies he owned to IKEA. At the time, this was a fairly common procedure which many entrepreneurs resorted to in order to reduce the capital gains tax burden. But when Kamprad was about to go ahead with the transaction, the government retrospectively changed tax laws to prevent him from doing so. He had no choice but to pay the taxes, but his resentment about the way successful entrepreneurs were treated in his country grew.

His government's short-sighted economic policies would eventually drive him out of the country. In 1974, Kamprad moved to Denmark and from there to Switzerland. It was only in 2013 that finally he returned to Sweden, to his birthplace of Älmhut, where he lived until his death in 2018.

Looking at IKEA's phenomenal success from the outside, people tend to forget how many setbacks and problems Kamprad had to overcome to get there. At one point, he decided to invest some of his profits in another sector and bought into a company that produced televisions. But the business never managed to break even, and finally Kamprad cut his losses. His adventure in another industry cost him dearly – he had invested over a quarter of the IKEA capital, which he was unable to recuperate.

According to Kamprad's philosophy, there was nothing wrong with making mistakes. "Making mistakes is the privilege of those who are willing to act," he would preach to his staff. "The fear of making mistakes is the cradle of bureaucracy and the enemy of any evolution. Nobody can ever claim to have decided on the only right solution. It's the willingness to act on a decision which makes it the right one."[63] That's why Kamprad insists that people must be allowed to make mistakes.

What first looks like a severe setback can often prove to be the seed of huge successes later on. Take the career of Michael Bloomberg, founder of the financial software, media and data company Bloomberg L.P. and the eponymous television station. With an estimated fortune of $53.4 billion in 2019, Bloomberg is one of the richest men in the world. Between 2001 and 2013, he was also mayor of New York City.

But it all started rather inauspiciously: he was fired from his job. When the commodity trading firm Philco Corporation acquired the Wall Street investment bank Salomon Brothers in 1981, he was told his services were no longer needed in the company. "One summer morning," he recalls in his autobiography, "John Gutfreund, managing partner of Wall Street's hottest firm, and Henry Kaufman, then the world's most influential economist, told me my life at Salomon Brothers was finished." Gutfreund told him: "Time for you to leave." For Bloomberg, this came as a complete shock. He remembers: "On Saturday, August 1, 1981, I was terminated from the only full-time job I'd ever known and from the high-pressure life I loved. This, after 15 years of 12-hour days and six-day weeks. Out!"[64] But if he hadn't been sacked that day, who knows what would have become of Bloomberg ...

Ten years on, Salomon was at the brink of the abyss. Warren Buffett owned a major share in the firm. In late 1986, when the company had been under threat of a takeover by the dreaded Ron Perlemann, Buffett had come to the rescue of his friend John Gutfreund. Not knowing what else to do, Gutfreund had called Buffett and begged him to invest in Salomon Brothers to save the company.

Never one to miss the opportunity inherent in every crisis, Buffett agreed under the condition that he and his company Berkshire were to invest $700 million for a guaranteed 15% profit. As part of the deal, Buffett and his partner Charlie Munger both joined the board of directors. It was a deal which would almost prove Buffett's downfall, plunging him into one of the worst crises of his life.

Like most dramatic events, this severe crisis seemed fairly harmless at first. In the afternoon of August 8, 1991 Buffett drove to Nevada with his girlfriend to spend the weekend there. That morning, he had received a phone call from John Gutfreund's office to let him know that Gutfreund was going to phone him in the evening. Buffett was having dinner at a Steak House restaurant when the director of Salomon's legal department, Don Feuerstein, called him. Gutfreund himself could not get to the phone because he was still on the plane.

Feuerstein told Buffett that there was a problem. Paul Mozer, a bond trader at Salomon whose name Buffett had never heard before, had repeatedly tried to hoodwink the mighty Federal Reserve. Salomon Brothers was one of only a few primary dealers authorized to buy bonds directly from the government, which gave them enormous power. Because Salomon had tried several times to monopolize the market, the share of treasury bonds individual companies were permitted to bid for had been restricted to 35%. Mozer had submitted two illegal bids for 35% each, using the names of two clients and then transferring the bonds to Salomon's account.

That didn't sound good but it hardly sounded dramatic. Later on, it turned out that the reality was a lot worse. Mozer had used the same trick several times; his bosses had known about his illegal bids for months and had tried to cover everything up. As happens in many crises, the truth only came to light bit by bit – and by trying to keep it under wraps, the Salomon executives made matters a lot worse for themselves.

A few days after Buffett first heard about the affair, the Federal Reserve Bank threatened to suspend all its business transactions with Salomon, which would have ruined the company for good. Understandably enough, the Federal Reserve Bank was not happy about having been hoodwinked by a bond trader, whose employers wouldn't even sack him when they found him out. Salomon had not exactly shown wisdom, responsibility or willingness to learn from mistakes.

If Salomon Brothers had failed, the results would probably have been equally devastating as those of the collapse of Lehman Brothers 17 years later. With an equity value of only $4 billion, $146 billion in liabilities, as well as derivatives worth several hundred million dollars and intricate links to other Wall Street investment banks, Salomon's balance sheet size was the second largest in the entire U.S. market at the time.

The Securities and Exchange Commission (SEC) launched an investigation. More and more details became public, with the media updating their reports on the scandal on a daily basis and speculating on the impending collapse of Salomon Brothers. Investors started taking flight and the company's stock market value dropped drastically.

They all knew that there was only one man who might be able to save them, a man who over the years had built up a reputation for being honest and straightforward as well as an incredibly clever investor. That man was Warren Buffett. The plan was to give the company a second chance and make him the interim chairman of Salomon Brothers.

For Buffett, deciding whether to go along with that idea was one of the hardest choices he would ever have to make. Alice Schroeder, his biographer, describes the situation on that Friday, August 16, as follows: "By this time, Buffett was the second richest man in the United States ... He was one of the most respected businessmen in the world. At some point during that long, horrible Friday, he recognized with a sickening jolt that investing in Salomon, a business with problems over which he had essentially no control, had from the beginning put all that at risk."[65]

Saving the badly damaged company at that point seemed almost impossible. Buffett was left with two options: He "could be a hero or he could fail. But he could not hide and he could not duck."[66]

Buffett decided to accept the challenge. But mere hours before the news was going to be announced in a press release which had already been prepared, information was leaked about a statement the Treasury Department was planning to release, banning Salomon Brothers from bidding for treasury bonds. With or without Buffett at the helm, the company's future looked bleak.

Buffett desperately tried to get hold of those responsible for the decision, and to convince them that they were not only signing the death warrant for Salomon Brothers, but triggering a devastating global financial crisis. He was willing to take responsibility in an all but hopeless situation, and to risk his most valuable asset, his reputation, which he had spent years building. However, he was not willing to commit professional suicide.

Buffett staked everything on a single chance – and he won. The Treasury Department reconsidered its position and agreed to some concessions. In the future, the company would no longer be allowed to bid on behalf of its clients, but it would be able to do so in its own name. For Buffett, that was a vital concession.

The task of cleaning up the chaos at Salomon Brothers, while following the legal proceedings and changing the company culture, took Buffett to the brink of exhaustion. "Events could do me in, and I couldn't get off the train. I didn't know where the train was going to go."[67]

Buffett's most difficult task consisted of creating a new corporate culture, one in which honesty and transparency were paramount. In a speech to his staff he said: "I want employees to ask themselves whether they are willing to have any contemplated act appear the next day on the front page of their local paper, to be read by their spouses, children and friends, with the reporting done by an informed and critical reporter."[68]

His employees were quite willing to comply. But when Buffett made substantial cuts to their bonuses because he thought it wrong that they got rewarded while the shareholders got penalized, many of them decided to leave the company and look for new jobs elsewhere. Once again, the future of Salomon was under threat.

Altogether, the affair cost the company an estimated $800 million in fines, penalties for breach of contract, legal fees and loss of revenue. But Salomon's eventual survival made Buffett an even richer man – and not only that, it added to his reputation as the greatest financial genius of all times.

To the superficial observer, the story of his success bears all the hallmarks of a singular and inexorable destiny. Somebody who had invested a thousand dollars with him when Buffett took over the fund would have made just shy of $17 million by 2018. Buffett himself has been ranked in the top three in the Forbes list of the richest people in the world for many years now. What this picture doesn't show is that above all, Buffett is a master of crisis management, who owes a large part of his success to his ability to excel in extremely difficult situations.

Take the example of his purchase of *The Buffalo Evening News*. Convinced that newspapers would make a good investment, Buffett had been looking for a suitable investment opportunity, which he finally found in 1977. He bought *The Buffalo Evening News* for $35.5 million, his most expensive purchase to date. But he could not even begin to guess how many headaches it would cause him in the near future.

In Buffalo, two papers were engaged in fierce competition. *The Courier-Express*, which came out on Sundays, had pretty much cornered the market for

Sunday papers. The owners brought legal charges against Buffett's plans to publish a Sunday edition of *The Buffalo Evening News*. He was painted as an outsider intent on ruining a local business rich in tradition by unfair practices.

In court, the Courier's lawyers quoted a statement in which Buffett had compared a monopoly on the local newspaper market with an unregulated toll bridge – both were equally covetable acquisitions. The court imposed completely unacceptable conditions on the publication of a Sunday edition. Buffett had been unable to argue his case persuasively.

Advertising clients remained loyal to *The Courier-Express*, and *The Evening News*, which had previously turned a profit, incurred losses to the tune of $1.4 million. "Buffett was chilled by the news," his biographer Alice Schroeder reports. "No business he had ever owned had lost so much money so fast."[69] Buffett was in a bad state, not least because his beloved wife Susie had just surprised him with the news that she was moving out of their home.

At that time, *The Buffalo Evening News* was Buffett's largest individual investment – and given the result of the lawsuit, everything was pointing towards a complete disaster.

Buffett was ready to give up, but his partner Charlie Munger talked him into persisting. After 18 months, the verdict against him was finally overturned by the Court of Appeal in April 1979. For Buffett, it was a belated victory – that came almost too late. Not only had he spent a lot of money on legal fees, the paper had also lost important advertising clients and kept losing millions of dollars every year. In late 1980, those losses amounted to a total of $10 million.

The final blow came with a strike organized by the drivers' union. After that, Buffett suspended publication and "told the union that the paper has a limited amount of 'blood,' and if it bleeds too much, it will not live anymore ... We're going to reopen only if there is a reasonable prospect of a viable operation."[70]

The unions got the message. Buffett was able to resume printing and the Sunday edition was no longer subject to restrictions. The rival paper, *The Courier-Express*, started losing its share of the market until it was forced to close down in September 1982. *The Buffalo Evening News*, on the other hand, was able to steadily increase its advertising revenue and circulation. A year after the strike, the paper was already turning a $19 million profit.

Buffett's story shows how even the most successful people are constantly confronted with huge challenges that may even threaten everything they have achieved so far. The same is true of Walt Disney. With almost 200,000 employees and an annual turnover of around $55 billion, the Walt Disney Corporation is one of the largest media empires in the world today. The story of its phenomenal success started in November of 1919, when two 18-year-olds, Walt Disney and Ub Iwerks, met while working for an advertising agency. When both were fired shortly after, they decided to form their own company, which they called Iwerks-Disney Commercial Artists. Business wasn't great, forcing Disney to take a job as an animation artist in order to ensure their new company's survival.

In May 1922, Disney created Laugh-O-Grams Films, Inc., a production company for animated films with seed capital of $15,000. Inexperienced in business matters, he agreed to contracts with extended payment periods. After his company was forced to file for insolvency in June 1923, Disney moved to Hollywood. As his biographer Andreas Platthaus points out, "the failed entrepreneur put several thousands of kilometers between himself and the investors who owned a share in Laugh-O-Grams. His investors had become his creditors and their demands for repayment would have made a new start in Kansas City impossible."[71]

In October 1923, Disney and his brother Roy founded Disney Brothers Cartoon Studio. One of their productions was *Alice's Wonderland*, which combined animation with real actors and actresses. In less than three years, they produced 34 Alice films. Eventually, Virginia Davis, who played the lead role, became too expensive for their budget. None of the actresses who replaced her were quite as good and in early 1927, Disney dropped the series and started producing films with animal protagonists.

Disney's approach was a novelty. Up to then, animals in animation films had not been 'human' enough to allow audiences to identify with them. He wanted his animals to talk and laugh, which at first earned him the derision and incomprehension of others.

The popular success of Disney's laughing rabbit Oswald soon proved them wrong. "Thanks to Oswald, Walt Disney appeared to have left his financial troubles behind him for the first time. But not for the last time, his new feeling of financial security would prove to be an illusion."[72] Disney had not taken into account that the distribution company retained copyright for the films, which permitted the company to move their production to another studio. When he attempted to raise his modest fee from $2,250 to $2,500 per film, the distribution company told him they were only willing to pay him $1,800 from now on. They also informed him that some of his closest and most talented staff had been approached, and were willing to take the Oswald animation to another studio.

Instead of buckling under their pressure, Walt Disney started looking for a new vehicle for his films and eventually settled on Ub Iwerks' Mickey Mouse, which would prove to be the making of him. The first film starring Mickey Mouse was called *Plane Crazy*, others followed and in 1932, Disney was rewarded with an Oscar for the creation.

Over the next few years, Disney added new characters such as Goofy in 1932 and Donald Duck in 1934. He also produced the first feature-length animation film, *Snow White and the Seven Dwarfs*, which won him another Oscar in 1937. In the post-war era, he produced a number of feature films such as *Treasure Island* and *20,000 Leagues Under the Sea*. The company came close to financial ruin several times before the box-office success of *Cinderella* saved it in 1950.

In 1948, Disney came up with the idea of building a Mickey Mouse theme park on 45,000 square meters opposite his studio to attract visitors. But he soon realized that the piece of land was nowhere near big enough, and started looking for alternatives. Eventually, he found a suitable piece of land in Anaheim, then a city of 20,000 inhabitants. He had trouble finding investors for his new project, which he called Disneyland, and was forced to put up his own savings instead. His brother Roy, who didn't think the studio was making enough money to finance his ideas, urgently advised him against attempting to realize them.

Instead of taking his brother's advice, Disney kept thinking up new ways to finance his pet project. He proposed a deal to the owners of the new television channel ABC: in return for their investment in Disneyland, he would grant them the right to produce a weekly show using his archive material.

It was an ingenious plan. Not only did it create a new market for Disney's short films, which were hardly ever shown in the cinema anymore – it also provided him with funding for his Disneyland project. ABC agreed to buy a 34.5% share in Disneyland Inc. for $500,000, and to act as a guarantor for loans up to $4.5 million. Disney also convinced other companies such as Ford and General Electric to finance attractions of their own in Disneyland – which in turn meant free advertising for them. More than just a gifted inventor of animal characters and film plots, Disney was also very creative at finding the money to fund his project.

The opening of the theme park was a big success, attracting over 28,000 visitors, 17,000 more than expected – but it was also a disaster in the sense that nothing seemed to work as it was supposed to. Disneyland was simply not prepared for so many visitors. The piece of land it was built on – an area of 170,000 square meters – soon proved to be far too small to accommodate them. Hotels and other businesses started sprouting up on both sides of the theme park, "robbing Disneyland of profits and rendering its creator's dreams of building a coherent kingdom of the fantastic meaningless."[73]

But once again, Disney refused to buckle under. Piece by piece, he bought up an area outside Orlando, Florida, during the 1960s, which was 650 times as large as the theme park in Anaheim. Walt Disney, who died in 1966, did not live to see the opening of the giant park in 1971. But his idea, for which he was ridiculed and which it took him a lot of effort to finance, proved to be an extraordinary success. Today, there are 13 Disney theme parks in four different countries on three different continents.

Disney wasn't the only successful entrepreneur to be confronted with huge difficulties which would later prove to be milestones on his road to success. Today, in 2019, Starbucks is a global brand with more than 30,000 branches all over the world and, in 2018, posted a net profit of $4.52 billion. But once again, the coffee chain's enormous successes grew from humble beginnings. Howard Schultz grew up in the projects of Brooklyn, the son of an unskilled laborer. As a youth, he was ashamed of living in a neighborhood that had an especially bad reputation. Picking up a girl from another part of New York for a date once, he had a brief conversation with her father, who was visibly displeased with the Schultz's answers to his questions: "Where do you live?" – "We live in Brooklyn." – "Where?" – "Canarsie." – "Where?" – "Bayview Projects." – "Oh." There was an implicit judgment in the older man's reaction, Schultz later remembered – "and it irked me to see it."[74]

Despite his humble background, Schultz was extraordinarily ambitious. The first of his family to go to college, he started working as a sales coach for Xerox after graduation and later for Hammarplast, the American branch of the Swedish Pestorp corporation, which made household appliances. Working as a salesman, he noticed that a small retailer in Seattle kept ordering large quantities of a particular kind of drip coffee maker, which simply consisted of "a plastic cone set on a thermos." Schultz became curious and decided to investigate: "I'm going to go see this company. I want to know what's going on out there."[75]

Setting foot in the original Starbucks store, he felt as if he was entering "a temple for the worship of coffee," he says in his autobiography.[76] There was a worn wooden counter, behind which coffee beans from all over the world were kept in bins: Sumatra, Kenya, Ethiopia, Costa Rica – at a time when most Americans still thought coffee was made from granules rather than from beans. The coffee in this shop tasted unlike anything Americans were used to at the time. Schultz was hooked.

At the time, there were only five Starbucks shops altogether. But Schultz saw a potential for growth, which the original owners had failed to recognize. He wanted to quit his job, move to Seattle and work for Starbucks. "Taking a job at Starbucks would mean giving up that 75,000 dollar a year job, the prestige, the car, and the co-op, and for what? Moving 3,000 miles across the country to join a tiny outfit with five coffee stores didn't make sense to a lot of my friends and family. My mother was especially concerned."[77]

For a whole year, he tried in vain to get Starbucks to hire him. After his interview with the company's founder and director, he had a good feeling. But then he got a call which shook him. "I'm sorry, Howard, I have bad news." After a long debate, the three owners of Starbucks had decided not to take him on. He could hardly believe what he was hearing: "Your plans sound great, but that's just not the vision we have for Starbucks."[78]

Schultz refused to take 'no' for an answer. "I still believed so much in the future of Starbucks that I couldn't accept 'no' as a final answer." Eventually, he did manage to talk the owners into hiring him. Later on, he would often ask himself: "What would have happened had I just accepted his decision? Most people, when turned down for a job, just go away." It would not be the last time his innovations were rejected. "So many times I've been told it can't be done. Again and again I've had to use every ounce of perseverance and persuasion I can summon to make things happen."[79]

At the time, Starbucks was quite different from what it is today. Shops only sold beans rather than actually serving coffee. During a trip to Italy, Schultz had enjoyed the atmosphere in the local sidewalk cafés. Watching his cup of coffee being prepared, he suddenly had a revelation. "Starbucks had missed the point – completely missed it." Serving coffee Italian-style was the way to go!

What seems so obvious today was a revolutionary idea at the time. "It was like an epiphany. It was so immediate and so obvious that I was shaking."[80]

Back in Seattle, he told the owners of Starbucks of his vision but they were strictly against it. Starbucks was a shop, they said, not a restaurant or a bar. Serving coffee would mean entering another industry. And after all, Starbucks had been making profits every year. Why take that kind of risk?

It took him a year to convince his employers to test his idea on a small scale. They finally gave in, allowing him to run a small espresso bar in the sixth Starbucks, which opened in central Seattle in April 1984.

The success of his experiment only made him more determined to try it out on a larger scale. Every day he would beseech Jerry Baldwin, one of the owners, to give him a chance. But Baldwin refused to budge. "Starbucks doesn't need to get any bigger than it is. If you get too many customers in and out, you can't get to know them the way we always have." His refusal was final. "I'm sorry, Howard. We aren't going to do it. You'll have to live with that."[81]

Feeling dejected and depressed, Schultz finally made the decision to quit and start his own coffee bar, which he was planning to name "Il Giornale." But he needed capital he didn't have. He had big plans and to realize them, he needed $1.65 million. Of the 242 investors he approached, 217 turned him down. They told him what he was planning was undoable.

"Il Giornale? You can't pronounce the name."

"How could you leave Starbucks? What a stupid move."

"Why on Earth do you think this is going to work? Americans are never going to spend a dollar and a half for coffee!"

"You're out of your mind. This is insane. You should just go get a job."[82]
The hardest thing of all was to keep his spirits up in the face of so much opposition. "You can't be dejected when you meet with a landlord to begin negotiations about leasing a location. But if you've had three or four fruitless meetings that week, how do you whip yourself up? You really have to be a chameleon. Here you are in front of somebody else. You're depressed as hell, but you have to sound as fresh and confident as you were at your first meeting."[83]

But he stuck to his guns and was finally able to win some investors for his project. The turning point came in March 1987. Jerry Baldwin and Gordon Bowker, the owners of Starbucks, decided to sell the Seattle branches, the roasting house and the Starbucks name. Altogether, they wanted $4 million.

Raising that kind of money after he had only just scraped together the capital for Il Giornale seemed impossible at first.

Then one of Schultz's investors announced that he was planning to buy Starbucks himself. The news was like a slap in the face for Schultz. His rival was a local business leader, who had probably already secured the support of the Seattle business community. In a meeting, he was told: "If you don't take this deal, you'll never work in this town. You'll never raise another dollar. You'll be dog meat."[84]

As he was leaving the meeting, he completely lost control and started crying, right there in the lobby. He did get the money together in the end. Refusing to give in to pressure or blackmail, he persisted. In his autobiography, he reflects: "Many of us face critical moments like that in our lives, when our dreams seem ready to shatter. You can never prepare for such events, but how you react to them is crucial ... It's during such vulnerable times, when the unexpected curve balls hit you hard on the head that an opportunity can be lost."[85]

In circumstances like these, our resolve is put to the test. There is no successful entrepreneur, no top athlete, nobody who is successful in other fields, who has not had to prove him or herself in these situations. If Schultz had given up, we would not be able to enjoy Starbucks coffee in Starbucks branches all over the world. And Schultz himself would have remained an employee of a small-time company rather than becoming one of the most successful and wealthy entrepreneurs in the United States.

Throughout my life, I have been confronted with various difficult situations. These experiences have taught me how important it is to ask myself, especially in a crisis, what the problem could be good for. In my autobiography – *Wenn du nicht mehr brennst, starte neu* – I tell the story of one such situation: in 2015, just three days before Christmas Eve, the closest employee of my then company Dr.ZitelmannPB.GmbH called me. I was just about to go through the baggage check at Frankfurt airport, as I had been doing almost every week for the past 15 years. Whenever I was on a business trip, it was entirely normal for me to speak with my closest colleague, Holger Friedrichs, the head of my company's PR department, about ten times a day. I had just told him some good news, about a client who had extended his contract for another two years. But Friedrichs brushed my news aside, replying instead: "I also have some news, but it's bad. I'm leaving the company. I'll be gone by the end of January."

What he said shocked me to the core. My professional partnership with Holger Friedrichs had lasted 15 years. And now this, totally out of the blue. Just three days before Christmas. My company had lost quite a few good employees that year, and it was mainly my fault. I had made a number of mistakes. I had stopped caring enough about the company; I had lost the requisite spark. My enthusiasm had waned and I had found more fulfilment working on my second doctoral dissertation. In any case, I know that I've always been a difficult boss, the kind many employees couldn't handle. But, throughout the years, there was one employee who had always remained loyal to me and had worked for the company day and night as if it were his own.

And now he was leaving. The employee on whom almost everything depended! He could do things I could simply never do. He was a PR genius with a sovereign natural ability for press and public relations work. I hired him on October 1, 2001, just one year after I had founded my company. As a good salesman, I had managed to win seven customers prior to launching the company. They had each signed contracts worth 120,000 deutsche marks a year. But after one year it dawned on me that my clients demanded more PR expertise than I actually had myself. Yes, I had been a successful and well-known journalist for several years. But, like most journalists, I didn't actually understand all that much about PR.

At that time, a young woman applied for a job with us, but finally decided on another job: "If you bring me someone who understands PR," I promised her, "then I'll give you a 1,000-deutsche-mark finder's fee as a reward." She brought Holger Friedrichs. I knew immediately: he was exactly the right man for the job. I liked the combination of subjects he had studied – philosophy and chemistry – and he had several years of PR experience.

Friedrichs is a quiet guy. Quite the opposite of me. He only talks about 10% as much as me. He laughs a little – and mostly only after you say that you've just told a joke. But he's the kind of person you can trust 100%. This is a quality we share, but it's not the only one. We are both industrious – and have a healthy dose of self-confidence. Now, here I was, standing in front of the baggage carousel at Frankfurt airport, and he drops the bombshell that he'll be gone in a few weeks. "What do you want to do?" I asked, but he didn't want to say anything about his plans.

Had he been poached by a client? Was he looking to launch his own PR company and perhaps take some clients and employees with him? Several clients even had exit clauses in their contracts that would allow them to terminate immediately if Friedrichs were to leave the company. My first thought was that he must want to go into business for himself. It had crossed my mind on occasion over the years, but I thought that as he hadn't done it before, maybe it wasn't something he wanted. Especially as we have always understood each other so well – and still understand each other very well to this day.

"Mr. Friedrichs, if you are leaving, please don't leave right away. There's no way we would survive. You know what a difficult situation the company is in. You leaving now would break the company." Of course, that was an exaggeration, but the situation without Friedrichs would have been very difficult in any case. Despite my pleading, he could not be talked out of it: January 31. Not a day longer. "Then I'm gone."

When you are confronted by a situation like this, there are different ways you can react, for example: "Why is this happening to me? What a mess! How ungrateful is he?! How can he let me down like this from one day to the next?" Fortunately, I am not in the habit of reacting like this. Especially not when things are really serious. Instead, I immediately think: "What could this problem be good for? How can I take advantage of the opportunity this problem presents?"

Two minutes after Friedrichs told me that he was leaving, I heard myself say: "What would you think if I sold the company to you?" The idea came to me spontaneously when I forced myself to think: "How can I turn this problem into an opportunity?" Yes, wasn't that a huge opportunity for me? Such a company, which bears its owner's name and which everyone believes is not worth much without its founder, is difficult to sell. You can only sell it to another company, but that company usually wants you to stay on board for a few more years. As an employee! For me that would be like getting divorced and the judge saying: "But the condition is that you live together with this woman for another four years." Many company bosses do something like that. For me that would never be an option.

And now my closest employee was resigning. That could be an opportunity ... Two days after the phone call we sat together with an auditor and two tax experts, followed by talks with the banks. We discussed how to structure and finance the sale. Five weeks later, we signed and notarized the purchase and transfer agreement for 100% of the company's shares, along with a consulting and cooperation agreement for the next three years.

I sold the company at a reasonable price, but it wasn't about getting the most out of it. I had earned a lot with the company over the previous 15 years – the average return on sales was an incredible 48%. I had invested the profits in the Berlin real estate market and earned many millions. Now it wasn't about one million more or less, but about getting out of the business cleanly. To give the employees a perspective and not to let the clients down. To give my closest employee, to whom I owe a lot, a chance. To give a future to the company that I founded and for which I had given everything for 15 years. And to become completely free myself. If I hadn't succeeded in selling the company, I would have had to wind it up in the worst case. All the employees would have been left without a job.

By selling the company I felt free, liberated. I wouldn't have to run from appointment to appointment anymore. For 15 years, every single day had been planned, mostly two to three months in advance. To say goodbye, the employees gave me a small book and worked out that I had flown 468,845.44 miles and traveled 129,142.94 kilometers by train. To acquire and look after 136 customers, 22 in Hamburg, 13 in Frankfurt, 23 in Munich, five in Stuttgart, seven in Düsseldorf, four in Cologne, three in Bonn, etc. The work had made me very happy, just like the other things I had done before in my life – as a historian, as an editor and as a journalist. But I had never wanted to do just one thing for my whole life. Today I have time for research, writing books and speaking engagements. The company my employee bought (which is now called PB3C) continues to do well and I have been advising them for three years now. The sale was a win-win situation for everyone.

Next time you are facing a huge problem, look for the opportunity within the problem. You must learn to accept that the more successful you are, the bigger the problems will become. As long as everything is running smoothly and without any problems, we are unlikely to make huge steps forward. Only in a crisis are we forced to try out new things and come up with innovative ideas.

You will be able to achieve larger goals only if your self-confidence grows. Strong self-confidence is an indispensable requirement for developing the courage to believe in yourself and set yourself larger goals. Your self-confidence is strengthened by mastering larger and larger problems.

Picture your self-confidence as a muscle that needs training in order to develop. The way to do this is by steadily increasing the weight it is required to lift. Your self-confidence will only grow by solving larger and larger problems. You can be certain that neither Ingvar Feodor Kamprad nor Warren Buffett nor Walt Disney were born with the kind of self-confidence that was to become their trademark. They had to develop it by tackling one crisis after another, by facing difficulties and new challenges head-on.

CHAPTER 4

Focusing

In early July 1991, Bill Gates senior had some guests over for dinner. Among them were his son, the founder of Microsoft, and Warren Buffett: two of the most successful men in the world, who, for many years, had taken turns at the top of the *Forbes* list of billionaires. The host asked his dinner guests: "What factor did people feel was the most important thing in getting to where they'd gotten in life?" Buffett immediately said: "Focus." Bill Gates junior agreed with him.[86]

Gates had been obsessed with computers since he was 13: "I mean, then I became hard core. It was day and night."[87] His parents were worried about him: "Although he was only in the ninth grade, he already seemed obsessed with the computer, ignoring everything else, staying out all night."[88] In the end, they would not even allow him to touch a computer for nine months.

"Bill had a monomaniacal quality," his college roommate remembers. "He would focus on something and really stick with it. He had a determination to master whatever it was he was doing."[89] An ex-girlfriend adds that he had always been extremely focused and intolerant of distractions. He didn't own a television and had even dismantled his car radio. She elaborates: "In the end, it was difficult to sustain a relationship with someone who could boast a 'seven-hour' turnaround – meaning that from the time he left Microsoft to the time he returned in the morning was a mere seven hours."[90]

Warren Buffett, too, had focused on a single goal for decades. Even as a child, his dream was to become rich and he had devoured a book on *One Thousand Ways to Make $1,000.* "Opportunity knocks," the reader is told on the very first page of Buffett's favorite read. "Never in the history of the United States has the time been so favorable for a man with small capital to start his own business as it is today."[91]

When he was 11 years old, Buffett announced that he would be a millionaire by the time he was 35. At 16, he had already saved up $5,000 from various enterprises. In today's currency, that money would be worth about $60,000 – not bad for a 16-year-old. His prediction was only off by five years: He had already made his first million when he was 30 – of course, a million dollars was worth a lot more then than it is now.

In *Think and Grow Rich*, Napoleon Hill says: "Every human being who understands the purpose of money wishes for it. Wishing will not bring riches. But desiring riches with a state of mind that becomes an obsession, then planning definite ways and means to acquire riches, and backing those plans with persistence which does not recognize failure, will bring riches."[92]

This does not mean resorting to unfair, let alone illegal practices to achieve your goal. Any so-called success you may achieve by doing harm to others or breaking the law will only ever be of a temporary, transitory nature. In the long run, you will be neither successful nor happy.

What is instrumental in achieving long-term success is focusing on a goal. Many people lose track along the way – their CVs give them away. They try first one thing, then another without ever finishing anything, and tend to become discouraged as soon as any problems arise.

You have to focus exclusively on a single goal – for at least a decade. Whatever it is you want to do – whether you aim to be an athlete, a musician, a scientist, an artist, a writer or a businessman – success will not come to you overnight, or even after a few weeks or months.

Boris Becker, the tennis player, also shared this ability to focus on a goal throughout his sporting career. When he was a child of three or four, he took one of his father's tennis rackets from the trunk of the car and started whacking balls against the wall at the tennis club, or against the blinds at home. His father would whisper to his mother: "He's not quite right in the head."[93]

Aged six, he joined the local tennis club in his hometown Leimen. Five years later, he was already selected for the German Tennis Federation's youth team. According to the officials, however, he would never make it to the top. "The so-called 'monitor reports' didn't rate me," Becker says. "I never fitted in, but the negative reports only served to spur me on. I wanted to prove them wrong."[94]

As a 17-year-old, he won a surprise victory at Wimbledon, beating Kevin Curren in four sets in the final. He was the first German and the youngest player ever to win the men's final of the most important tennis tournament in the world and the youngest winner in any Grand Slam tournament.

Becker talks about the extreme concentration that was an important factor for his success in this as in other matches. In the changing rooms before his first Wimbledon final, he greeted his opponent with a curt "Hi" – not a single word more. He never spoke to his opponents before a match – except once to his fellow countryman Michael Stich. "We know the result. I was talking, and he won."[95]

Sitting in the changing room, Becker feels "as if I'm in a tunnel." His vision shrinks to something he himself calls "this tunnel vision": "But I am wearing blinkers and sitting there like a zombie. That is my way of coping with the pressure, of concentrating. Nothing else interests me. I have to get myself into this trance, this total isolation."[96]

Then he goes out on the court – self-confident and fearless – with his "head held high, chest out." Before a match, Becker says, he would feel extremely nervous, scared even. But his fear always went as soon as he set foot on the court. "I feel no fear. I feel like a racehorse at the starting gate. My mind is so occupied with the match that hasn't even begun yet that I don't look behind or in front of me."[97]

In the third set of the now legendary Wimbledon final of 1985, the umpire announced: "Championship point Becker." The 13,118 spectators shouted out as one. "I can't hear anything anymore. At least, I hear sounds, but not words, not even those voices shouting from above: 'Boris!'"[98] Becker won the match. He went on to win 49 singles titles in all, among them six Grand Slam tournaments, three of them at Wimbledon, as well as 15 doubles titles.

Becker describes the mental and emotional state that helped him win so many matches: "I don't reflect any more. I simply let myself go, right up to the dive roll to the net at the end. I don't hear the umpire. I don't even look at the scoreboard – I keep count of the score myself. When I reach the climax of this trance-like state, the 'zone,' the only thing I'm aware of is the onlookers."[99] Whether they were for him or against him didn't matter to him. "In every match I reached a point where I faced the wall, and managed to jump over it – concentration and willpower made it possible."[100]

Becker got as far as he did by focusing exclusively on a single goal for almost three decades – between the age of four and 32. In his youth, he used to play soccer as well as tennis, and in retrospect he believes that he was equally talented at both. But very early on, he started to focus on the single most important part of his life – playing tennis.

Unfortunately, Becker did not succeed in transferring the attitudes that had made him so successful in sport to other areas of life. At the end of his sporting career, he became involved in a variety of investments and companies. Ultimately, these were not successful. At the same time – like many successful athletes – he had become accustomed to a very high-cost way of life. His expenditure far exceeded his income. High living, an expensive divorce and a string of bad investments finally led to him losing the triple-digit million fortune he had earned during his sporting career.

What tennis was for Boris Becker, soccer was to Oliver Kahn. He, too, had set himself a definite goal at a very early stage: "I wanted to become the best goalkeeper in the world ... A tremendous vision, tremendously far from reality at the time, a hyper-hyper-goal. Somehow it wasn't nebulous at all, but very concrete."[101] Kahn did win the title of Best Goalkeeper in the world three times, in 1999, 2001 and 2002. He was Best European Goalkeeper four times and German Soccer Player of the Year twice.

Kahn describes his trancelike state during a match. "My brain is focusing at the very highest level. Focusing any harder would be unimaginable. Complete obliviousness to any disruptive influences."[102] He would notice neither the audience in the stadium nor any other external influences. "When I'm standing on the pitch, something goes 'click!' – and I'm one hundred percent in the moment, one hundred percent focused. Then every game becomes a kind of final."[103]

The 2001 Champions League final was one of those moments when Kahn succeeded in focusing 100%: "I noticed nothing anymore except for the ball and the player kicking it. It felt as if I was inside an empty, silent room. The audience of 80,000 in the stadium might as well not have been there."[104] As a goalkeeper, he had developed a way of training his ability to focus. "I started to keep my eyes on the ball during a game – without ever shifting my gaze even for a single second. At every moment of a game, even when my own team had scored a corner, when the ball was further away from my goal than at any other point of the game, I didn't allow my eyes to drift even for a second. My eyes, my focus, my concentration remained trained on that small white dot."[105] In a penalty shootout, he would focus so much that nothing else existed: "If the world was to end at that moment, I wouldn't notice."[106]

Even in the run-up to an important game, Kahn was already completely focused. "During those phases, I was oblivious to almost everything else, I retreated into my tunnel, and nothing existed for me but my complete focus on the road to success."[107] He tried to control every detail, leaving nothing to chance and making sure nothing got between him and his 'campaign.' "I would even get nervous if I noticed, or even just got the impression that my team mates were preoccupied with trivialities which in my view were not conducive to their focus."[108]

For successful men such as Oliver Kahn or Bill Gates, the term 'focus' has a double meaning. On the one hand, it means the ability to concentrate on a single goal for several decades, on the other hand it means concentrating on something so hard that everything else ceases to exist.

I want to tell you the story of another man who has spent the last three decades focusing on one thing and one thing only, and whose ability to focus has brought him enormous success – for his clients, but also for his company and for himself. His name is Christoph Kahl, the German founder of the German-American company Jamestown.

Jamestown raises capital from German investors in order to buy real estate in the U.S. By issuing shares in close-end investment funds, Jamestown has been able to buy U.S. real estate worth more than $11 billion since 1984. The majority of their commercial property funds have been liquidated by now. The worst-performing of them paid out 8.5% annually on average, the best-performing almost 35%. On average, investors made over 19% a year. No initiator of close-end real estate funds in Germany has ever been able to secure similarly sensational profits for investors.

What is the secret of his success? I have known Christoph Kahl for more than 20 years, and it has been my privilege to serve as his advisor for 15 of them. As a result, I think I know a thing or two about the secret behind his success. His first secret is focus. Many other funds managers spread themselves too thinly in the 1990s, issuing various different types of funds – shipping funds, real estate funds, media funds and so on. But Christoph Kahl has chosen another way. Focusing exclusively on commercial real estate in the United States for many decades, he has gained specialist knowledge of the subject, which has in turn enabled him to position himself distinctly from many of his competitors. After all, people trust an expert to know more about a particular field than almost anybody else.

There are other factors which contribute to Kahl's success. In addition to his clear focus, his success is based on transparency, controlled risk-taking and caution, even in the face of success. This last point – the ability to remain cautious despite his success – is of particular importance to him. When I interviewed him for this book, he said: "You are writing a book about those who have had success. You might also write one on those who have been successful initially, only to fail later on. And you would probably find that over-confidence played a major part in their failure."

With success comes self-confidence. And that is a good thing. Self-confidence makes us strong enough and brave enough to take on larger projects, as Christoph Kahl did. In 1984, he bought office and warehouse space in Nashville, Tennessee, for $3.5 million. At the time, 82 investors bought shares in his fund. In the next few years, he carried on buying U.S. real estate mostly below the ten-million-dollar mark. In 1999, he risked his largest venture to date, buying an office tower in Manhattan which is part of the Rockefeller Center complex. The fund was worth $650 million, 185 times the value of his first fund.

To finance the project, he had to put up $300 million in equity, most of which he had to advance or to guarantee loans for. "If I hadn't succeeded in raising those 300 million from investors, I would not have been able to survive financially," Kahl admits.

The whole thing proved even trickier than he had anticipated. In 1999 and 2000, when he was attempting to sell the shares, investors were simply not interested in 'boring' real estate. Germany was in the midst of a stock market bonanza. In those two years, German investors spent $100 billion on equities. As any television program or newspaper article would tell you, the stock market was the most progressive and sophisticated form of investment. In 1999, investors in the German stock market made profits of 39%. An American real estate fund which paid out all of 7% seemed boring and unattractive in comparison – not to mention the rising dollar rate, which made the American market even less of a winning proposition.

Selling his fund proved an arduous and difficult task – and Kahl had risked $300 million. "If an idea doesn't work, you have to exercise your imagination, that's when the time has come for product innovation," Kahl says. He solved his problem by inventing a so-called reinvestment model, which proved so successful that he would use it again and again, even when funds once more became easier to sell. He eventually managed to launch his fund, which made investors more than 34% a year until it was dissolved in 2006.

Over the next few years, when investors sobered up and started to rediscover the merits of real estate, Kahl was able to sell even larger funds. In 2005, he bought about 50% of the General Motors Building in Manhattan, which was then worth $1.7 billion.

One success after another can easily lead to over-confidence, which according to Kahl is one of the greatest dangers for successful people. There is a thin line between healthy self-esteem and dangerous over-confidence – as thin as the line between the desire for financial independence and bottomless greed.

Listening to the critical opinions of others, and taking them seriously, helps. After a successful start, too many people tend to surround themselves with sycophants. I have attended a lot of Jamestown management meetings, and I know that this is one company whose managers are encouraged to voice criticism or disagreement with their boss. "In my company," Kahl says, "the people who will get far are the ones who stand up for their opinions and are willing to contradict me."

A company which rewards independent thinking will foster a corporate culture which helps the successful entrepreneur to remain grounded in reality instead of overestimating his own abilities. Most importantly, Kahl says, successful people have to recognize the danger of over-confidence, which is one of the greatest risks they are faced with.

Transparency is another secret of Kahl's success. He ran into problems shortly after buying an office tower in Boston for $416 million in 2001. Two days before the 9/11 attacks, I was in Boston with him and on the evening of September 11, we met in Berlin. At the time, all of us were so shaken by the attacks, we hardly considered the economic repercussions.

Those were massive and they certainly affected the financial services industry in the United States. The demand for office space in Boston's financial district fell drastically. It soon became clear that Jamestown would only be able to pay out dividends of 6.5%, 1.5 points less than the expected 8% the company had forecast for investors. For other fund managers, this minor discrepancy might not have been worth mentioning – but it was the first time in the history of Jamestown that one of their funds was not performing as well as they had led investors to expect. Without a moment's hesitation, Kahl took the earliest opportunity to advise investors very openly on the problems he was expecting. By demonstrating his willingness to communicate bad news, he won the trust of investors and sales partners alike. The story eventually had a happy ending: at the height of the real estate boom in 2006, Kahl was able to sell the office building for $100 million more than he had paid for it.

Another fund was also cause for concern. In the space of a few months in 2006, Kahl had raised $648 million for his Co-Invest 4 fund. It was the largest closed-end real estate fund ever launched in Germany. But because of the financial crisis, the value of U.S. real estate dropped dramatically. Kahl soon realized that for the first – and to date the only – time in the company's history, investors were likely to lose some of their money. Again, he informed them very early and openly. While not happy about the news, investors still appreciated his honesty. Thanks to Kahl's intensive efforts, the fund was able to pay back investors' initial stakes in 2016.

Trust is built when things aren't going as well as expected – by letting those concerned know as soon as possible and without glossing over the bad news. Many providers of financial instruments hide away when there are problems, or attempt to cover them up. In the long run, this type of behavior will lose them the trust of investors.

Kahl has always been particularly inventive in times of crisis. When German media were full of reports about the real estate crisis in the U.S. after 2008, for several years sales of closed-end real estate funds collapsed completely in Germany. With the market as depressed as it was, no initiator was able to raise equity funds for investments in the U.S. from private investors. Across the market, business got worse every year and several former market leaders had to stop business altogether.

Faced with this situation, Kahl decided to expand into institutional business. He continued to pursue the same investment strategy in the U.S., but instead of raising capital from private investors in Germany, he now targeted institutional investors such as pension funds worldwide – in the U.S. as well as in Australia and Europe.

In late 2011, Jamestown launched the Jamestown Premier Property Fund, its first fund for institutional investors. By the end of 2018, Jamestown had already succeeded in raising $4 billion in equity while the performance of its fund significantly exceeds the benchmark.

In 2010, a couple of years after the financial crisis, Kahl made headlines by closing a deal that was to be the largest single asset transaction of the year in the New York real estate market and part of the largest ever fund liquidation in the German closed-end fund industry. Jamestown sold the building at 111 Eighth Avenue in New York to Google for $1.8 billion. In 2004, when the Jamestown fund launched with a total volume of $1.03 billion, the property was valued at just below $800 million. The fund also sold its remaining properties at high profits, securing its investors a net pre-tax return of over 18% per year.

Kahl made another sensational deal with the Chelsea Market office building in New York, in which he acquired 75% of the shares in 2003 on the basis of a property valuation of $280 million. Because the 25% co-owner was able to force a sale in 2011, Kahl sold the building for $795 million from one of the funds for private investors to the institutional PPF fund. This sale, together with other distributions from the fund, brought the private investors an annual pre-tax profit of 28.6%. That was sensational, but even more so was the fact that in 2018, he managed to sell the property to Google for $2.4 billion.

I have invested in several of Jamestown's mutual funds, including the fund that bought and sold the Chelsea Market property. The annual returns for investors in these funds after U.S. taxes were 13.4%, 14.8%, 17.5%, 21% and 29.1%, respectively. My returns were actually much higher than those of the other investors, who had invested 100% at launch and whose annual returns were correspondingly lower due to the longer holding period. I had acquired the funds on the secondary market several years after their issue, which meant that my annual returns, even though I bought into some of the funds above nominal value, were boosted by the shorter term to maturity. The returns I achieved with these funds were 23.8%, 25.4%, 25%, 29.4% and 44%, respectively.

At the time, I wrote to Kahl to tell him that my only regret was that I hadn't invested larger amounts. Over the past few years, however, I've invested seven-digit amounts in Jamestown's PPF fund, which sold Chelsea Market to Google, among others.

The bedrock of Kahl's success was his focus. Not only has he focused all of his attention on a single project – U.S. real estate – for decades, he also looks into every legal, economic, technical and fiscal detail of each and every one of his investments. When I asked him whether his perfectionism sometimes gets in the way of getting things done, he admitted that I might have a point, but added that he would rather focus on a few large projects that are worth the effort and attention invested into them.

Focusing means setting yourself goals in life – and pursuing them persistently over many years. Many successful people have dedicated their entire lives to the pursuit of a single goal. Others, including Arnold Schwarzenegger, have pursued, and achieved, a succession of goals. According to his biographer Marc Hujer, Schwarzenegger would never plan more than one project at a time. "In America, they call somebody like him a 'one-issue man,' somebody who completely throws himself into one thing at a time and then looks for the next thing."[109]

As soon as Schwarzenegger reached one of his goals, he would start focusing on the next one. But focus also means concentrating completely and exclusively on a given task. In weight training, it means becoming at one with the weights and focusing only on finishing the set and on improving his performance.

Warren Buffett focuses on everything he does. Playing bridge is one of his few hobbies. Bill Gates had previously attempted to talk him into buying a computer by promising that he would send the most beautiful girl working at Microsoft to teach him how to use it. Buffett refused his offer because he did not see the point of owning a computer.

Only when his girlfriend told him that he would be able to play his favorite game online did he change his mind. But he insisted that he only wanted to learn about the features he needed for playing bridge. Beyond that, he was not interested in the computer or any of its functions. He could do his tax return in his head, Buffett said, he didn't need a computer. But playing bridge on his own – now that he did need a computer for.

He soon grew to enjoy his online games, playing with so much focus and dedication that nothing could have distracted him. Once a bat flew into his house and started flapping around in his den. His girlfriend screamed: "Warren, there's a bat in here!" But he was so intent on his game he did not even look up. All he would say was: "It's not bothering me any."[110]

After some training sessions with two-time world champion Sharon Osberg, Buffett entered the world championship with her – highly unusual for somebody who had never even played in a championship tournament. Buffett sat down at the table and appeared to ignore his surroundings completely – as if he was the only person in the room. The other players were far more experienced than he was, "but he was able to focus as calmly as if he were playing in his living room ... Somehow his intensity overcame the weakness of his game," his biographer says.[111] It was the same kind of intensity which allows wiry karate athletes to smash a row of bricks where a bulky weight lifter would fail. Focus – which martial artists perfect with the aid of meditation – can compensate for the lack of brute muscle power.

To everyone's surprise, Buffett qualified for the final of the bridge world championship in his first tournament ever. But his superhuman effort had taken its toll. After focusing so hard for one and a half days, he was too exhausted to compete in the final and had to pull out.

Buffett does not do anything by halves, even when it's 'only' a hobby. IKEA founder Ingvar Kamprad took an even more extreme line: he disapproved of his leading executives having any hobbies at all lest they become distracted from focusing on their real goal of developing the company. He once said in a television interview: "I expect my enthusiastic staff not to have any larger interests or hobbies outside of the company."[112]

Well, there are different schools of thought on this. On the one hand, focus is important and spending too much time on other things may not be conducive to achieving your chosen goal. On the other hand, having a couple of outside interests or hobbies will help you recharge your batteries and gain perspective, as playing bridge did for Buffett.

A well-known sports psychologist, who used to look after the German soccer team among others, explained the importance of creating a parallel universe in which top athletes immerse themselves in order to switch off and cope with the enormous mental pressure they are under. He said they found it easiest to switch off by focusing their attention on another activity.

Are you familiar with the so-called flow state – focusing all your attention on a single thing to the exclusion of everything around you? Successful people have a gift to focus longer and harder than others. Most of us focus only 80% of our attention on one thing. We may be working or studying, but at the back of our minds, we are thinking about other things – what we are going to do later on, what we left unfinished earlier today, what happened to us yesterday. However, somebody who focuses 80% of their attention on something will not achieve 80% of their potential, but only about 30% or 40%. That's why the ability to focus is such a crucial precondition of success.

No writer or journalist will be able to compose a good text if he or she is constantly being interrupted. To write well, you have to focus exclusively on the task at hand. Do not allow yourself to be distracted by phone calls, emails or colleagues dropping in on you.

Whenever I explain this in one of my lectures, somebody in the audience will tell me that they need to be constantly available to their clients or other people. That may well be true – but only if you work for the fire brigade or the emergency services. Generally, not a single house is going to burn down and nobody is going to bleed to death just because you let a few hours pass before returning a call. Can you imagine a soccer player running to the side line during a match in order to phone his tax accountant? Of course not. Instead, players do what all high achievers do: They focus 100% on a single thing, in their case winning the game. And afterwards, they return their phone calls.

In an era of information overload due to cell phones and email, creating the right conditions to follow your own agenda is more important than ever. In the end, you have two choices: either you are your own boss, defining your own goals and priorities, or you take orders from others. Even as an employee, you probably have more leeway to define your priorities and your working rhythm than you are currently using. At the end of the day, what counts is the results you achieve, not your ability to multitask.

Once you have identified the decisive factors that will bring you closer to your goal, you have to do everything to focus precisely on these factors. The ability to focus is not necessarily something we are born with – it can be acquired. We all tend to spread ourselves too thinly, to lose track of our priorities and to focus on trivialities. Every once in a while, we need to take a step back and take a long hard look at our lives. Ask yourself: "Am I really doing the important things, which will get me closer to my goals? Or am I frittering my time away with marginal activities, which will at best contribute in a very minor way to my eventual success?"

Only somebody who is able to focus, both in the sense of concentrating on a single goal – or on a limited number of goals – for many years, and in the sense of focusing 100% on these goals at all times, will be able to achieve more ambitious goals.

CHAPTER 5

Dare to Be Different

People who are extraordinarily successful are different from those who have little or no success in life. If you think and act like everybody else, you will only ever be as successful as everybody else. To be more successful, you have to think and act differently, and to do that, you must dare to be different. You need the courage to swim against the tide and to question assumptions that are firmly rooted in popular opinion. Any new idea or innovation passes through four stages: first, it is ignored. Then it is ridiculed. Next, it is violently opposed and finally it is accepted as being self-evident.

The men and women portrayed in this book have all dared to be different. Time and again, Warren Buffett, George Soros and Prince Alwaleed, all of them successful investors, resisted the pull of popular opinion and pursued contrarian investment strategies – again and again, they did so successfully. In this chapter, you will meet some women who have shown particular courage. These women all lived in different time periods and they were quite different characters – but the one thing they did have in common was the courage to be different.

First of all, let me tell you the story of a woman who had to fight over 2,000 lawsuits brought against her – and who all her life dared to be completely different from everybody else. Let me tell you about the life of Beate Uhse, who started from scratch to create what was to become the largest adult-entertainment emporium in the world. Even if – like me and many other people – you are no great fan of Beate Uhse and her products, I am sure that you will come to admire her, once you know more about her.

German-born Beate Uhse had always been ambitious. At 15, she won the regional javelin championship in her native Hessen. She left school at 16 because she wanted to fly airplanes – a remarkable career choice for a girl of her time. She was still only 17, the only female in her class among 59 men, when she went on her first training flight. "After 213 take-offs and landings, as well as target-approach and high-altitude flights and a long-distance flight over 300 kilometers, I got my A2 pilot's license in October 1937. It arrived by registered mail on my 18th birthday at my home in Wargenau."[113]

In August 1938, she passed her stunt-pilot test after having already won second place a month earlier in the reliability test-flight for female amateur pilots. Three weeks later, she placed first in her category and second in the overall ranking in an air race in Belgium. When she was offered a work placement in the Buecker aircraft plant, her father was "utterly appalled": "His daughter amongst 2,000 male production workers and mechanics, the only female on the factory floor. He didn't like it at all."[114]

Needing pilots for stunt work, the UFA film production company approached the company where Beate Uhse worked. One day she was asked to fly a stunt for her idol, the actor Hans Albers, in one of his 'Watch out, here I come' roles. Towards the end of the war, she flew in the Luftwaffe's aircraft ferrying squadron. On April 22, 1945 she was the last woman to fly out of Berlin when the Red Army invaded the German capital. "At 5:55 a.m., we tried our luck. The plane was totally overloaded."[115] Her plane was hit but she was lucky – the damage was only to the undercarriage fairing. "We were climbing slowly, torturously slow. But we made it, we escaped from the beleaguered city. We were the last people to get out by plane."[116]

After the war, she ended up in a prisoner of war camp with her son, who was born in 1943 when she was 24. Her first husband had died in a plane crash shortly after his birth. Uhse herself was severely injured in an accident while still in the POW camp. "No job, no money, no parents, no husband, no home anymore – and now I might be crippled for the rest of my life. Survived the war, only for this to happen after three days of peace. My private reckoning: a disaster."[117] How on Earth, she wondered, was she going to support herself and her child?

Within a short period of time, she was approached for help by three female friends, all of whom had become pregnant when their husbands returned from the war. In the immediate aftermath of the war, when everybody was struggling to survive, most couples did not want a child. They wanted to know how to prevent unwanted pregnancies – condoms were not available at the time and the contraceptive pill was another 15 years in the making.

Beate Uhse sat down in front of her typewriter and designed a brochure, which for want of a better title she called Schrift X (Document X). In it, she described the Knaus-Ogino method of contraception, which is based on the different phases of the menstrual cycle. In exchange for five pounds of butter (money was worth nothing in those days), a printer volunteered to produce a print run of 2,000 brochures and 10,000 mail circulars. It all went according to plan. Selling her brochure for one deutsche mark apiece, she received plenty of orders. In 1947, she already had sold a whopping 37,000 copies.

"More and more customers wrote to me to ask if I couldn't get items for them which had existed before the war, meaning condoms and sex-ed books, titles like van de Velde's *The Perfect Marriage* or *Love Without Fear* ... I was a babe in the woods, a complete innocent, when I started my trade."[118]

She started selling sex-education books and condoms through her new company. "I was living hand-to-mouth. Whenever there was a little money, I got new promotional material printed, copied out addresses from telephone directories which I had organized and sent out letters advertising our range of products."[119]

Her new partner was very supportive. "He told me about his terrible time in Russian captivity. In order not to go mad, he had focused all his thoughts on a single project: In his head, he had founded and run a mail-order business."[120] Although he had never intended to enter the adult-entertainment industry – his idea had been to sell hair tonics – the new company certainly benefited from these plans.

However, at the time anything to do with sexuality was a taboo subject. Soon Uhse was summoned by the police for the first time. "On May 25, on your own initiative, you sent a brochure containing obscene material to Professor Such-and-such. Why?"[121] One day, three policemen came to see her to write down the addresses of 72 customers who had ordered condoms. She was charged straight away. The prosecution argued that there was a possibility the condoms had been sent to customers who were not married. Since the law prohibited sexual intercourse between unmarried couples, selling condoms to unmarried customers was considered aiding and abetting fornication. Fortunately, she was able to prove that each and every one of the 72 men who had bought condoms from her was married.

The prosecutor's office kept filing new charges against her. She was accused of "artificially over-stimulating" her customers' sex drives. One attorney in the prosecutor's office in particular had trained his sights on her. He expostulated: "In advertising psychology, the fact that desire, i.e. a feeling of lack, can be artificially stimulated is a well-known phenomenon. The average American is convinced he would not be able to achieve anything without the aid of chewing gum. Fashion is a result of the same phenomenon. That is where the greatest danger of erotic writing lies: The emotional compass is distorted and value coordinates start shifting."[122]

Times were different then. Beate Uhse received thousands of letters asking her for advice in sexual matters. One of the questions was: "I would like my wife to get on top but she refuses because she thinks it would be unnatural. Is it?"[123]

Beate Uhse had obviously hit a gold mine with her business idea. By 1953, her company had 14 employees and a turnover of 365,000 deutsche marks. One year later it passed the half-million mark, climbing steadily to 822,000 deutsche marks in 1955, 1.3 million in 1956 and two million in 1957. In 1958, the figure rose by another 64%. The company now had over 600,000 customers and 59 employees.

But the prosecutor's office would not give up. Beate Uhse had extended her range to nude photography – harmless images by today's standards. The prosecutor examined each photograph conscientiously. He was looking for a particular facial expression that he referred to as a "lewd smile." Unlike more noncommittal expressions, lewd smiles were punishable by law because they constituted an act of "solicitation to commit fornication." But this time, Beate Uhse was lucky – having inspected the evidence, the judge found in her favor: "Try as I might, I can detect no differences between the ladies' facial expressions."[124]

The Catholic church railed against Beate Uhse, too. The Cologne diocese provided forms that churchgoers could use to press charges against her for the unsolicited delivery of licentious material. One claimant described his ordeal to the court: "When I came home, there was a letter in the hallway. When I touched it, I could feel evil." What did evil feel like, the judge wanted to know. "Well, now, you can sense it … As soon as I opened the letter, I saw filth. I threw it in the garbage straight away."[125] However, the judge argued that the claimant could hardly have felt offended by the contents of a brochure he had not even looked at. Beate Uhse was acquitted on all 82 counts.

In 1962, Beate Uhse opened her "specialist shop for marital hygiene" in the northern German city of Flensburg. It was the world's first stockist of erotic articles. Fearing opposition from the good citizens of Flensburg, she waited until just before Christmas – in the season of peace people might be less inclined towards violent protest, she thought. In the next few years, she turned over millions upon millions and expanded in many countries worldwide. In May 1990, the company went public. There was such a run on the shares that Commerzbank, which was in charge of the initial public offering, had to bring the end of the subscription period forward by four days. Even so, the shares were over-subscribed by 63 times, and went up by 80% on the very first day. Beate Uhse died just two years after the IPO. In the years that followed, the company's stock price steadily declined and competition from internet-based rivals proved too much to overcome. As a result, the company was forced to register its insolvency in 2017. Nevertheless, the company still exists today, simply under a different name.

'Rebelliousness' and the courage to be different were hallmarks of Coco Chanel's life, too. The French fashion designer was born Gabrielle Chanel in 1883, the illegitimate daughter of a door-to-door salesman. After her mother's death when she was only two years old, she grew up in an orphanage. She was nicknamed Coco for two songs she sang during her unsuccessful stunt as a chanteuse, "Ko Ko Ri Ko" and "Qui qu'a vu Coco."

Between 1906 and 1910, she lived in Royallieu in the Compiègne region. This was when she started designing hats for her female friends and eventually opened her own shop. Thanks to her lover, rich British mine owner Boy Capel, who gave her a loan and a guarantee, she was able to open her first fashion boutique in Paris. Only five years later, she had 300 seamstresses working for her and, much to Capel's surprise, paid back the money he had lent her. Now she was truly independent – free at last!

Twenty years later, she had 4,000 employers and was selling catwalk fashion globally. And in 1955, she was awarded the fashion Oscar for the "most influential fashion designer of the twentieth century." She was also the only representative of the fashion industry to make it into *Time* magazine's top 100 most influential people of the twentieth century. The original bottle of

Chanel No. 5, the perfume she created in 1921, is on permanent exhibition in the Museum of Modern Art in New York.

The clothes she designed were revolutionary. Chanel created a new functional style with clean lines and no frills. "And for the first time," her biographer emphasizes, "a revolution in feminine attire, far from following any whims or caprices, consisted essentially and unavoidably in abolishing them."[126]

In the 1920s, she invented the 'little black dress.' The Chanel tweed suit became the uniform of business women all over the world. Her designs flew in the face of all convention – and yet they were perfectly suited to the spirit of the time. "Creation is an artistic gift, a collaboration of the couturier with his or her times," Chanel says.[127] Her skirts were so short as to be considered scandalous at the time, she dressed women in trousers, shoes with ankle straps and knitted swimsuits. She broke another taboo by using jersey fabrics to show off the female body.

Soon there were copy-cats who tried to imitate her style. Where another fashion designer would have been outraged, Chanel was pleased. The fact that others would even want to copy her designs she saw as proof of their popularity. "But of course: once an invention has been revealed it is destined for anonymity. I would be unable to exploit all my ideas and it's a great pleasure to me to discover them realized by others, sometimes more successfully than me."[128] The fear of plagiarism was a sign of "laziness ... unimaginative taste ... lack of faith in creativity," Chanel adds.

Coco Chanel was as successful as she was because she had the courage to be different. "No intrusion of culture or erudition in the style she created, no historical reminiscences," as her biographer puts it. "Her creative act was a subversive act."[129] Her private life, as well as the fashion she created, was testimony of the courage to resist norms and conventions. She had countless affairs with men but never married. Rebelling against all conventions, she simply sensed the spirit of the times before others did. Her predecessors, Chanel claimed, "hid away, like tailors, at the back of their shops, whereas I lived a modern life, I shared the habits, the tastes and the needs of those whom I dressed."[130]

Embodying 'modern life' and daring to be different – if that was Coco Chanel's motto, it was shared by another woman born 75 years later. With 350 million records sold, Madonna is the most successful pop star in the world. However, she is more than just a pop star. In June 2007, Forbes nominated her the third most influential person in the world. Even at the age of 60, she is still earning $75 million a year, more than other successful musicians such as Lady Gaga or Beyoncé. With a fortune of $600 million, Madonna is one of the richest musicians in the world.

Her success certainly wasn't due to any extraordinary musical talent. Camille Barbonne, her manager who paved the way for her early successes, commented: "She had just enough skill to write a song or play guitar. She had a wonderful sense of lyric, however ... But more than anything, it was her personality and that she was a great performer."[131]

Anthony Jackson, a session musician who has worked with Madonna, says: "She knows she's not the greatest singer, but she knows how to get the music down. She's got style, and a way of choosing songs and guiding the way they go."[132] Before playing the title role in the screen adaptation of Andrew Lloyd Webber's musical *Evita*, she had to take professional singing lessons for three months because Lloyd Webber had insisted on recording the soundtrack live with an orchestra. Her rendition of the ballad *You Must Love Me* would win her an Oscar in 1997.

When she was taking singing lessons in the fall of 1995, Madonna was already one of the best-known and most successful female artists in the world. She had achieved this much by embodying the dreams and the self-perceptions of many women of today. Although regarded as a radical feminist and proud of it, she has nothing in common with those feminists who take an aggressive stance against men and reject heterosexuality. The question of whether Madonna was 'one of us' or whether she was a 'traitor to the cause' was the subject of many a heated debate in feminist publications. Feminine and desirable, yet strong, belligerent and self-confident, Madonna refused to fit into any simplistic categories.

Her very resistance to conventional roles made her the template for women's longings and desires. Texan folklorist Kay Turner's book *I Dream of Madonna* bears witness to this. Women from various age groups and social backgrounds talk about what Madonna means to them. Some see her as a liberator, others as a comrade-in-arms, a seductress, or simply as the only woman who really 'gets' them. In her 400-page biography of Madonna, Lucy O'Brien says: "She has an everywoman quality, and what was remarkable at the time was the extent of her influence."[133]

Madonna was born in 1958. At just five years of age, her mother died. In high school, she became interested in drama and decided to become a dancer. She started studying dance at the University of Michigan but then dropped out, much to her father's distress. When he tried to talk her into continuing her education, she shouted: "Stop trying to run my life for me!" and threw a plate of spaghetti against the wall.[134]

Madonna moved to New York with $30 in her pocket. She worked as a waitress and modeled for nude photographs. "She was a street-savvy kid who'd pick up someone to go home with if she was hungry and needed a meal," Barbonne says. Madonna claims not to have felt exploited because "I let them take advantage of me."[135]

Above all else, she wanted to become famous. "She'd do anything to be a star," says her ex-boyfriend, DJ Mark Kamins. "She was on a mission."[136] British musician Dick Witts remembers Madonna being "brash in her lust for fame."[137]

What exactly she wanted to be famous for she did not know herself. At 19, she wanted to be an acclaimed dancer, later on she pictured herself as a successful actress, until she finally discovered that music was the most promising ticket to superstardom. Music, Madonna said, is "the main vector of celebrity. When it's a success its impact is just as strong as a bullet hitting the target."[138]

A journalist who interviewed Madonna early on in her career said of her: "She had long-sightedness, she was clear about where she was going ... She struck me as someone who was ultra-determined in an almost 1980s yuppie 'Greed is Good' way." In the interview, Madonna talked about producers, about markets, about who she wanted to work with in years to come. "She was thinking ahead all the time."[139] Interviewed on *American Bandstand* in January 1984, she predicted: "I'm going to rule the world."[140]

Madonna used deliberate provocation as a means to become famous. In her stage show, she often linked sexual and religious imagery in order to cause outrage. The Catholic church obliged by repeatedly calling for boycotts of her concerts. The Canadian police threatened to arrest her on an obscenity charge. In 1992, her book of erotic photography, which she simply titled *Sex*, caused a major controversy. It was published in a limited edition of a million copies on October 22 and sold out immediately. Commercially, Madonna's provocative book was a huge success and it brought her into the spotlight of the media, but her audiences took affront and started staying away from her shows. With her popularity at an "all-time low,"[141] she was accused of courting scandal for scandal's sake. Her book was regarded as the expression of a deeply disturbed psyche.

Unlike other artists who thrive on provocation, Madonna has always been willing to concede some ground rather than fight an unwinnable war of attrition. Whenever she felt she had gone too far, she would appease her mainstream audience by performing innocent acts like her "Girlie Show" tour in 1993.

Madonna has always understood the importance of reinventing herself and changing her image constantly to avoid being type-cast. After her successful album debut, she tried something completely different, much to the chagrin of her record label, Warner Brothers. Jimmy Bralower, who played drums on the *Like A Virgin* album, explains: "When you have three hits in a certain vein, you do the same thing again. If it ain't broke, don't fix it. Madonna was bucking all normal trends, she was fighting trends."[142]

She shed the funk influences of her debut in favor of radio-friendly pop numbers such as *Like a Virgin*. Later on, she would increasingly incorporate jazz or soul elements into her music and borrow ideas from hip hop. Like the Rolling Stones, she constantly adapted to new trends in popular music, rather than releasing the same album over and over again.

This approach required a good deal of courage. During live performances, her audiences kept wanting to hear their favorite hits but Madonna would rarely grant them their requests. Her career has always been a tight-rope walk between provocation and mainstream, between riding popular trends and assuming an attitude of avant-gardist disdain. She has often been accused of 'stealing' from other musicians and has been involved in numerous lawsuits. She has always adapted different influences and has not been afraid of copying what worked for other artists.

Above all, she has always been willing to learn new things, and has never stayed in the same place for long. Pat Leonard, who has worked with Pink Floyd and Michael Jackson amongst others, recalls: "At one point, she asked to do some vocal take-downs with me, her and the vocal coach. Some singers feel they don't have to do much, but she did."[143]

Her eagerness to learn, to change, to develop, to try out new things and break with conventions and taboos has stood Madonna in good stead throughout her career, helping her to achieve her dreams of fame and riches more successfully than any other woman of her time.

Those who dare to be different have a very different perspective on crises and problems, too. Where others despair and panic, they thrive on unprecedented opportunity. They have the strength not to become affected by the general mood and they enjoy doing things differently from everybody else. That's why they succeed and prosper.

People who have the courage to be different also evaluate crises very differently from the majority. In situations that terrify most people, they flourish and see special opportunities. Arnold Schwarzenegger certainly knows how to handle a crisis, as his biographer concludes: "Schwarzenegger has always been able to turn problems into opportunities. During the economic crisis of the 1970s, real estate speculations made him a millionaire. The Californian budget crisis made him governor, the ecological crisis secured him a second term ... Schwarzenegger, the profiteer."[144]

Prince Alwaleed, sometimes referred to as the "Warren Buffett of the Middle East," is another prime example. Born in Saudi Arabia in March 1957, the investor became one of the 50 richest men in the world, with an estimated fortune of just over $15 billion in 2018. The cornerstone of Alwaleed's fortune was not oil, but real estate deals and development projects. In the late 1980s, he found a large undeveloped piece of land in the Olaya district of Riyad. Apart from the odd shop selling jewelry or electric items, there wasn't much happening in that part of town at the time. Prince Alwaleed contacted the owners but they were asking the equivalent of $1,600 per square meter, which he thought was too much.

When the Iraqis invaded Kuwait in 1990, the entire region was in a state of panic. Fearing that Saudi Arabia might be the next target, many investors withdrew their capital from the country. Real estate prices started plummeting and Alwaleed was able to buy the land he wanted for $533 per square meter, a third of the original asking price. He used a third of the area to build the tallest building in the whole of Europe, the Middle East and Africa, which he named Kingdom Centre. The rest he sold four years later at a 400% profit. Although he was happy that the previous owners had sold him the land at such a good price, he did not really understand why they had done so: "What did they think – America was not going to defeat Saddam?!"[145]

This would become his strategy, which he applied again and again – he always saw crises as opportunities for successful investment. In the early 1990s, Canary Wharf, the largest real estate project in Europe at the time, was under development in east London. Unfortunately, when the new office complex occupying more than 34 hectares was finished, real estate and rental prices had plummeted to a low and because of the lack of infrastructure in that part of London, no investors were interested in 160,000 square meters of empty office space at the London docks. Paul Reichmann, the initiator of the ambitious project, lost his investment.

Alwaleed bought a 6% share in the Canary Wharf company and made Reichmann chairman of the board. Four years later, the real estate company went public. The shares reached their highest price in 2000. In January 2001, Alwaleed sold two-thirds of his stake in the company, which had originally cost him $66 million, for $204 million. Over five years, he had made an average annual profit of 47.7%. His investments in Apple and Murdoch in the late 1990s, when both companies were in severe financial trouble, also made him several hundred million dollars.

Alwaleed made his largest investment in 1991 after the stock market value of Citigroup, for a time the largest bank in the United States, had dropped to a low. He invested $800 million in the distressed company, the biggest investment of any individual shareholder. The value of his share rose to $10 billion before dropping drastically during the financial crisis in 2008.

One man who made a lot of money by swimming against the tide is Jim Rogers, one of the best-known investors in the world. He studied history and philosophy at Yale and Oxford before he took a job on Wall Street in 1968. He succeeded in laying the foundations for his wealth and success during what proved to be hard times for the U.S. stock market.

Rogers met George Soros at the Arnhold and S. Bleichroeder investment bank and went on to found the Quantum Fund with him. Although hedge funds are common today, at the time theirs was one of only a handful. Bonds were far more popular than shares, while large-scale investments in commodities or currencies were almost unheard of. Moreover, most Americans invested almost exclusively in domestic securities and showed little interest in other countries. Short-selling, too, was far less common at the time than it is today.

Rogers and Soros tore up the rule book, buying shares, commodities, currencies and bonds from all over the world and resorting to strategies such as short-selling. They made investments nobody else would have dreamt of at the time and discovered new and interesting markets worldwide.

Defying received wisdom, Rogers frequently bought shares in companies that were in dire straits. In the mid-seventies, for example, he bought vast amounts of shares in the aircraft manufacturer Lockheed. He told me the story of a typical encounter at a fancy dinner with bankers and investors. One of them had got wind of the fact that Rogers had been buying Lockheed shares – at a time when the company was embroiled in a number of scandals that made negative headlines on an almost daily basis and had already seen its share price plummet. "Who would invest in companies like that?" he wondered aloud – loudly enough to make sure everybody could hear him. The other guests were laughing with him. Rogers felt humiliated – after all, he was the butt of their joke.

"He who laughs last, laughs longest" – the old adage would hold true once more. Rogers had done his homework and his positive analysis of the company's prospects was to prove completely on the mark. Subsequently the share price shot up and his fund made a huge profit. During a period when the S&P 500 Index only rose by 47%, the Quantum fund managed by Rogers and Soros climbed by a staggering 4,200%. "When other people are laughing at you," Rogers says, "you know you're going in the right direction. The more people are laughing at you, the more likely you'll turn out to be right."

"When I was a young man," he told me, "that wasn't easy for me. I didn't necessarily enjoy going against the tide and when everybody tells you you're wrong, you're bound to start doubting yourself even if you do get a kick out of being in a minority of one." Even he has had times when he was unable to escape being affected by the general panic. For example, he had been short-selling oil in the immediate run-up to the war between Iran and Iraq. When war broke out and the oil price shot up, he got caught up in the general panic and closed his positions. This proved to be a mistake, as the oil price was to drop sharply later on.

Over time, as Rogers became more experienced, he was less bothered by other people's jibes. "I realized the importance of sticking to my guns and believing in an analysis I knew to be correct even if things seem to be going against me at first," Rogers says. "Today it's more likely to be the other way round: if everybody suddenly agrees with me, I start doubting whether I'm right or whether it might be time to start selling."

In the 1980s, *Time* magazine dubbed him the "Indiana Jones of Wall Street" because he invested in countries that were unknown territories to most Americans. "I'd buy shares in Portugal, Austria, in African countries and South America. Ninety-nine per cent of U.S. investors hardly knew these markets existed. Most didn't even invest in Germany. I bought Siemens shares instead of General Electric – and I was right about that too," Rogers says.

In the late 1990s, at the height of the 'new economy' boom, the prestigious Wall Street firm Merrill Lynch closed down its commodities trading department. At a time when investing in internet start-ups was all the rage, few people were interested in commodities. Rogers, on the other hand, had long taken an interest in the commodities market. In the same year Merrill Lynch closed its commodities operations, Rogers set up the Rogers International Commodity Index (RICI), which is today the best-known commodities index worldwide.

"Your success in life and on the stock market depends on your ability to anticipate change," Rogers states. He had realized that the collapse of communism and the economic rise of China and other emerging markets would lead to an enormous demand for commodities while supply would continue to decrease. From 1990 to 1992, Rogers and his girlfriend went on a two-year motorbike trip around the world, covering 100,000 miles on six continents and making it into the *Guinness Book of Records*. His record of that trip in his book *Investment Biker* makes fascinating reading. Between January 1, 1995 and January 5, 2002, Rogers went on another round-the-world trip with his wife, this time covering 150,000 miles in 116 countries.

Whenever young people ask him for his advice on the best way to become successful, he tells them to follow in his footsteps and study history and philosophy. "They then reply: but I want to make money and become rich, like you did. They really think studying economics will help them get there." Rogers finds their naivety amusing. "Studying history has helped me understand that everything changes all the time, that everything is in flux. Things are happening today that most people wouldn't have believed possible even 30 or 40 years ago. The collapse of the Soviet Union, the American decline, the unstoppable rise of China, the worldwide web – who would have been able to predict any of that? Permanent change is the only historical constant," says Rogers. "And understanding that is more important for your success as an investor than any detailed knowledge they'll teach you in economics classes at university."

Studying philosophy was equally useful, he claims. "It helped me to develop a healthy scepticism. You can't take everything at face value, not even if the media and pundits keep repeating it over and over again. Think for yourself, have the courage of your convictions and get to the bottom of things, even if you go against conventions and prevailing opinions," Rogers says.

In December 2007, Rogers sold his luxury townhouse in New York City for over $16 million and left the U.S. for Singapore, where he still lives today. When I met him there in 2013, he told me that Asia was the place to be today, just as London had once been in the 19th century and New York in the 1920s. The future, he said, was not in the U.S. or in Europe, but in Asia, and he wanted his two children, who were born when he was already in his sixties, to grow up speaking Mandarin.

When I first met Jim Rogers, we got along so well because we both recognized the importance of swimming against the tide. In my autobiography, I detail my investments in the Berlin real estate market. Here's an example of how I turned zero euros into four million euros – because I was willing to swim against the tide.[146] In 2004, I bought a building with 24 apartments in the then unfashionable district of Berlin-Neukölln. Everyone at the time advised me against it – except the estate agent Jürgen-Michael Schick, who sold it to me and brokered it to another investor 11 years later for four times the price. When I told my acquaintances, who included many real estate experts, that I wanted to buy an apartment building in Neukölln, they were unanimously negative. Deutsche Bank even turned down my financing application because they considered Neukölln too risky a location.

It's worth looking back through some old newspapers, because today, with the Berlin residential real estate market widely regarded as the most attractive in Europe, it's hard to imagine how absurd an investment in Berlin-Neukölln had to seem at that time. The Berlin *Tagesspiegel* of March 20, 2002 reported on a "Berlin Future Panel" organized by the German Institute for Economic Research (DIW). The DIW stated that while Germany was regarded as bringing up the rear in terms of growth in Europe, within Germany, Berlin was even further behind. Tourism was in decline and retail sales had collapsed. The *Berliner Morgenpost* of August 22, 2003 stated that the vacancy rate on the Berlin housing market had "risen to record levels." A total of 160,000 apartments were vacant. There was a dispute between the building senator, Peter Strieder (SPD), and Gernot Klemm of the left-wing PDS: According to the newspaper, they were arguing about whether the oversupply of housing meant that they should demolish some of the city's post-war, prefabricated buildings, or whether it also made sense to also demolish pre-war apartment buildings in the city center, as the PDS demanded.

On February 10, 2004 the leading specialist journal for the German real estate industry published an article on the city's 130,000 vacant apartments under the headline: "Berlin housing market under pressure." The newspaper referred to a study from a bank which reported that property prices for owner-occupied homes were still falling. The bankers predicted that prices would continue to fall in typical residential neighborhoods. Condominiums were selling for between €1,000 and €5,000 per square meter, but 'almost nobody' wanted to buy newly built apartments, or apartments with more than two rooms.

In November 2004, *Spiegel TV* reported: "Neukölln is regarded as the poorhouse of Berlin. The district has more than 300,000 inhabitants, but almost a quarter of them are unemployed. This is the area with the highest density of social welfare recipients in Europe." The headline of the *Berliner Zeitung* in January 2004 was: "Neukölln – On the brink of being ungovernable." And *Die Welt* ran an article on September 9, 2004: "Neukölln: Center of Poverty – Welfare is the new normal."

Hadn't I read the newspapers and the negative research reports about Berlin at the time? Yes, I had. But I was convinced that the bad news and opinions were more than priced in. The apartment building in Neukölln was extremely cheap, precisely because nobody else wanted to buy it. Real estate prices are calculated according to a price-to-rent ratio that divides the price by the annual net cold rent. The annual net cold rent amounted at that time was €151,000, and I acquired the property for €1.02 million. That was actually a bargain price, because I bought it for a price-to-rent ratio of 6.8, or with a gross initial yield of almost 15%!

Including the costs for the broker and the land transfer tax as well as for initial maintenance measures, I paid a total of €1.22 million. Fortunately,

I had a clever banker, who understood that what a bargain this was and that I could not go wrong with this investment. The bank lent me €1.164 million to cover the purchase and the acquisition costs, as well as another €78,000 to modernize the building. Altogether, they lent me €1.24 million, €27,000 more than I needed for the purchase, acquisition costs and the modernization. So, I bought the property with zero equity.

However, I did agree to a very high initial repayment rate of 6%. The residual debt by the end of March 2015 was just €224,000. With prices on the Berlin real estate market skyrocketing, and some investors paying sums that I simply could not understand, I decided to sell the building, for which I received €4.2 million. In the ten years I held the property, I had raised the rents only moderately, but while I had bought the apartment building in 2004 at 6.8 times the annual net cold rent, I was able to sell it at a price-to-rent ratio of 24 in 2015. So, this is how I managed to turn zero euros into four million euros in about ten years. It was an extraordinary real estate investment, the kind that only rarely succeeds. Nevertheless – or even precisely for this reason – there is a great deal you can learn from this investment.

When you buy a property, as with any other investment, you need a vision of the future. At the beginning of the millennium, like others, I saw the problems on the Berlin real estate market: high vacancy rates, stagnating and falling rents. At the same time, however, I also saw the inherent opportunities. As early as April 18, 2000 I published an article in *Die Welt* with the headline: "Prices will double in ten years." In view of the gloomy state of the market – the article referred to price slumps of up to 50% for apartments in mid-market residential areas – there were few who accepted my assessment.

But I had logic on my side: "There is a housing shortage on the horizon," I argued in my article, "because housing construction and modernizations in Berlin have always been tax-driven. When the special depreciation allowance expires at the end of 1998, for the first time ever, investors will have to survive without specific tax advantages. However, given the fact that rents are so low, this is often not worth it." My conclusion: the supply of housing would decline and rents and prices would rise significantly in the medium to long term.

It's never easy to identify the perfect time for an investment. When prices are down, I feel pretty safe. As soon as they start to rise and the mood turns, I become nervous. Neukölln is a good example. The boom there began a few years ago. From price-to-rent ratios of between nine and ten, prices initially rose to 12–13 times net annual cold rent. That seemed too expensive to me: "Would I be crazy to buy at a ratio of 13 in Neukölln? That's almost twice as much as I paid first time around!" But my reluctance to pay higher prices was thoroughly wrong. What I wasn't expecting was that prices would keep on rising, year in year out and even explode. If I had bought at that time at a ratio of 13, I could probably sell again today at more than twice the price.

However, this is something that contrarian investors simply have to accept. As a contrarian investor, it is highly likely that you will sell prematurely and then watch prices continue to rise. Or you will stop buying before prices have bottomed out. But I did not regret it for a second, that's not my mentality. I think we all have enough to do with dealing with the present and planning for the future, and it would be a waste of energy to worry about missed opportunities that will never reappear. The experience I made with my small-scale investments has been repeated time and again by the big investors.

For contrarian investors, crises and collapses offer golden opportunities. At a time when other investors are busy licking their wounds, contrarians prosper. There is never a better time to buy than during the panic of a market crash. Warren Buffett sometimes spends years observing a particular company whose business strategy he likes, waiting for an opportunity to buy the company at a good price. During times of rising stock market prices and general euphoria, these opportunities are rare. During times of rising despair and general malaise, when shareholders are trying to get rid of their stock as fast as possible – that's when contrarian investors grab their chances.

To a man like Warren Buffett, even tragedies such as the 9/11 attacks present themselves as opportunities. Ajit Jain, the manager of his insurance interests, immediately started selling insurance cover against terror attacks, filling a gap in the market that the destruction of the World Trade Center had made tragically evident. Jain insured the Rockefeller Center and the Chrysler Building in Manhattan, a South American oil refinery, an oil platform in the North Sea and the Sears Tower in Chicago. Buffett's Berkshire company even insured the Olympic Games against the risk of cancellation or non-participation of American athletes. The Winter Olympics in Salt Lake City were covered by Berkshire policies, as was the soccer World Cup.

Buffett was no less shocked by the atrocities than other Americans. However, he did not let personal outrage get in the way of his business interests. "Cash combined with courage in a crisis is priceless," he says.[147]

Fund manager John Paulson certainly shares Buffett's beliefs. While the majority of Americans kept counting on rising house prices, Paulson saw early on that in the years of cheap credit in the wake of the 9/11 attacks, a real estate bubble was expanding to gigantic proportions and waited impatiently for it to burst.

He wasn't the only one to realize that the bubble would burst. But he was one of only a few people who started thinking about how to cash in on this knowledge. Which financial instruments might be used to bet on the outcome he predicted? When was the right moment to start betting? How to win other investors at a time when everybody else was still full of euphoria about the future of the real estate market?

Paulson first tried profiting from dropping share prices by short-selling shares of companies engaged in real estate development. When this strategy failed, Paulson and some fellow investors started looking for a better way of profiting more directly from the expected slump in real estate prices.

They eventually decided on so-called CDS contracts, which insured bundles of subprime mortgages against default of payment. Since most market players did not believe in a default, insurance premiums were ridiculously low.

Investors who bought these subprime mortgages blindly relied on the evaluations of rating agencies, which were in turn based on calculations of the risk of default. But Paulson was not so easily fooled. He knew that these calculations were based on historical data from a time when house prices were still on the rise and the percentage of subprime mortgages offered to home owners with a dubious credit rating was much lower. He doubted that reliable predictions for the future were possible on the basis of these data.

At first, Paulson had great difficulty finding investors who were willing to bet on the real estate bubble bursting. Most investors do not pursue a contrarian strategy – in fact, it would be a contradiction in terms if they did. Once he had finally raised enough capital, he was faced with another problem. Instead of rising as other market players started recognizing the risk of default, as he had hoped, prices for CDS contracts kept falling. Many of his investors started questioning his strategy and wanted their money back.

Paulson would not budge. He studied the mortgage market inside and out, constantly on the lookout for bad credit ratings and high-risk mortgages, the ones systematically ignored by more optimistic market players. He spent a lot of time on identifying the local real estate markets in the United States where speculation and questionable mortgage-lending practices had led to the worst excesses.

U.S. banks had indiscriminately granted mortgages to people who had neither income nor capital, sometimes without even asking for proof of income. Interest rates on these mortgages remained extremely low for the first two years, but rose sharply from then on. It was a gamble that paid off only for as long as interest rates were low and house prices continued to rise.

Paulson did not think this could go on for much longer. He was convinced that sooner or later, many of these mortgage holders would default on their payments. His strategy paid off in the long run. When the real estate bubble did burst, triggering a global financial and economic crisis, investors in his fund made $20 billion from what the majority of market players perceived as a catastrophe of unprecedented dimensions. Paulson himself took a 20% share, $4 billion. There is a book about him called *The Greatest Trade Ever* – it really was the greatest deal ever made in the history of finance.

Recognizing an opportunity in what others perceive as a crisis takes particular mental strength. You have to have the courage to act against popular opinion. No matter how convinced you are of your own strategy, you are bound to start doubting yourself at some point: is it really the majority of others who are in the wrong, or have I become fixated on something to a point where I cannot see the flaws in my own thinking? Or might it be possible that I really have realized something the majority of market players haven't yet noticed?

The ability to swim against the tide is something all successful entrepreneurs and investors have in common. When Howard Schultz was devising a strategy for the expansion of Starbucks on a national level, he could have found countless good reasons why his plans were far too ambitious and unrealistic. "From Day One, Starbucks was bucking the odds."[148] Seattle, where Starbucks originated, was in the grip of a severe recession in the early 1970s. Boeing, the city's largest employer, lost so much business the company was forced to reduce its workforce from 100,000 to 38,000 over the course of three years. Many people moved away. Around the time Starbucks opened its first shop, a billboard near the airport quipped: "Will the last person leaving Seattle – turn out the lights?"

In any case, it was hardly an auspicious moment to create a coffee chain. Overall coffee consumption in the U.S. had been dropping steadily for the previous decade. If the founders of Starbucks had commissioned a focus-group study, the result would have been discouraging. But they weren't interested in market research and did not waste time on finding reasons why their idea was bound to fail. Of course, it makes sense to weigh the pros and cons of any goal you have set for yourself. But unless you actually try it out, you'll never know whether your plan will work or not. Trying and failing is far better than not trying at all – if you don't try, you have already failed.

Adverse conditions can be regarded as opportunities, too. Take the history of Google, which was undoubtedly part of the internet hype in the late 1990s. At the time, many prophets predicted the dawn of the age of cyberspace. New companies were formed on a daily basis, most of which would end up losing huge sums of money. In 2000, about 18 months after Google was founded, the dot-com bubble burst. The market reacted as it always does – excessively. Suddenly anything to do with the internet was regarded as risky business, leading to mass redundancies in Silicon Valley. Fortunately, Google founders Larry Page and Sergey Brin proved immune to the general malaise.

Both saw the crisis as a unique opportunity to recruit first-rate talent from other companies at reasonable salaries. Software designers and mathematicians who had previously been unaffordable for a new company like Google, were suddenly begging Page and Brin for jobs. They were able to hire the best and the brightest and their company developed at a speed that would have been unthinkable if it hadn't been for the crisis.

To sum up: successful people have the courage to think and to act differently from the majority. They are self-confident enough to disregard the opinion of others. At times, they may even gain pleasure from acting against mainstream opinion. And even in the midst of a severe crisis – or rather, especially in the midst of a severe crisis – when others feel scared and desperate, they are able to summon the courage to focus on the opportunities brought about by this very crisis.

Some people have trouble accepting that they are different from others. Are you one of those people? If you are, take courage from the fact that few successful people conform to social norms and conventions. On the other hand, some people claim not to care what others think of them. I find that hard to believe. None of us are completely oblivious to the opinion of others. However, there is one important difference: some people can handle rejection and disapproval, others can't. The latter often indicates lack of self-esteem. But if you use the opinion of the majority of those who are unsuccessful as your yardstick, you will remain as unsuccessful as they are. By thinking and acting like everybody else, you will only achieve as much as everybody else. To aim higher than the majority, you must learn to think independently in order to act independently and to achieve more than others.

CHAPTER 6

Learn to Stand Your Ground

Nobody likes arguments. Except for the notorious troublemakers among us, we all try to avoid them. Arguments cost time and energy – in any given situation, always ask yourself whether an issue is worth arguing about or not. However, those of us who avoid arguments at any cost will never move anything or change anything.

At managerial level in particular, there are two different types: the 'cuddly', harmony-seeking boss who would prefer everybody to agree on everything, and who above all wants to be liked by his staff; and the tough, success-oriented executive who is quite prepared to put up with significant clashes of interest in his company for the sake of change and progress.

Jack Welch is a prime example of the second type. In his 20 years as CEO of General Electric (GE) from 1981 to 2001, he increased the company's turnover from $27 billion to $130 billion, while annual profits went up by 600% to $12.7 billion. In late 2000, GE was the most valuable company in the world with a market capitalization of $475 billion. He also reduced GE's workforce of 400,000 employees by a quarter. As you can imagine, his style of leadership led to massive arguments and confrontations. In 1999, Welch was voted "Manager of the Century" by *Fortune* magazine. His leadership principles are well worth examining.

One of Welch's most striking characteristics was his willingness to take on anybody in an argument. Of course, he did not start arguments for the sake of arguing, but he soon realized that the only way forward for the giant yet sclerotic corporation was by changing its structures completely. He knew that in order to make his company fit for the future, he would have to fight against the influences of special interest groups, against nepotism, excessive bureaucracy and laziness.

After he had been made CEO, he was invited to address the Elfun Society, an exclusive gathering of ambitious white-collar workers at GE.

They were in for quite a shock when he started his first speech by saying: "Thank you for asking me to speak. Tonight I'd like to be candid, and I'll start off by letting you reflect on the fact that I have serious reservations about your organization."[149] Never one to mince his words, he explained to his audience that he considered their group to be an outdated concept with which he held no truck. When he had finished, his illustrious audience was speechless.

He shocked them even more by drawing a diagram of three circles denoting the different divisions of the multinational conglomerate. All divisions outside the three circles – including many with long-standing traditions and a lot of employees – were slated for restructuring, sale or closure. This included divisions such as small household appliances, central air-conditioning, television man-ufacturing, audio products and semiconductors, all areas in which Welch did not think GE would be able to hold out against Asian competitors in the long run. The executives and employees working in these divisions were outraged. More than one said: "Am I in a leper colony? That's not what I joined GE to become."[150] In the first two years of Welch's reign alone, he sold 71 divisions and product lines, increasing productivity dramatically but also triggering huge resentment. Many other executives might not have gone ahead with these radical changes in the face of so much opposition.

When Welch sold off the housewares division, he was bombarded with angry letters from outraged employees. "If email had existed," Welch realizes, "every server in the company would have been clogged up." The letters all expressed similar sentiments: "What kind of a person are you? If you do this, it's clear you'll do anything!"[151]

In the space of five years, Welch fired 118,000 employees from unprofitable divisions. "Throughout the company, people were struggling to come to grips with the uncertainty," Welch remembers.[152] Instead of hiding away, he confronted his workforce openly, holding fortnightly round-table discussions with around 25 employees. "I wanted to change the rules of engagement, asking for more – from fewer. I was insisting that we had to have only the best people."[153]

Welch did not just confront the executives and employees of his own company. He also took on union leaders, mayors and politicians who were trying to put pressure on him. On a visit to the governor of Massachusetts, Welch's host voiced his hope that GE would create more jobs in his state. "Governor," Welch replied, "I have to tell you. Lynn is the last place on Earth I would ever put any more work." The plant in Lynn had been the only one to hold out against the national contract GE had signed with the unions. "Why should I put work and money where there is trouble, when I can put up plants where people want them and deserve them?"[154]

Fortune magazine named Welch as number one among the "Ten Toughest Bosses in America." In a feature on him, employees who wished to remain anonymous said: "Working for him is like a war. A lot of people get shot up; the survivors go on to the next battle." The article claimed that being bombarded with questions by Welch was paramount to a physical attack.[155] On the other hand, he was generous with praise, acknowledging good work and rewarding outstanding employees with bonuses.

He refuted any criticism of his 'tough' approach. In his autobiography he even says: "I shouldn't have agonized as long as I did on so many people who weren't going to cut it. The consistent lesson I've learned over the years is that I have been in many cases too cautious. I should have torn down the structures sooner, sold off weak businesses faster than I did."[156]

Welch was equally uncompromising towards employees who did not share the company values, no matter how good the results they achieved. His advice to other executives was not to fire them surreptitiously, using excuses along the lines of "Charles left for personal reasons, to spend more time with his family."[157] Instead, he recommended being upfront about the fact that an employee had been fired for their refusal to comply with the company values. "You can be sure that Charles' replacement will act differently, not to mention anyone else doubting your commitment to the values."[158]

Welch could not stand grumblers who kept complaining about everything that was wrong with the company and about not being valued and appreciated enough. Bosses whose employees acted in this way had only themselves to blame, he claimed, because they had created a culture of entitlement, fostering in their employees "a classic entitlement culture, in which your people have the deal exactly backward. They think you work for them."[159] His advice to 'soft' executives was: "You are running a company, not a social club or a counselling service."[160] He recommended they change the culture within their company as fast as they could, and told them to stand their ground: "Without doubt, you will hear yelps of pain as you dismantle your entitlement culture. Indeed, some employees that you like and value may leave in protest. Take the hit and wish them well."[161]

Above all else, Welch preached a culture of communication. That way, he said, each and every employee knew what was what and whether their performance was up to scratch. Many companies made the mistake of indulging "the very human tendency to soften hard, urgent messages with false kindness or phony optimism."[162] Too many bosses pulled their punches rather than "com[ing] right out and tell[ing] underperformers how badly they are doing until, in a burst of frustration, they fire them."[163] Managers prided themselves on being too 'kind' or too 'nice' to tell their employees "exactly where they stand – in particular, the real losers."[164]

This is because they are not able or not willing to stand their ground. It is easier to avoid arguments than to fight them out. Fighting costs time and energy and often involves risk because the outcome of an argument is always open.

However, most people instinctively sense when they are dealing with somebody who is overly concerned with harmony, consensus and conciliation. They are right to consider this trait a weakness. Seeking harmony is a good thing but as with most good things, you can have too much of it. An exaggerated yearning for harmony usually results from fear. People who are scared of rubbing others the wrong way and are afraid of disagreement and disapproval often suffer from low self-esteem. Lacking the confidence to think that they can win an argument, they avoid arguments altogether. By doing so, they have lost already. People with low self-esteem, who are usually reluctant to stand their ground and engage in confrontation, will rarely win the respect of others. If you consider yourself weak, others will do the same.

In companies with functioning hierarchies, this kind of person will not be promoted to a leading role. After all, who would want to entrust leadership functions to somebody who avoids confrontation and values harmony above all else? Other employees might like that person but they would not respect him or her. How would a boss who wants to be liked by others more than anything else ever be able to enforce the necessary measures, or to conduct open and unpleasant appraisals with employees who are falling short of expectations?

What to do if you are a natural born harmony-seeker? First of all, you need to make an effort to change your nature, secondly you need to hire managers who are willing to engage in confrontation and can compensate for your own weakness. You would be able to delegate these unpleasant tasks to them to a certain extent.

The ability to stand your ground is the precondition for asserting yourself against others. Arnold Schwarzenegger's biographer claims: "He always wants to be different from everybody else, he refuses to assimilate to the world around him and so he creates an environment which assimilates to him rather than the other way around."[165]

Self-help books on dealing with others in the vein of Dale Carnegie's classic *How to Make Friends and Influence People* have traditionally favored a different approach. "The only way to get the best of an argument is to avoid it," Carnegie concludes in a chapter headed: "You Can't Win an Argument."[166] Elsewhere, he advises his readers: "Show respect for the other person's opinion. Never say, 'You're wrong.'"[167]

Carnegie's book contains a lot of useful advice on the do's and don'ts of criticizing people. Many managers would achieve far better results by following his suggestions. Warren Buffett even devised an individual training program on the basis of Carnegie's philosophy – and he went on to become one of the most successful investors and managers of all time. However, people who shy away from confrontation tend to take a one-sided view of Carnegie's advice, using it as an excuse to avoid arguments at any cost. We all know that real life doesn't work that way.

Those in positions of authority are respected only if they have a track record of risking confrontation, if and as necessary, for the sake of doing what needs to be done. That doesn't necessarily mean rising their voices and getting tough but it does mean prioritizing the enforcement of legitimate goals and expectations. If this can be done the gentle way, good for you. But every manager knows that it can sometimes become necessary to voice criticism unequivocally. If you are unable to do so, you will have trouble asserting yourself, leading others and getting their respect.

Books on leadership often paint an unrealistic picture of the successful manager. He or she is always slow to criticize and generous with praise, never raises his or her voice and never dresses an employee down in the presence of others. These ideal entrepreneurs and executives are certainly out there – but just as certainly, they are outnumbered by the vast majority of others who are quite different from the prototype depicted in books and seminars on leadership.

Analyses of successful entrepreneurs have shown that there is a negative side to the ability to engage in arguments: a way of dealing with employees which is far from exemplary, but rather counterproductive since it leads to demoralizing, or even losing, valuable staff members.

Take Bill Gates, one of the most successful entrepreneurs in history. In some respects, he is the exact opposite of the executive championed in books on leadership. Gates was notorious for sending emails to his employees in the middle of the night (often, they would still be at work). A typical missive would start: "This is the stupidest piece of code ever written."[168] His employees referred to them as "flame mail" – they were "blunt and often sarcastic."[169]

Even before he founded Microsoft, he was well known for his tantrums. When he was working with Micro Instrumentation and Telemetry Systems (MITS) he would frequently blow his top. The boss of MITS remembers "him coming into my office that first summer and screaming and yelling at the top of his lungs that everyone was stealing his software, and he was never going to make any money, and he wasn't going to do another thing unless we put him on the payroll."[170]

Like many bosses, Gates lacked patience, and he would often express his impatience in a way that others found offensive. A former Microsoft manager remembers Gates bursting into his office during his very first week with the company, and shouting: "How can you possibly take this much time working on this contract? Just get it done!"[171] In discussions, "he wielded his formidable intellect like a blunt instrument. He could be rude and sarcastic, even insulting, when he wanted to make a point ... Once the flaw was pinpointed, he would rip the person to shreds."[172] Gates would often rock back and forth in his chair, staring into space as if his thoughts were elsewhere. "Then suddenly, when he heard something he didn't like or didn't agree with, he would stop rocking, sit up straight, and become visibly angry, sometimes throwing his pencil. He often yelled or pounded his fist on the table."[173]

A Microsoft line manager remembers: "He would browbeat people. Just imposing your intellectual prowess on somebody doesn't win the battle, and he didn't know that."[174] When one of his managers told him he couldn't simultaneously manage a project and write the code, Gates erupted, slamming his fist on the table and shouting at the top of his voice.[175]

A female employee recalls that aggression was Gates' default setting. "I'd just wait for him to get finished ranting and raving and when he got tired we would talk. He would on occasion send me just rabid emails."[176] To his secretaries, too, he "was often condescending." His temper "was upsetting to staff workers unfamiliar with his confrontational style." Another employee recalls that everybody was "always relieved when he was out of town."[177]

Gates had a strange sense of humor. A visitor to the company remembers: "We were walking out of the building about 8 o'clock at night, and a programmer was just signing out for the day. He said: 'Hey Bill, I've been here for 12 hours.' And Bill looked at him and said, 'Ahhhhh, working half-days again?' It was funny, but you could tell Bill was half-serious."[178]

Although Gates was far from easy to get along with, his employees appreciated the fact that they always knew where they stood with him. Says one member of his staff: "A lot of people don't like their jobs because they don't get any feedback. There was no problem there. You would know exactly what Bill thought of the work you were doing."[179]

And of course, the anecdotes about Gates' notorious temper only tell one side of the story. He knew better than any other entrepreneur how to inspire and motivate his staff to achieve a shared goal. Nobody can get excellent performance from employees only by putting pressure on them. Even though Bill Gates was notorious for his aggressive attitude towards others, he also knew how to encourage his staff by giving them a lot of leeway to develop creatively. The pioneering spirit and inspiring atmosphere at Microsoft attracted many intelligent and ambitious young people to the company.

Bill Gates is not the only business leader to behave in such a seemingly contradictory manner. Rupert Murdoch's biographer claims that the media tycoon with a net worth of $19.2 billion "does not need to be liked – does not, it seems, even like to be liked."[180] He was nevertheless able to motivate his staff to an extremely high degree. "To his employees ... he can be cold, impatient, all business, even cruel. And yet among them there's a sense of excitement and opportunity about working for him – and this at a time before he's done much to suggest great excitement or opportunity."[181]

Apple founder Steve Jobs is another prime example. Working for him, his biographers write, was like being on a seesaw between "finding Steve annoying, frustrating, intolerable, and yet answering his clarion call, marching to the beat of his drum, willingly, even gladly."[182] Jobs did not mind people contradicting him – but "this only applied to people he respected, people who had a real contribution to make and whom he could look upon in certain respects as his equal. For anyone else who tried to talk back to Steve, his time at the company would probably come to an abrupt end."[183]

Some of the rules Jobs insisted on were quite absurd. Writing on the whiteboard was a privilege he reserved for himself alone. When Alvy Ray Smith, who would go on to co-found Pixar, took up a marker pen in violation of this rule, Jobs blew his top, shouting: "'You can't do that!' Alvy was stunned and speechless as Steve leaned into him until their noses almost touched and hurled insults meant to demean, belittle, and wound." Smith quit his job. "He had given it 15 years of his life, but he was willing to give it all up rather than continue to have Steve Jobs in his life."[184] This story shows the damage men like Jobs can do to themselves and their company with their behavior.

Jobs, his biographers say, was surrounded by an "aura of fear … like a dark cloud. You didn't want to be called in front of him to do a product presentation because he might decide to lop off the product, and you with it. You didn't want to encounter him in a hallway because he might not like an answer you gave and would say something so demeaning that it could undermine your confidence for weeks. And you sure as hell didn't want to be trapped in an elevator with him because by the time the doors opened, you might not have a job."[185] But let me repeat: fortunately, this is only one side of the story. Anybody who has ever seen Steve Jobs give one of his electrifying speeches can easily imagine how he has always managed to create an inspiring and challenging atmosphere in his company, motivating his employees to do their very best in spite of his tantrums. However, if you lack Jobs' charisma, you would be well-advised not to test your staff's patience to such an extreme extent.

Working for marketing guru David Ogilvy was no picnic either. As his biographer reports, Ogilvy "had no qualms about imposing his standards." One of his copywriters says: "You had to have the hide of a rhinoceros to survive a meeting with Ogilvy, or have done your homework in depth and executed your strategy impeccably … He was not above the ad hominem method or any other attack that he felt would get through to the sinner. And, like De Gaulle, he felt that praise should be a rare commodity lest you devalue the currency."[186]

When Ogilvy edited something one of his staff had written, it felt, "like being operated on by a great surgeon who could put his hand on the only tender organ in your body. You could feel him put his finger on the wrong word, the soft phrase, the incomplete thought."[187] His brother Francis, who ran the agency before him, was a similar type. "People would come in on Monday morning and find 'From F.O.' notes on their desk: 'You promised a note on ... Pray expedite.' Or 'I asked for ... Pray explain why you have not yet ...'"[188]

Working with billionaire investor George Soros, his employees report, was hard because "you felt like you were constantly being second-guessed." He would treat his staff like high school students who were a bit slow. "It was very easy for him to lose his temper. He had a way of looking at you with such penetrating eyes that you felt you were under a laser gun ... He always felt he wanted you around, but he never thought you were going to get it right: he would just tolerate you, almost like you were a lesser being."[189] So convinced was Soros of his own extraordinary intellectual capacities, he "had a hard time abiding people he thought less gifted."[190]

Ray Kroc, the man behind the success of McDonald's, has been described as "something of a benign corporate dictator" with "the appearance of an autocrat." He had very clear ideas on the standard of grooming he expected from his staff. He hated dirty or chewed fingernails, creased suits, short-sleeve shirts and unkempt hair and could not stand employees who chewed gum, smoked a pipe, read the comic pages, or wore white socks.[191] Kroc believed "that a clean and tidy appearance said something about the strength of someone's character."[192] "He even wanted his employees to keep their automobiles clean."[193] He would sometimes order managers to trim their nose hair or brush their teeth.

Anybody who violated these rules was given the boot. An employee who picked him up at the airport wearing cowboy boots and driving a dirty car was fired on the spot. There were times when Kroc would gladly have fired all his managers – but his anger would pass as quickly as it flared up. One morning, somebody he had sacked the day before was just clearing out his office when Kroc came in and asked him: "What are you doing?" When his employee reminded him that he had been fired the night before, Kroc told him to unpack his stuff and start working.[194] "In fact, most of his 'firings' were never carried out because those designated to perform the deeds realized that the founder was merely venting steam."[195] Kroc "had a temper and was capable of blowing up at any moment," but he was quite willing to listen to reason and admit that he had made a mistake.[196]

Henry Ford, the father of the American automobile industry, was another boss who was not at all interested in harmony. He stuck resolutely to his Model T brand, despite the fact that everyone around him was telling him he needed to move with the times and make changes. When one of his employees took advantage of Ford's absence to start developing a successor model, which he proudly presented upon Ford's return, Ford flipped out, as one witness recounts: "He takes his hands out, gets hold of the door, and bang! He ripped the door right off! God! How the man done it, I didn't know! He jumped in there, and bang goes another door. Bang goes windshield. He jumps over the back seat and starts pounding on the top. He rips the top with the heel of his shoe."[197]

August Oetker, founder of the German food giant Dr. Oetker, was very keen on tidiness and cleanliness and would throw a tantrum if somebody did not abide by his rules. A female employee remembers: "One day, a mat had been moved in a room and you could see that the floor wasn't quite clean underneath. It didn't escape the doctor's notice and he went off on one, using the worst swearwords." A workman who stood on a marble top without taking his shoes off first was sent packing by Oetker himself.[198]

Of course, none of these entrepreneurs were successful *because* of their inconsiderate behavior towards others – but they certainly were successful *in spite of* it. Their willingness to confront others, which is in principle a positive character trait, comes at a price. And don't forget that we might be willing to forgive a charismatic business genius such as Gates or Jobs for some things that would be a lesser man's professional downfall. It is unlikely that somebody in a managerial position would ever climb very high up in the company hierarchy if he or she treated their staff the way Gates or Jobs did. Those who would have the power to promote that person would see him or her as a difficult character who has trouble fitting in and getting on with other employees.

Men like Soros, Jobs or Gates do not have to care about how they are being perceived by their bosses because they are their own bosses. But even Steve Jobs was forced out of his own company for many years largely because of his style of leadership. Other entrepreneurs have escaped a similar fate only because they own the company and cannot be fired.

Many of the entrepreneurs in this book have always been difficult. Even at an early age, they found it hard to fit into existing structures and were not willing to accept anybody else's authority. This experience may well have been a key factor in their decision to become entrepreneurs.

In my book *The Wealth Elite,* I conducted interviews with ultra-high-net-worth individuals. Many of my interviewees saw themselves as difficult people who are too nonconformist to integrate themselves into prescribed structures or subordinate themselves to others. In some cases, they expressed this in quite drastic terms: One said that he would have had to be given "pills" to function as an employee. He was too rebellious and too much of a know-it-all. Another said that he would have been driven "crazy" working in a publicly owned company, and that he would not have been able to bear that in the long run: "I would have ended up in the loony bin." Another reported that the idea of potentially working for a boss to whom he felt superior, and that he would be forced to "kowtow to" or parrot the words of, was repugnant to him. Yet another quit the company he was working for after just four weeks. He sees himself as an "alpha type" and had the feeling that the company wanted to start out by "knocking him down a peg or two."[199]

Many successful people learned in their childhoods and as young adults to assert themselves in major arguments with domineering figures of authority – an ability which benefited them greatly in later life. Tennis star Boris Becker says: "Over the years I had many arguments with my father. Often we wouldn't talk for months on end. He'd assume rights that he wasn't entitled to, even as a father."[200] After Boris won Wimbledon for the first time, his father helped a TV station arrange a victory reception for him in his hometown of Leimen although Boris had told him he did not want one. He ended up having to go along with it so his father would not lose face. After the first time, he warned his father: "Well, Dad, it was all right this time, but please, never again, OK?"[201]

After Becker's second Wimbledon win, his father did organize another party without asking his son beforehand. Boris told his father to cancel the arrangements he had made. "Too late," his father claimed. "How could you do such a thing? You don't respect me," Boris replied. He had come back to Leimen for some peace and quiet, not to rehash over and over again what his victory meant to him. "That's it. I'm not talking to you for at least six months."[202] His father did not believe him but Boris stuck to his promise and did not speak a word to him for six months.

Prince Alwaleed's aunt remembers the legendary billionaire's childhood: "He was a rebel, because of the divorce between his mother and father, and he took the side of his mother, more than once, and this made him, in a sense, an outcast."[203]

Aged 13, Alwaleed played truant so many times he had to be forced into going to school. "Eventually," Riz Khan writes in his biography of the prince, "his father intervened. The young prince was dragged off to Saudi Arabia to attend the King Abdul Aziz Military Academy, in the hope of instilling some discipline into him ... He was being sent there to be disciplined, which went against all his rebel instincts."[204] There could be no doubt, Khan says, that "when he was young, Alwaleed was different and somewhat troubled."[205]

The real trouble started when he punched a teacher in the stomach. Alwaleed had been caught looking at a classmate's paper during an exam. The teacher said that he would give him an 'F' on the test and told him to leave the room. Alwaleed denied that he had cheated and reminded the teacher that he was the grandson of King Abdulaziz and of Riad El Solh, the first Lebanese prime minister. The teacher replied something along the lines of: "To hell with your grandfathers." Prince Alwaleed stood up and said: "Before I leave, I have a message for you from my grandfathers."[206] With that, he hit the teacher so hard he suffered from a severe contusion. It wasn't the first time Alwaleed had misbehaved and his teachers had had enough. The headmaster, who was a family friend, had no choice but to expel the young prince.

Steve Jobs, too, was a rebel in his youth who kept picking fights with his parents and teachers. Because of his bad behavior and unruliness, he was repeatedly suspended from school. He refused to do his homework, which he considered a waste of time. "I was pretty bored in school, and I turned into a little terror," Steve Jobs confesses. He was the leader of a gang that planted bombs and put snakes into classrooms. "You should have seen us in third grade," he recalls. "We basically destroyed the teacher."[207]

His parents didn't know what to do. When he announced that he wasn't going to go to school any more, they made the decision to move. "At 11 years old," his biographers write, "Steve was already able to demonstrate enough strength of will to convince his parents to resettle. His trademark intensity, the single-mindedness that he could apply to remove any obstacle to his progress, was already evident."[208]

When Jobs was 16, he wore his hair down to his shoulders, took drugs and hardly ever went to school. Then he decided to enroll at Reed College in Portland, Oregon, the first liberal arts college in the Northwest. His parents were shocked – not least by the fees, which were more than they could afford, and by the distance from home. His mother said: "Steve said that Reed was the only college he wanted to go to, and if he couldn't go there, he didn't want to go anywhere."[209]

His parents used up their savings to send him to college. The dean remembers: "Steve had a very inquiring mind that was enormously attractive ... He refused to accept automatically received truths. He wanted to examine everything himself."[210] Eventually, he dropped out of Reed College, too, although he continued to live there at the school's expense.

Like Jobs, Larry Ellison, who founded the Oracle company and is today one of the richest billionaires in the United States, was adopted as a child. He and his father were constantly arguing. "Apparently the only thing Ellison and his father did was disagree," his biographer says.[211] According to Ellison, his father was a complete conformist. "My father was not rational. My father believed that if the government said something, the government was always right. And if the police arrested someone, the person was always guilty."[212] As far as his father was concerned, the teachers were always right, too.

The lack of respect was mutual. Ellison's father had little confidence in his adoptive son's abilities. He told him over and over again that he would never get anywhere in life. For Ellison, his father's lack of confidence in him was all the motivation he needed. His friends felt the tension between him and his father. "He hated his father. It wasn't a pleasant homelife for him at all," one of them said.[213]

The arguments continued at school, where Ellison would stand up to his teachers. He was not willing to learn anything he could not see the point of and would sabotage whatever he did not want to put up with. After he had finished school, his attitude kept getting him into trouble at the companies he worked for. He eventually realized that his only option was to form his own company where he would be in control of how things were done.

Bill Gates did very well in school, especially in math, but he was known for his "hard-nosed, confrontational" behavior towards his teachers. In tenth grade, he had a blazing row with his physics teacher. "The two were heatedly arguing with one another, jaw to jaw, in front of the class on a raised stage that was used for class demonstrations. Gates was yelling at the top of his lungs, waving his finger, hammering away at (the teacher), telling him he was wrong about a physics point ... and Gates was winning the argument."[214] His biographers say: "Gates was impatient with those not as quick as he was, teachers included."[215]

Bill Gates had a better relationship with his parents than most other future successful entrepreneurs, but his decision to drop out of Harvard was the cause of a serious argument. Gates said he had come to Harvard hoping to meet people who were intellectually superior to him but had yet to find them. He had decided he would be better off forming his own company and moving to Albuquerque, New Mexico, to do so.

His parents did everything they could to stop him from going through with what they thought was an absurd idea. They asked a well-respected successful businessman of their acquaintance to meet with their son and talk sense into him. Gates told the man about his plans and about the revolution in personal computing, which was just around the corner. One day, he said, everybody would own a personal computer. The acquaintance who was supposed to talk Bill out of his plans ended up supporting him.[216] His parents were appalled when he did drop out of university in order to form Microsoft, which was to make him the richest man in the world.

Ted Turner, the creator of the 24-hour news channel CNN, today the biggest property owner in the United States and several times a billionaire, had a similar history of serious confrontations with his father and his teachers. His parents enrolled him at McCallie, an exclusive all-boys' school in Chattanooga, Tennessee, which was amongst the strictest boarding schools in the southern United States. Turner says about his school days: "I did everything I could to rebel against the system. I was always having animals in my room and stuff like that and getting into trouble one way or another, and then having to take my punishment like a man." He even forced the school to review its entire disciplinary system. "I had more demerits than anyone in the history of the school ... For every demerit, you had to walk a quarter of a mile. Well, there was only so much time you could walk on any weekend and anything left over was carried over." In his first year at the school, Turner had already collected more than 1,000 demerits, which corresponded to more miles than it was possible to walk. "So they had to devise a new system where you couldn't get a limitless supply of demerits."[217] Turner's career as a troublemaker continued when he was a student at Brown University in Providence. He had already been suspended once for his countless infractions when he was caught with a girl in his dorm room – a serious violation of school rules, for which 21 other students had already been suspended – and was kicked out of college for good.

This episode was preceded by a serious argument with his father about his choice of a major. In a letter, his father wrote: "My dear son: I am appalled, even horrified, that you have adopted classics as a major. As a matter of fact, I almost puked on the way home today ... These subjects might give you a community of interest with an isolated few impractical dreamers and a select group of college professors."[218] His letter ended with a warning: "I think you are rapidly becoming a jackass and the sooner you get out of that filthy atmosphere, the better it will suit me."[219] Turner took revenge by having his father's letter reprinted verbatim on the editorial page of the *Daily Herald*. Although this was done anonymously, his father was furious.

Warren Buffett also had a lot of fights with his parents and his teachers – he even got into trouble with the police. Looking back on his youth, he readily admits he was "antisocial": "I fell in with bad people and did things I shouldn't have. I was just rebelling. I was unhappy."[220] Warren's parents were appalled by his behavior. By late 1944, his biographer says "he had become the school delinquent."[221] He kept getting bad grades, and he was so difficult to get along with that his teachers ended up leaving him in his room by himself, shoving "my lessons under the door like Hannibal Lecter ... I was really rebelling ... I set the record for checks on deficiencies in deportment and all that," Buffett remembers.[222] On graduation day, Buffett refused to wear the obligatory suit and tie. "They wouldn't let me graduate with the class ... because I was so disruptive and I wouldn't wear clothes that were appropriate."[223]

'Rebellion' was the guiding principle by which French fashion designer Coco Chanel lived her life, as well. She writes in her autobiography: "I was a rebellious child, a rebellious lover, a rebellious fashion designer, a true Lucifer."[224] It was her pride that made her a rebel. Pride, Chanel says, "is the key to my bad temper, to my gypsy-like independence, to my antisocial nature; it is also the secret of my strength and my success."[225]

Her own experience has taught her that "a rebellious child makes for a well-prepared and very strong human being."[226] "I cannot take orders from anyone else," Chanel claims.[227] "I am, people frequently say, an anarchist."[228] Assertiveness, that much is true, does seem to be a quality honed in confrontation with others, especially during childhood and youth. Rebellion against authority reinforces a sense of independence and self-confidence that is indispensable for future success – Chanel's life is a prime example.

David Ogilvy's school report credited him with "a distinctly original mind" and the ability to express himself well in his native language, but expressed concern about his inclination "to argue with his teachers and try to convince them that he is right and the books are wrong; but this perhaps is only a further proof of his originality. It is a habit, however, which it would be wise to discourage."[229] Much later, after Ogilvy had become famous, he gave a speech at his old school's Founder's Day celebration in which he confessed: "I detested the philistines who ruled the roost. I was an irreconcilable rebel – a misfit ... There is no correlation between success at school and success in life."[230]

Many of the successful personalities featured in this book – men like Warren Buffett, Bill Gates or Steve Jobs, and women like Coco Chanel – probably considered themselves their teachers' intellectual superiors and in most cases they may well have been right. Garry Kasparov, the most successful chess player of all time, remembers his teacher phoning his parents to complain that he questioned what she was teaching the class. Such behavior was practically unheard of in the Soviet school system. The teacher told Kasparov to stop acting up – he was making it seem as if he thought he was cleverer than everybody else, she said. To which Kasparov replied: "But isn't that true?"[231]

Billionaire Richard Branson had a hard time at school as well, mainly because he was dyslexic. Unlike most of the individuals featured in this book, he always had a very good relationship with his parents, who supported him in any way they could. But what they taught him was fundamentally different from what most children learn from their parents. His mother would constantly repeat mantras such as "The winner takes it all" or "Pursue your dreams." Even when he was still a child, she put him through all kinds of ordeals which he had to master in order to gain self-confidence. "My first lesson in self-sufficiency was when I was about four years old. We'd been out somewhere and on the way back Mum stopped the car a few miles from our house and told me to find my own way home across the fields ... As I grew older, these lessons grew harder."[232]

When he was 12 years old, his mother shook him awake in the early hours of the morning, telling him to get dressed. It was winter, it was bitterly cold and pitch-black outside. His mother gave him a packed lunch and sent him on a 50-mile cycle ride towards the coast. "It was still dark when I set off on my own with a map in case I got lost. I spent the night with a relative and returned home the next day." He was proud of what he had accomplished and looked forward to his mother's praise. But all she said was: "Well done, Ricky. Was that fun? Now run along, the vicar wants you to chop some logs for him."[233]

Branson claims that he owes his success to his parents' "tough love" approach to child-rearing. "Those early lessons, which increased as we grew, were because my parents wanted us to be strong and to rely on ourselves, to be free, independent spirits."[234] Unlike many other high achievers, Branson could always count on his parents' unconditional support – even when he left school early to devote himself to his projects: publishing a national student newspaper and starting up a mail-order record business.

Branson is a rare exception. Many of the successful men and women featured in this book grew up without even knowing their real parents. And most of them – future entrepreneurs in particular – rebelled against anyone in authority, especially against parents and teachers. Those very arguments and confrontations gave them the confidence and inner strength to go their own way later on in life.

As we have seen, a rebellious personality will often lead people to start their own business. Refusing to tolerate structures and restrictions imposed by others, they decide they want to be their own boss. However, we have only looked at the careers of people who would later become successful – because they possessed other special talents and mental resources. Of course, not everybody who has trouble conforming to other people's rules and standards and who keeps getting into fights with authority figures will become a success – quite the contrary. Many of them will fail because a certain willingness to conform and compromise is a necessary quality for a career in management, for example.

What does all this mean for you? In order to achieve higher goals, you need a high degree of assertiveness. If you are a harmony-seeker by nature, you must learn to stand your ground. Assertiveness is less an innate gift than an acquired skill. Like confidence, which we have already mentioned in a previous chapter, assertiveness is like a muscle that needs training and the way to train it is by engaging in confrontation. Of course, that doesn't mean you should pick fights for their own sake. Arguments cost time, strength and energy. Above all, you have to learn not to let others draw you into unnecessary confrontations. "I choose my own fights" – that was one of the mottos my father taught me. In other words: just because somebody else is trying to engage you in a confrontation doesn't mean that you have to jump through their hoop. Do not allow others to impose confrontation on you and thereby to determine what you invest your time and energy in. In many cases, it might be more sensible to avoid a confrontation – and to save your strength for other, more important arguments, which will get you closer to the goals you have set for yourself.

CHAPTER 7

Never Take 'No' For an Answer

For those of us who remember the 1980s, Steve Jobs was the man who invented the Macintosh; the first commercially successful computer with a graphic interface. It amazed consumers and experts alike when it was launched on the market in 1984. Younger people know him as the creator of the iPhone.

Steve Jobs' company, Apple, had already made him a millionaire by the time he was 24. After he pulled off the most successful IPO in the history of finance in December 1980, his fortune was estimated at $217.5 million. At the time of his death in 2011, his wealth was estimated at around $8.3 billion. He was one of the richest men in the United States, and for many the marketing genius of our time. In the year before he died, Apple was the third-most valuable company in the world. He had created a company that, even after his death, remains extremely successful. In 2018, Apple was the first trillion-dollar company in history, making it the world's most valuable company.

As we have already seen in the last chapter, Steve Jobs always possessed a quality that many other successful personalities share: He was a difficult, polarizing character whom others either worshipped or detested. And he would never have been half as successful if he hadn't always refused to take 'no' for an answer.

In the spring of 1974, 18-year-old Steve Jobs applied for a job with Atari, which had just launched a popular video game. The company was advertising for people who wanted to "have fun and make money." The idea appealed to Jobs. One day, the personnel manager told Al Alcorn, the head of the engineering department: "We've got this weird guy here. He says he won't leave until we hire him. We either call the cops or hire him."[235]

At the time, Jobs was a hippie who experimented with drugs and, together with a few other technology freaks, had just invented an illegal device for tricking the phone company and using their phone lines for free. Needless to say, he did not strike them as a very promising candidate for a job. Alcorn remembers him as being "dressed in rags basically, hippie stuff. An 18-year-old drop-out of Reed College. I don't know why I hired him, except that there was some spark. I really saw the spark in that man, some inner energy, an attitude that he was going to get it done." Alcorn's colleague asked what on Earth was he supposed to do with Jobs. "He has b.o., he's different, a goddamn hippie."[236] They eventually agreed to let Jobs work nights so his presence wouldn't offend anybody.

About two years later, in April 1976, Jobs and his friend Steve Wozniak founded Apple. The owner of a computer shop ordered 50 units of their first prototype, which they had dubbed Apple I, for $500 each. It was a huge success for the two young entrepreneurs, but the question of how to finance the necessary investments remained unsolved. The two friends had formed their company with $1,000, which they had raised by selling a Volkswagen van and an electronic calculator. Jobs' various attempts to find somebody willing to put up the money remained unsuccessful until he finally met Bob Newton, the manager of an electronics company who promised to contact the owner of the computer shop and ask for confirmation of the $25,000 order.

Jobs' biographers Jeffrey S. Young and William L. Simon comment: "Anyone less determined would have said, 'Okay, I'll call back in a few days,' and left. Steve refused to leave until Newton made the call."[237] Newton eventually agreed to a credit line of up to $20,000.

Shortly after launching Apple I's successor, the Apple II, Jobs saw an advertising campaign for Intel that he thought was great. Immediately obsessed by the idea of launching a similar campaign for his new computer, he contacted Intel's marketing department and was told that their campaign had been created by the Regis McKenna agency. Jobs phoned the director and was referred to the project manager in charge of new clients instead, who informed him in no uncertain terms that a new company such as Apple would never be able to afford Regis McKenna's services.

Jobs wouldn't accept this. He kept calling every day until the project manager agreed to come to the garage that served as the 'headquarters' of Apple and to take a look at the computer Jobs had been waxing lyrically about on the phone. "As I was driving over to the garage, I was thinking, 'Holy Christ, this guy is going to be something else. What's the least amount of time I can spend with this clown without being rude and then get back to something more profitable?'"[238]

He was impressed by Jobs' persistence – but not impressed enough to actually accept the job. Most people would have given up at this point and decided to look for another agency – after all, there were tens of thousands of them in the United States. But Jobs had his heart set on hiring the same agency that had created the Intel campaign he admired so much. He still refused to take 'no' for an answer. He started calling the director's office three to four times a day until McKenna's secretary was so fed up with answering his calls she talked her boss into speaking to Jobs himself. Jobs succeeded in arranging a meeting with McKenna.

But even when Jobs and Wozniak met face to face with the director of the advertising agency, he would not be swayed. "When McKenna proved reluctant," Jobs' biographers write, "Jobs pulled his now-customary tactic of refusing to leave the office until McKenna consented to handle the account. Steve was so persuasive that Regis McKenna, in a decision which would turn out to be hugely beneficial for all of them, agreed to accept Apple Computer as a client."[239]

There was just one problem: how was Jobs supposed to pay for an advert in *Playboy*, as McKenna suggested since the target group was predominantly male? McKenna suggested that he talk to Don Valentine, who had formed a venture capital company in the early 1970s which specialized in funding promising new start-ups in the electronics industry.

Valentine liked Jobs and his Apple computer but he wouldn't invest in the company unless Apple took an experienced marketing professional on board. Jobs asked him to recommend a few people, which Valentine refused to do. Once again, Jobs didn't take 'no' for an answer. He kept calling Valentine three or four times a day until the entrepreneur finally gave him some names, among them Mike Markkula. On January 3, 1977, Wozniak and Jobs met Markkula at his home to sign the documents that turned Apple into a joint-stock company. Each of them owned a share of 30% and, in the early days, Markkula was also Apple's largest investor.

Once again, Jobs' stubbornness had carried the day and got him what he wanted. His staff frequently found him hard to cope with. When Apple's next big project, the Macintosh, was in the planning phase, he showed up at a meeting with a phone directory, which he tossed on the table: "That's how big the Macintosh can be. Nothing any bigger will make it. Consumers won't stand for it if it's any larger."[240]

His employees looked at the phone directory in utter shock. Jobs was asking the impossible. The book was half the size of the smallest computer ever built at the time. The electronic parts, the technicians agreed, would never fit into a casing of that size. It was obvious that Jobs knew nothing about electronics, they thought, or he would never have made such a ridiculous demand. "Steve wasn't someone who took no for an answer," his biographers state drily.[241] He insisted: his staff would have to find a way to build a computer that size.

The Macintosh was supposed to hit the market on January 24, 1984. Apple had launched a huge advertising campaign to that effect, which was covered by every television channel in America. But on January 8, his software designers told him they couldn't possible meet the deadline. They only had another week in which to solve the remaining technical problems – it was impossible, they told him firmly. Jobs had to understand that the product launch must be postponed!

Jobs did no such thing. Hearing that something was 'impossible' made him aggressive. But for once he surprised his team by not throwing a tantrum. Instead, he explained calmly that they were great and that everybody in the company was counting on them. They had to meet the deadline because the alternative, delivering a demo version, really was impossible. He said that he had faith in his team, he knew they could do it. Then he put the phone down. The software designers were speechless. They had already given it their all and were about ready to break down from exhaustion. But there was nothing else for it. They got up, returned to their workstations, and at the very last moment, in the early hours just before dawn on January 16, they did the 'impossible,' which Jobs had asked them to do.

But people who keep pulling off the 'impossible' against all odds can easily let success go to their heads. They start thinking they are infallible and always right about everything. This is what happened to Steve Jobs, who had been right so many times. He had predicted that he would sell 70,000 units of the Macintosh within the first 100 days. Everybody thought he was crazy. But once again, he was right. Shortly after, the tide started to turn. IBM launched a PC that had far more useful features and functions than the Macintosh and also came at a lower price. Apple's sales declined rapidly. Most of the 200,000 units they had optimistically produced had to be sold off at a huge loss. There were internecine fights within the company and many blamed the problems on Jobs, whose style of leadership had not endeared him to his staff.

His fellow executives ganged up against him, forcing Jobs, the founder of the company, to move out of his office and into a small building across the street, which Jobs nicknamed 'Siberia.' Shortly after, John Sculley, whom Apple had poached from Pepsi, declared: "There is no role for Steve Jobs in the operations of this company, either now or in the future."[242] Jobs felt as if he had been punched in the stomach. He sold all of his shares, which were worth a lot less now than they had been when Apple first went public, and formed a new company, which he called NeXT. He also bought the Pixar computer animation company from film producer George Lucas, who urgently needed money to pay for his divorce.

At first, both companies were anything but successful. Month after month, year after year they operated at huge losses. The computers they produced didn't sell and Jobs finally decided to get rid of Pixar's hardware branch and focus exclusively on computer graphics. He eventually succeeded in coming to an agreement with the Disney corporation, which commissioned Pixar to produce several animated films. Disney's CEO Michael Eisner felt that his company was increasingly being outdone by producers like James Cameron, who used computer animation to great effect in films such as the Arnold Schwarzenegger vehicle *Terminator*.

Pixar was commissioned to produce *Toy Story*, for which Disney invested $100 million in advertising – three times the film's production budget. *Toy Story* became a runaway box office success, and an excellent calling card for Pixar's IPO in December 1995.

In previous years, the company had incurred huge losses. This was a few years before investors started buying into a good 'story' of a technology start-up even though the numbers weren't right. But the success of *Toy Story* generated a lot of good press for Pixar and inspired the imagination, which is a key factor in stock market success, as Jobs had predicted correctly.

Jobs wanted to float his shares at an opening price of $22, which his advisors and investment bankers thought was far too high. They recommended an opening price of $12–$14 instead. At $22, they warned him, there was a high risk that the shares wouldn't sell. Yet again, Jobs refused to take 'no' for an answer, and insisted on an opening price of $22.

When trading started, all Pixar executives were glued to their screens. After half an hour, the shares traded at $49. By the end of the day, the price had dropped slightly but, at $39, it was still a lot higher than expected. Steve Jobs was a billionaire – at least for that one moment. The company, which had been a complete failure for many years, started producing one box-office success after another, setting new standards for the computer animation industry. With a turnover of $2.5 billion, it was soon the most successful Hollywood studio in history. In late January 2006, Disney announced that it was going to take over Pixar for $7.4 billion. Steve Jobs joined the Disney board of directors. With a share of 50.1% in Pixar, he was Disney's largest individual shareholder.

Ten years earlier, he had achieved a comeback with Apple. In 1996, he had sold his company NeXT to Apple for $402 million. The following year, he joined the board of directors and was soon promoted to interim CEO. By launching new products like the iPhone or the iPad, he turned the company's fortunes around and brought it back from the brink of bankruptcy to become one of the most successful corporations worldwide.

Remember how it all started: with one man's refusal to take 'no' for an answer. You don't need to be a Steve Jobs to draw some important lessons from his story. Most of us give up too easily when confronted with rejection and with a 'no' which appears to be final. The next time somebody tells you 'no,' ask yourself: "Wait a moment – why should I accept this as a final answer? Let's see if there's a way of turning 'no' into 'yes.'" This strategy doesn't just work for Steve Jobs – it works for you and me, too.

If somebody turns you down, try first of all to put yourself in their place and to disregard your own interests completely for a moment. This approach has frequently served me well in contract negotiations. I might say: "Let me sit where you're sitting for a moment and look at things from your point of view." And then I will do so. Once you have understood the whole picture and taken on board the other party's interests, you will often be able to negotiate successfully.

Dealing with people who always say 'yes' can be far more treacherous than dealing with those who always say 'no.' What do I mean by this? I used to sell life insurance, because I thought that would be the best way to learn about sales. My colleague and I went from door to door, 'cold-calling' on people. Were people waiting for us to ring their doorbells? Of course not. The trick was to carry on regardless of every time you had a door slammed in your face.

Let me tell you about the man who said 'yes.' He had been kind enough to listen to me extol the benefits of life insurance for almost 45 minutes, nodding his approval and interrupting me at intervals with phrases such as: "That sounds good!" Confident that I had made a sale, I started filling in the application form for an insurance policy. My interlocutor, who had acted so polite and interested up to that point, asked me curtly: "What are you doing?" Self-consciously, I explained that I was just entering some information, just in case ... He wouldn't even let me finish my sentence. "That's completely out of the question for me in any case."

Since then, I have learned that from a salesperson's point of view, people who say 'yes' to everything are much more difficult to handle than those who raise objections and express their concerns. They say 'yes' in the hope of avoiding confrontation and getting rid of the salesperson as soon as possible. They keep their thoughts to themselves ("let him talk, with any luck I'll soon be rid of him"), not giving their interlocutor any opportunity to refute their arguments and objections. Experience has taught me that they have to be drawn out of their shells before they will tell you what they really think and why they have reservations.

I have often seen similar situations in my work as a business networking consultant. One important part of my work is facilitating talks between executives from real estate companies who I believe have shared interests. These talks frequently result in takeover bids, joint ventures and deals worth tens of millions of euros. In the initial round of talks, participants mostly swap pleasantries and emphasize the interests they have in common. That's fine as far as it goes, but experience has taught me that you get a lot further a lot faster the sooner you address the disagreements and objections which might stand in the way of collaborating on a project.

If each party keeps their reservations to themselves, there is never an opportunity to discuss them. That's why, in those talks, it is frequently up to me to say: "I am glad that you have found you have so much in common. That's exactly what I had expected and hoped for. But now I would like to ask you to state the three most important arguments against a collaboration." There are times when I need to be patient and keep silent until somebody speaks up. Frequently, nobody 'dares' to mention more than one objection, which more often than not isn't even their main concern. So, I insist: "Is there anything else which from your point of view might speak against this project?" I will not let it go until I am satisfied that all potential objections have been raised.

Good salespeople have to learn to deal with a non-committal 'yes' as well as with a resolute and decisive 'no', which seems to forestall any objection and to leave no room for discussion. Frank Bettger, who was for a time the most successful insurance salesman in the United States, shares his strategies in *How I Raised Myself from Failure to Success in Selling*.

If somebody told him 'no', he would usually simply change the subject of the conversation. This is how he did it. One day, acting on an acquaintance's recommendation, he went to see the director of a large construction company. He was in the habit of having mutual acquaintances write letters of introduction for him. When he showed the letter to the director, his prospective client replied: "If it's insurance you want to talk to me about, I'm not interested. I just bought more insurance about a month ago." He sounded as if he had made up his mind once and for all and Bettger would just be wasting his breath on him. Instead, he asked: "Mr. Allen, how did you ever happen to get started in the construction business?" He then listened to the other's life story for three hours – and a few weeks later the company director and some of his staff bought insurance policies worth $225,000 from Bettger, which was a whole lot of money at the time.[243]

"How did you get started?" was one of Bettger's favorite conversational gambits, which he used to break the ice and try a different tack. Successful entrepreneurs in particular enjoy telling the story of their humble beginnings and of the difficulties they have had to overcome. Bettger won sympathies by showing an interest and proving himself a good listener. He also picked up a lot of information about his client-to-be which was instrumental to selling insurance cover. "The most important secret of salesmanship is to find out what the other guy wants, then help him find the best way to get it," Bettger advises.[244]

Here are some simple rules that will help you change a 'no' into a 'yes':
1. Instead of prematurely accepting 'no' as a final answer, consider it an interim stage of your negotiations.
2. Try to understand the other person's point of view. Sit in their chair and look at the issue at hand from their perspective. Look for creative solutions to make both parties' interests coincide. Use your imagination!
3. Give the other person an alternative, so that they can change their mind without losing face. Nobody wants to lose out in a deal and it is up to you to make the other person feel that they have won.

4. In negotiating, the magic word is 'fair.' If you really are trying to come to a fair solution for both parties, this little word can work wonders. Propose a compromise, then point out: "Neither of us is going to be 100% happy, that's the nature of a compromise. But I think this solution is fair to both parties."

5. Ask the other person to understand your own situation and your attitude towards it. You sat in their chair, now ask them to sit in yours and see things from your point of view. Help the other person by highlighting emotional as well as rational aspects of your position and your perspective.

6. Many people make the mistake of approaching a negotiation too 'openly,' without having set a clearly defined goal in their own mind. Before entering into negotiation, you have to be entirely sure of what you want and you have to be sure of how far you are willing to compromise. The other person has to realize that you mean every single word you say.

CHAPTER 8

Programming Your Inner GPS

The people around Oracle founder Larry Ellison frequently wondered why he would quote numbers and make claims that were blatantly untrue. His staff finally came to the conclusion that Ellison was living in the future rather than in the present, let alone the past. "He had a problem with tenses," a member of his staff recalls. "It was like, we will have 50 employees, so we might as well say we have them now." His long-term personal assistant adds: "He doesn't live in today, because there are problems today, and there are solutions tomorrow."[245]

Successful people are constantly focused on the future. They do not waste their time with regrets. They are able to learn from past mistakes and then move on. "We just figure there is so much to look forward to that there is no sense thinking of what we might have done," Warren Buffett says. "It just doesn't make any difference. You can only live life forward."[246] Buffett never dwelled on unpleasant aspects of life. He compared his memory to a bathtub: "The tub filled with ideas and experiences and matters that interested him. When he had no more use for information, whoosh – the plug popped up, and the memory drained away ... Certain events, facts, memories and even people appeared to vanish."[247]

The same is true of Arnold Schwarzenegger who, according to his biographer, never wasted his time thinking about things he could not change in any case. "Even as a teenager he chose never to look back at what was unpleasant, whether specific episodes in his past or the psychological realities of his own life."[248] Instead of dwelling on the past, he would visualize his goals for the future. He started seeing his biceps as a mountain landscape rather than as flesh and blood.[249] He approached his financial goals in the same way, picturing himself as a successful millionaire long before he was one in order to motivate himself.[250]

In this chapter, you will learn how to program the goals you have set for yourself into your subconscious. I will focus on one particular technique of self-hypnosis that will make this process much easier for you. Without this technique, I would never have reached many of my own goals. But you don't have to take my word for it – let me tell you the story of a German physician, Dr. Hannes Lindemann, who in the 1950s became the first person to sail across the Atlantic single-handedly in a small collapsible boat, setting a record that remained unbeaten until 2002. He was able to do this by using a technique that was pioneered by the German psychiatrist Johannes Heinrich Schultz in the early 1930s. This method, which Schultz called "autogenic training," allows the conscious mind to program goals into the subconscious while the body is in a state of deep relaxation.

Six months before he was planning to start the crossing, Lindemann started programming certain set phrases into his subconscious. "I will make it," was one of them. He would start his days early in the morning by repeating this phrase to himself, and continue to do so during the day and especially in the early afternoon.

"After living with the resolution 'I will make it' for about three weeks, I 'knew' that I would survive the crossing and return safe and sound."[251] During the Atlantic crossing, this resolution would come to him automatically at various points. When his boat capsized on day 57 and he had to spend the night lying on the slippery deck before he could put the boat upright again at dawn, the resolutions he had drummed into his subconscious surfaced in his conscious mind and helped him get through the ordeal.

The famous Tyrolean mountain climber Reinhold Messner has a similar story to tell. A few years ago, I heard him give a lecture in which he told of a close encounter with death after he had fallen into a crevasse. He decided that in the unlikely case that he could make it out of the crevasse after all, he would turn back immediately. But once he had gotten out, he felt an inner compulsion to continue the climb. "There was nothing else I could do, because I had woken up every morning with this very goal and gone to sleep every night with it and had programmed it into my subconscious again and again, day after day," Messner said. His subconscious had not allowed him to give up until he reached the summit.

But let's go back to Hannes Lindemann and his Atlantic crossing. His most important resolution was "Due west." As soon as he deviated off his course even slightly, his inner voice was to remind him: "Due west." He started suffering from hallucinations due to severe sleep deprivation. But as soon as he heard "west," he would snap awake and he was able to adjust his course immediately. "This example demonstrates how formulaic resolutions are able to penetrate even hallucinations – a novelty in medical research. But it also shows that formulaic resolutions can have as strong an effect as post-hypnotic suggestions."[252]

In fact, Professor Schultz's mental self-coaching technique originated in hypnosis. In the early years of the 20th century, Schultz worked in a hypnosis lab and his early writings on hypnosis laid the groundwork for his pioneering study on autogenic training and meditative relaxation (*Autogenic training: a psychophysiologic approach in psychotherapy*, 1959).

Strictly speaking, autogenic training is a kind of self-hypnosis. Schultz had discovered that the formulaic phrases hypnotists employ can be administered by the subjects themselves in order to induce a state of deep relaxation in which the depths of the subconscious can be accessed.

By mastering the art of autogenic training, you will not only learn an extremely effective relaxation technique, you will also be able to program goals into your subconscious, just as you can program a destination into your GPS. Just as your GPS will calculate and display a route for you to follow, your subconscious will help you navigate towards a goal which you have programmed into it during autogenic training.

I myself have been practicing autogenic training for around 40 years, including many phases of my life during which I have done so daily. But I have met very few people who have truly mastered the technique. That's not because autogenic training is hard to learn. In fact, learning this technique is very simple. However, you have to be prepared to practice at least twice a day without fail for the first nine months – something for which most people lack the necessary discipline. It may take longer, or it may take less time – depending on the individual person. Some people notice appreciable results after only a few weeks, for others it takes many months. Schultz himself commented: "There is nobody who hasn't learned it after practicing 600 times."[253] Once you have mastered this technique, you have mastered it for life – like knowing how to read and write, or how to ride a bike.

You can take lessons or teach yourself from a book. I have taught several classes myself, as well as giving private lessons. Lying or sitting down in a meditative posture, you then have to recite certain phrases several times. You start by telling yourself: "I am completely calm," then you proceed to the next exercise: "My right arm is heavy, both my arms and legs are heavy." Once you have mastered the technique, this will induce a pleasant feeling of heaviness. All your muscles will be completely relaxed.

Next you induce an equally pleasant feeling of warmth as the blood flows to your limbs. Then you tell yourself: "My right arm is warm; both my arms and legs are warm." There are more phrases to recite: "My heartbeat is calm and regular," "My breathing is calm and regular," "My abdomen is warm," "My forehead is pleasantly cool."

The effects are measurable. Around the world, more than 60 different tests and experiments have been used to measure the physical and psychological changes brought about by autogenic training. Thermographic readings and other scientific measurements have confirmed changes in body temperature, heart rate and breathing rhythm.

Once you know how to use these basic phrases to induce a state of deep relaxation, your subconscious is very receptive to suggestive phrases. In this sense, autogenic training is very similar to hypnosis. These phrases have a particularly strong effect if they have been repeatedly programmed into the subconscious in a state of complete relaxation. This is the most effective kind of autosuggestion.

I myself have built a fortune simply by programming new financial goals into my subconscious every year. To this purpose, I use phrases such as: "I make X euros a year, my subconscious shows me the way," or "On December 31 of this year, I will be worth X euros, my subconscious shows me the way." My accounts, which I have kept for over ten years in order to compare the goals I have programmed into my inner GPS with the actual results, show a success rate of 85% – despite the fact that I set myself very ambitious goals and raised them considerably every year.

Why does this work? In his 1962 classic *The Power of Your Subconscious Mind*, Joseph Murphy explains how autosuggestion can help you to achieve your goals. "Decree health, and the subconscious mind will establish it," Murphy writes. "Do not be concerned with details and means, but know the end result. Get the feel of the happy solution of your problem, whether it's health, finances, or employment."[254]

You may think this sounds strange. Most people immediately start reviewing critically and with their conscious minds whether and how a goal might be attained. They imagine all kinds of obstacles and look for reasons why they could fail. But we know from experience that the way to a goal programmed into the subconscious mind does not have to be known to our conscious mind. The important thing is to imprint your goal on your subconscious by constant repetition. Our subconscious is cleverer than our conscious mind, and will always find a way to reach a goal.

In the third chapter of his self-help classic *Think and Grow Rich*, Napoleon Hill identifies autosuggestion as the key to success. He advises readers to relax and then to imagine certain goals in graphic detail – as if they had already been realized. Hill considers this the only way to achieve financial or other goals.

Many people are skeptical about these techniques, although they experience the effects of the constant repetition of key phrases on our actions on a daily basis. The power of advertising is only one example of this effect.

Many of the interviewees I spoke with prior to writing my book *The Wealth Elite* emphasized the importance of setting goals in writing. They set themselves precise financial goals and exact deadlines for achieving them. An astonishing number of interviewees described a process of detailed goal-setting, which they carried out once a year. They took the time to define milestones for the next year, while also reviewing the goals they had set for the previous year in order to assess what they had achieved.

Many described the detailed visualization techniques or other rituals which they are convinced help them to reach their goals. One interviewee had worked with a Feng Shui consultant to create a 'wealth corner' in his house, where he prayed every day for the achievement of his financial goals, and one had fixed his aspirational "1,000,000,000" in large figures above his office door.

Authors such as Murphy and Hill have given some important clues for achieving goals. But neither of them has provided an effective technique for programming your goals into your subconscious. Autogenic training is one such technique because it allows you to access the very deepest layers of your subconscious by relaxation and then to program goals into it with the constant repetition of certain key phrases. Of course, you can 'mentally recite' goals, images and resolutions to yourself without any formal autogenic training. In the 19th century, Emile Coué was the first to develop autosuggestion techniques.

While acknowledging the importance of his predecessor's contribution, Schultz pointed out that Coué cast the "seeds" of his positive thoughts into the wind. Only some of them sprouted and bore fruit because he lacked the knowledge required for a successful "cultivation of the soil." "Unlike the formulaic resolutions and mottos used in autogenic training, the 'Coué method' consists of persuading and convincing oneself of a desirable state of affairs without having 'prepared the ground.' It lacks the gradual preparation by self-coaching, which is characteristic of autogenic training."[255]

Similar to hypnosis, autogenic training is a means of suppressing or even suspending critical thinking and value judgments for a certain time period in order to gain direct access to the subconscious. As important as analytical thinking may be, it is also extremely limited. Human behavior is often guided by subconscious impulses rather than conscious decisions. Frequently, the latter are only belated rationalizations of the former. Our subconscious holds a store of information, the products of implicit learning processes, that we are unable to access with our conscious minds. If you manage to program your goals into your subconscious, it will be able to retrieve the information necessary for achieving these goals by itself. And you will soon see that people and situations that can help you achieve your goal will begin to materialize for you, as though attracted by a magnet.

Is it really possible to program 'all' your goals into your subconscious, and to attain them, by using autogenic training techniques? Only if you believe in your own goals. If you try to program your inner GPS to become president of the United States next year, or to fly to Mars the year after, you would not be able to believe in your own goals – and consequently, you would not be able to attain them.

But we rarely set our goals 'unrealistically' high. Most people set their goals far too low. Hardly ever will you achieve more in life than you were planning to achieve. Wouldn't it be depressing to reach the end of your life and to realize that you might have achieved so much more – if only you hadn't set your goals quite so low?

How high you set your goals is always up to you. If you are overweight, you can set yourself the goal of losing a few pounds – or you can set yourself the goal of having a perfect figure. I am convinced that, in some respects, higher goals are even easier to achieve than more modest ones because you will be much more motivated and enthusiastic the higher you aim. I also think that in the final count, setting yourself very ambitious goals and attempting to achieve them is no harder than putting up with a mediocre and boring life. And above all: you will never know whether you have any hidden talents and whether you might be able to achieve more in life after all unless you try.

The goals you program into your inner GPS have to be clearly defined, ideally quantifiable and with a deadline. No one would contact Amazon and ask them "please send me something nice." The online retail giant wouldn't know what to do with such a request. Neither can your subconscious process non-specific requests along the lines of "I want to become rich," "I want to have a better body" or "I want to be successful." But if you define precisely how much money you want to have by a certain date, your subconscious will know what to aim for. And you will be able to monitor and measure whether you have achieved your goal or not.

Always write your goals down. The importance of this has been demonstrated by a survey of Harvard graduates who were asked whether they had a goal that they had written down. In the survey, 84% of respondents said they had no specific goals for the future at all. Another 13% did set themselves goals but "only in my head." Only 3% had one or more goals that they had put down in writing. Ten years on, the same persons were interviewed again. The 13% who had set themselves goals (albeit not in writing) were earning twice as much on average as the 84% who had none. But the 3% who had written down their goals were earning ten times more than the rest.[256]

The relevance of goal-setting to entrepreneurial success has also been examined by scholars. The theory of 'goal-setting' developed by Edwin Locke (University of Maryland) and Gary P. Latham (University of Toronto) is of central importance.[257] In 1981, they published a review of the research findings on this topic from the 1970s. In 90% of the studies on this topic, they reported the following finding: "Specific and challenging goals lead to higher performance than easy goals, 'do your best' goals, or no goals ... Goal setting is most likely to improve task performance when the goals are specific and sufficiently challenging." They also examined how specific and how difficult the goals were to achieve. The result: more challenging and more specific goals lead to better results than easy and vaguely formulated goals.

Goal-setting theory was developed inductively, both in field tests and experiments, from studies involving 40,000 participants in eight countries. Ambitious and specific goals are so important because, according to Locke and Latham, they focus an individual's attention on the activities that are relevant to the goals and because individuals increase the intensity and the duration of the effort required to achieve them. They work harder and longer to achieve their goals than people who do not have them.[258]

The surest and fastest way towards achieving high goals is by writing down a few major goals, then dividing them into annual goals and 'programming' them into your inner GPS every day. You don't have to practice autogenic training to achieve your goals, but I am convinced that you will get there much faster if you program auto-suggestive resolutions into your subconscious by using this technique.

I would recommend that you reread this chapter after finishing this book. It teaches you a good and reliable way to put into practice what many other authors have already urged you to do, that is to mobilize the power of your subconscious in order to achieve your goals. Are you one of those few people who have the discipline to spend many months learning autogenic training techniques and then using them day after day to program your goals into your inner GPS? Or are you among the many skeptics who won't even try it, or among those who lack the discipline to practice day after day? The answer to this question may well determine how much you will achieve in the next ten years.

Once you have programmed your inner GPS, you are ready to take the next step and learn another formula that will get you closer to achieving your goals: stamina + experimentation. All great inventors, entrepreneurs, athletes and artists have used this formula, whether consciously or unconsciously.

CHAPTER 9

The Formula for Success: Stamina + Experimentation

Garry Kasparov played his first chess world championship tournament in 1984. His opponent was the chess genius Anatoly Karpov. Kasparov was only 21 years old when he challenged him. The tournament started on September 10 and was played by the same rules that had been in force since the world championship in 1978. The title went to whoever was the first to win six games.

Although Kasparov was full of confidence, he lost four games in quick succession and was "only two defeats away from a humiliating rout."[259] After analyzing the way the games had gone up to this point, Kasparov decided to change his tactics radically and immediately. "I switched to guerrilla warfare in game after game, reducing risk, waiting for my chance."[260]

The next 17 games were all draws. The tournament went on for months and months. During the hundreds of hours he spent in front of a chessboard and in preparation for the next game, Kasparov worked on his moves and on his thinking, analyzed mistakes, kept varying his tactics. At first, things seemed to go according to plan for him. But then he started losing. At five-nil for Karpov, it looked as if the veteran champion was on course for victory.

The nervous tension was unbearable for both men. Karpov was physically and mentally exhausted, he lost almost 30 pounds and had to be hospitalized several times. Kasparov had better nerves and managed to close the gap to five-three. Finally, on February 15, 1985 five months and more than 300 match hours after it had started, the match was stopped.

Kasparov had applied a formula for success that all successful people use: stamina plus experimentation. His stamina was nothing short of phenomenal. No world championship had ever gone on for this long – three months had been the previous record. But his willingness to learn even while he was playing was just as important. "The world champion had been my personal trainer for five gruelling months. Not only had I learned the way he played, I was now deeply in touch with my own thought processes. I was increasingly able to identify my mistakes and why I had made them."[261]

Being successful requires stamina – but stamina alone is useless if it means making the same mistakes over and over again. It needs to be accompanied by a highly developed willingness to experiment: "You won't find new ways of solving problems unless you look for new ways and have the nerve to try them when you find them," Kasparov wrote. "They won't all work as expected, of course. The more you experiment, the more successful your experiments will be. Break your routines, even to the point of changing ones you are happy with, to see if you can find new and better methods."[262]

One year after his match against Karpov, 22-year-old Kasparov became the youngest chess world champion in history. He retained his title for 15 years. When he retired from professional chess in 2005, he had the highest ranking in the world.

In the business world, the same combination of stamina and a willingness to experiment is a key to success. The story of the Barbie doll, probably the best known and most successful toy in the world, shows this.

New York, 1959: Ruth Handler was sitting in her hotel room and crying. She had had such high hopes of the toy industry trade fair where she was planning to present the latest product of her company Mattel, the Barbie doll. This doll was completely different from any others that were on the market at the time: it did not look like a child, but a woman. People laughed at Ruth Handler: what mother would want to buy her daughter a doll with large breasts, an extremely small waist and legs up to her armpit? Industry experts representing the large chains thought the same thing – Mattel received hardly any orders for the doll. Ruth Handler started to panic and sent a telegram to Japan, asking her suppliers to cut production by 40% – overly optimistic, she had ordered 20,000 dolls a week for the next six months.

The idea for the doll had first come to Ruth Handler in the early 1950s. She had observed how much her daughter Barbara, who the doll was later to be named after, and her friends enjoyed playing with cut-out paper dolls, which they kept dressing and undressing. She had noticed that the girls preferred one model in particular, that of a grown woman. They identified with her. They wanted to be like her when they were adults: attractive, well-dressed and wearing make-up. Wouldn't it be much more interesting for the girls, Handler thought, if they had a real, three-dimensional doll to play with instead of paper cut-outs? "I knew that if only we could take this play pattern and threedimensionalize, we would have something very special."[263]

The idea stayed with her, but the kind of doll she had in mind was nowhere to be found – not until she went to Europe for six weeks in 1956. In the Swiss city of Lucerne, she saw a doll called Lilli in a shop window. Lilli was one foot tall and had a blonde ponytail. Ruth and her 15-year-old daughter Barbara had never seen another doll like her. Lilli was not meant for children, though. She was based on a cartoon in the German tabloid *Bild* and marketed as a novelty gift item for men. Handler bought her anyway. She knew: Lilli was exactly what she had been looking for. This was the doll she was going to manufacture for young girls.

Easier said than done. The doll was supposed to look as real as possible, with glued-on eyelashes and an entire wardrobe of outfits. Handler soon found out that production costs would be far too high. She knew she would have to have the dolls made in Japan, where the cost of labor was very cheap at the time. She traveled to Japan and got different toy manufacturers to experiment for several years until they managed to produce a doll for about three dollars. Add to that the cost of the doll's dresses, which were extremely expensive to make. The average white-collar worker in the U.S. was earning little more than $200 to $300 per month at the time, which meant that the first Barbie dolls were luxury commodities that only members of the middle and upper classes could afford.

In 1945, Ruth Handler had co-founded a company with her husband and a third partner. They started out producing picture frames but then turned to making furniture for dollhouses. Her husband had a gift for invention and innovation, but he was very introverted and selling definitely wasn't his strong suit. Ruth, who was a natural at marketing and advertising, looked after that side of the business. Her company was the first toy manufacturer to run television commercials all year round. They started in 1955 with a nationwide campaign on Disney's *Mickey Mouse Club*, the most popular children's program at the time.

Their campaign revolutionized the toy industry – from then on, it wasn't the parents who chose toys for their children. Instead, children would keep whinging until their parents bought them the toy they had seen advertised on television.

So far, Handler had focused on selling and marketing, leaving the invention of new toys to her husband. Barbie was her first creation. She paid a lot of money for an expert's report by Ernest Dichter, an authority in the field of marketing psychology at the time. His survey of 191 girls and 45 mothers showed that most of the girls loved the doll, while the mothers hated her. Dichter's wife later said: "He interviewed girls about what they wanted in a doll. It turns out that what they wanted was someone sexy looking, someone that they wanted to grow up to be like. Long legs, big breasts, glamorous."[264] Dichter suggested making Barbie's breasts even bigger – finally she had a 39-inch bust, 18-inch waist and 33-inch hips. But was this really what young girls wanted?

In the television adverts, the young girls' dreams were expressed in the lyrics of a song: "Someday I'm going to be just like you, 'till then I know what I'll do ... Barbie, beautiful Barbie, I'll make believe that I am you."[265] Mattel's competitors ridiculed the campaign at first: "Can you believe what that crazy Mattel did? They went on TV and expected moms to buy whorelooking dolls for their kids."[266] They were not the only ones to be skeptical. Even Handler's own employees had little faith in the success of her seemingly crazy idea.

For all their doubts and skepticism, Barbie became a resounding success, making Mattel one of the largest toy manufacturers in the United States. Only a year after launching the doll, the company went public. Five years later, Mattel had an annual turnover of $100 million and was listed among the Fortune 500 enterprises for the first time.

Ruth Handler was successful mainly because she stuck with her idea against all odds. Her husband had been opposed to it, as had her staff and almost everybody else she talked to. Even if consumers wanted a doll like that, they argued, it would be impossible to manufacture at a reasonable price. Being told that her plan was 'impossible' made Handler even more determined to go through with it and to prove to everybody that it was possible. Handler succeeded by combining stamina and experimentation, which is the formula for success of any kind. She needed stamina because it took her almost ten years to turn her idea into reality. She spent three years improving the doll she had seen in Switzerland. She paid close attention to every detail – from Barbie's fingernails to her make-up and wardrobe, which would prove to be an essential factor in the doll's phenomenal commercial success. Proud Barbie owners would keep asking for new outfits so they could dress her in the latest styles.

Her competitors' failed attempts to copy her success she attributed to their lack of stamina and attention to details, which might seem irrelevant, but were in fact instrumental to her success.

Howard Schultz's patience was tested, too. When he took over Starbucks, the company had been turning a profit year after year. But there were only five Starbucks shops altogether – while Schultz was planning to start a nationwide chain. "It didn't take long for me to realize that we couldn't both sustain that level of earnings and build the foundation we needed for fast growth." He told his staff and his investors that he expected to run the company at a loss for the next three years.[267]

That's exactly what happened. In 1987, Starbucks suffered a loss of $330,000. A year later, that number increased to $764,000, reaching $1.2 million in the third year. In the year after that, the company was back to making a profit. Schultz remembers: "That was a nerve-wrecking period for all of us, filled with many white-knuckle days. Although we knew we were investing in the future and had accepted the fact that we wouldn't be profitable, I was often filled with doubts."[268]

There was one month when losses were four times the amount budgeted for. As it happened, a meeting of the advisory board was scheduled for the week after that. Knowing that he would be called on to account for his actions, Schultz didn't sleep a wink. He was scared of the board members' reactions. At the meeting, the mood was as tense as he had expected. "Things aren't working," one of the board members said. "We will have to change strategy." Schultz was shaking inside and had to muster all of his willpower in order to convince them to stick with the original plan. "Look," he said, trying his hardest to keep the panic out of his voice, "we're going to keep losing money until we can do three things. We have to attract a management team well beyond our expansion needs. We have to build a world-class roasting facility." And finally, he added, they needed an IT system "sophisticated enough to keep track of sales in hundreds and hundreds of stores."[269] Did he really mean "hundreds and hundreds" of stores? Some investors were skeptical. Starbucks only had 20 branches at the time. And now this Schultz guy wanted to invest huge amounts of money in a computer system that was able to manage hundreds of shops?

And why on Earth, the skeptics asked, did he want to hire experienced and expensive executives who would be woefully overqualified for the job? In his autobiography, Schultz reflects: "Hiring ahead of the growth curve may seem costly at the time, but it's a lot wiser to bring in experts before you need them than to stumble ahead with green, untested people who are prone to making avoidable mistakes."[270]

But the company kept swallowing money. After all the trouble he'd had raising the $3.8 million he needed to buy Starbucks, he now had to find another $3.9 million to finance his ambitious plans for expansion. In 1990, the company needed even more capital, which he got from a venture capital fund. A year later, Schultz had to raise another $15 million. Altogether, there were four rounds of so-called private placements of company shares before Starbucks went public in 1992.

Imagine how much stamina it must have taken to get through that time. Wouldn't Howard Schultz's life have been so much easier if he had set his sights lower and kept costs down? He would have been able to turn a profit a lot sooner, which would have saved him a lot of trouble dealing with his investors and their critical questions. Was he really on the right path? Wasn't he increasing the risk with every million he spent?

Schultz didn't look at it that way. From where he was standing, the larger risk lay in not investing enough. "When companies fail, or fail to grow, it's almost always because they don't invest in the people, the systems, and the processes they need. Most people underestimate how much money it will take to do that. They also tend to underestimate how they are going to feel about reporting large losses."[271] Large investments in the company's early days not only resulted in high annual losses – they also meant that the founder had to give up more and more of his share in the company. But Schultz was willing to pay the price – and his stamina would be rewarded in the end.

Schultz has the following advice for other would-be entrepreneurs: "When you're starting a business, whatever the size, it's critically important to recognize that things are going to take longer and cost more money than you expect. If your plan is ambitious, you have to count on temporarily investing more than you earn, even if sales are increasing rapidly. If you recruit experienced executives, build manufacturing facilities far beyond your current needs, and formulate a clear strategy for managing through the lean years, you'll be ready as the company shifts into ever higher gears."[272]

The kind of stamina Schultz demonstrated depends on two key factors: a high tolerance for disappointment and a truly high goal. Only a high goal will motivate you enough not to give up in spite of defeats and lean periods. But the key to success is a high tolerance for disappointment. Schultz had to develop his early on in his career when he was working as a salesman for Xerox.

For six months, he knocked on the doors of every office on his territory in Manhattan between 42nd and 48th Street, from the East River to Fifth Avenue. "Cold-calling was great training for business," he remembers. "So many doors slammed on me that I had to develop a thick skin and a concise sales pitch for a then new-fangled machine called a word processor."[273] He became a very successful salesman. "I sold a lot of machines and outperformed many of my peers. As I proved myself, my confidence grew. Selling, I discovered, had a lot to do with self-esteem."[274]

This kind of self-confidence is a necessary requirement for developing enough stamina to bounce back from defeat. However, the more stamina you develop, the more your self-confidence will grow. If you have stamina and a high tolerance for disappointment, and if you end up being successful because of those very qualities, your self-confidence is bound to increase. Only then will you be able to set your goals even higher and to overcome the obstacles on the road to success, which will in turn grow higher and higher. No wonder, then, that many of the personalities featured in this book were good salespeople above everything else – a job which, as much as empathy and assertiveness, requires a high tolerance for disappointment.

Without stamina, you won't make it in the business world. Michael Bloomberg spent 15 years working for Salomon Brothers before he was fired and decided to start his own company. In his autobiography, he writes: "Thank goodness, every time another firm came to hire me away, I said no. I always found a reason to stay, some fresh outlook on my Salomon life that made me recommit myself to the firm."[275]

Bloomberg's patience was frequently tried to its limits and beyond. After six years with Salomon, things were going great for him. He was the darling of Wall Street and feted by the media. He was making good money and there was only one accolade he was still waiting for: He still hadn't made partner in the company. The prestige that came with being a partner "mattered more than everything in the world to me," he wrote. "I'd earned this partnership, and now I wanted the public acknowledgement of my value once and for all, as a big fish in the big pond."[276]

The list of new partners was published in August 1972. Bloomberg, who had counted on being on it, and wanted it more than he had ever wanted anything else, was devastated to find his name wasn't on the list. He had been passed over in favor of colleagues who had done nothing to deserve this honor. "I had been passed over and, with such a big group accepted, humiliated as well." Bloomberg was gutted. He had tears in his eyes. And he started plotting his revenge. "I searched for someone to blame. 'I'll quit,' I told myself, in the first of many crazy mutterings. 'I'll kill them.' 'I'll shoot myself.'"[277]

Most people would have reacted the same way and blamed their defeat on others who had failed to recognize their achievements or had conspired against them. But Bloomberg soon came to his senses. From now on, his motto was: "Screw 'em!" He worked even harder than before, became even more focused and gave everything he had to give. And he kept telling himself: "Screw 'em!" Three months later, he got his long-coveted partnership.[278]

When he formed his own company in 1981, his patience and his stamina were tested all over again. He had been richly rewarded for his stamina by Salomon Brothers, who sent him on his way with a golden handshake worth $10 million. He founded his own company with a few colleagues. To start with, they rented a small office – about 30 square feet – on Madison Avenue in Manhattan. "In our broom closet of an office, we celebrated our start on day one with a bottle of champagne."[279]

Bloomberg, who had always worked hard, put in 14 hours a day, six days a week, during this period. Then he came up against the same hard truth that Howard Schultz had: "I had committed nowhere near enough money to fund development."[280] His expenses were far higher than he had originally expected.

There was no way of predicting whether clients would be prepared to pay for the product he was planning to sell – a completely new kind of computer terminal for the display and distribution of financial information. He even started wondering whether risking his fortune and his good name was a good idea. After all, he had already spent $4 million of the $10 million he had received from Salomon Brothers. And his new business was still running at a loss. "Fortunately, however, even had I wanted to leave this enterprise behind, there was no graceful way to exit (thank God for ego!), so we ploughed ahead."[281] Stamina and tolerance for disappointment are of major importance but they won't get you far unless you are willing to experiment and open to new ideas.

If you stick to a rigid plan no matter what, all your stamina will get you nowhere. Michael Bloomberg doesn't believe in detailed planning: "You'll inevitably face problems different from the ones you anticipated. Sometimes you'll have to 'zig' when the blueprint says 'zag.' You don't want a detailed, inflexible plan getting in the way when you have to respond instantly."[282]

Let me repeat it once again: stamina will lead to success only if it is accompanied by a willingness to experiment. Thomas Edison, one of the greatest inventors in history, had the stamina to conduct 10,000 different experiments before he succeeded in inventing the light bulb. How many of us would have given up after a hundred, or a thousand, failed experiments?

Those who act proactively and are able to learn quickly from mistakes tend to be more successful than others who keep working on perfecting their ideas, but hesitate to put them into action. "We made mistakes, of course," Bloomberg admits. "Most of them were omissions we didn't think of when we initially wrote the software. We fixed them by doing it over and over, again and again. We do the same today." While his competitors were still busy trying to come up with the perfect final design, he was already working on his fifth version of the prototype. "It gets back to planning versus acting. We act from day one; others plan how to plan – for months."[283]

If you are starting a new company, don't try to stick slavishly to a plan, but always be willing to learn and to experiment. Bloomberg has always stressed that predictions about new business ideas are mostly useless and meaningless, however much banks and other investors may insist on them. "The noise in the assumptions you have to make is so great, and the knowledge you have of strange areas so limited, that all the detailed analysis is usually irrelevant."[284]

An entrepreneur who is just as skeptical as Bloomberg when it comes to rigid plans, and who has shown what the combination of perseverance and experimentation can do, is Jack Ma, the founder of Alibaba. In the U.S. and Europe, Amazon may still be better known than Alibaba, but a comparison of the two companies illustrates the importance of Jack Ma's e-commerce giant. Singles' Day is celebrated on November 11 each year and serves to illustrate Alibaba's market power. In 2009, Jack Ma had the idea of making this date a day for special offers. The four 'ones' in the date symbolize the single people who are expected to give each other gifts on Singles' Day – and they do. On November 11, 2016, the campaign flushed €15.1 billion into the cash registers of merchants on Alibaba.com. In 2018, the figure rose further with Alibaba reporting turnover of $30.8 billion on Singles' Day. In comparison, online retailers in the U.S. turned over a combined $7.9 billion on Cyber Monday, Black Friday, Thanksgiving and Prime Day.

In 2018, Alibaba's brand was worth $113 billion – ahead of well-known American corporations such as IBM ($96 billion), Coca-Cola ($80 billion) and Disney ($54 billion). Through his company, Jack Ma has risen from his beginnings as a simple schoolteacher to one of the richest people in the world. In October 2018, the Chinese *Hunrun* magazine reported that he was the richest man in China, with assets of $39 billion. According to *Forbes*, in 2018 he was one of the 20 richest people in the world. A year earlier, *Fortune* had crowned him second in its World's 50 Greatest Leaders list, and in *Forbes* he has been ranked as one of the "most influential people" in the world for years now.

Ma stands as an excellent example of what the combination of perseverance and experimentation can achieve. Jack Ma was born in 1964. As a boy, he did everything he could to learn English. He was an avid reader of Mark Twain's books and used every opportunity to improve his English. Aged 12, he had an idea of how he could improve his English skills: every morning at five o'clock he rode his bicycle for 40 minutes to an international hotel in his hometown and waited there for tourists. When he approached them, he suggested a deal: he would show them around the city as a travel guide and they would teach him English in return. Whether it was snowing or raining, he waited outside the hotel day after day, morning after morning, year after year. One day he met an Australian family with whom he made friends and who invited him to Australia, where he was impressed by the high standard of living that people there enjoyed compared with China.

His English was improving constantly, but he was so weak in mathematics that he failed the standardized university entrance test – he only achieved one out of 120 possible points. He tried again, and this time he achieved 19 out of 120. His overall results were so bad that the university turned him down. Still, he did not give up and at some point he managed to get into Teachers' College – although he admits that it was the least respected university in his city. In 1988, he obtained a bachelor's degree in English and found a job as an English teacher.

A trip to Seattle in 1995, where a friend showed him the internet for the first time, proved to be decisive in shaping his future life. He was immediately interested and intuitively recognized the role the internet would play in the future. That same year, he founded the company *China Yellow Pages*, which struggled to eke out an existence. He had spent almost all of his money on registering the company, which left little for anything else. The company's office consisted of a single room with a workstation in the middle, where a very old PC stood.

The biggest problem was that it was not possible to access the internet in his hometown of Hangzhou at that time. Given such circumstances, anyone else would have given up on the idea of setting up an internet company there. But Jack Ma was different. He told all his friends about the possibilities of the internet and was able to convince some to commission him to design websites for them. He asked them to send him documents about their company, which he translated into English and sent by post to Seattle, where the websites were actually created. The friends in Seattle took screenshots of the websites they were working on and sent them back to China, where he showed them to his clients. The fact that he even managed to find companies in his hometown who were willing to spend the not insignificant sum of 20,000 renminbi (about $2,400) is testament to his enormous persuasiveness. "I was treated like a con man for three years," is how Jack Ma remembers those early days.[285]

Over the next few years, Ma repeatedly changed his business model – combining experimentation with perseverance. In 1999, he founded the Alibaba Group as a business-to-business e-commerce platform. Things were by no means easy at first. Jack Ma later remembered: "First week, we have seven employees. We buy and sell, ourselves. The second week, somebody started to sell on our website. We bought everything they sell. We had two rooms full of things we bought for no use, all garbage, for the first two weeks – in order to tell people that it works."[286] From the outset he thought big and set himself very ambitious goals. Shortly after he founded his company, he told a journalist: "We don't want to be number one in China. We want to be number one in the world."[287] He was so convinced of his future success that he even had a meeting filmed in his modest apartment in February 1999 – as a document for the company's later history. During the small meeting, he posed the question: "In the next five or ten years, what will Alibaba become?" Answering his own question, he said that "our competitors are not in China, but in Silicon Valley ... We should position Alibaba as an international website."[288]

Ma tried to raise money from venture capitalists in Palo Alto, Silicon Valley. The investors he met expected him to present a fully developed business plan. But, much like Bloomberg, the Google founders and so many other successful company founders, Jack Ma did not have a business plan. His motto was: "If you plan, you lose. If you don't plan, you win."[289] Unfortunately, the investors had a hard time understanding Ma's approach. "We don't really have a clearly defined business model yet," he conceded. "If you consider Yahoo! a search engine, Amazon a bookstore, eBay an auction center, Alibaba is an electronic market. Yahoo! and Amazon are not perfect models and we're still trying to figure out what's best."[290] Thanks to his charisma, he nevertheless managed to persuade the employee responsible for China at Goldman Sachs to invest $5 million in his company.

Jack Ma's example shows that entrepreneurial intuition and, above all, the willingness to be open to new ideas, and to always be ready to adapt a business model, are much more important than book knowledge of the kind taught in business administration courses around the world. In a lecture, he said: "It is not necessary to study an MBA. Most MBA graduates are not useful ... Unless they come back from their MBA studies and forget what they've learned at school, then they will be useful. Because schools teach knowledge, while starting business requires wisdom. Wisdom is acquired through experience. Knowledge can be acquired through hard work."[291]

What Jack Ma says is confirmed by entrepreneurial research: entrepreneurial success is not the result of explicit, academic learning and book knowledge – it is the product of implicit learning processes that manifest themselves in intuition and gut feeling. However, this is not something irrational or mystical; it is accumulated experience, which in turn is the result of a combination of perseverance and the willingness to experiment. I have written more on this very subject in my book *The Wealth Elite*.

As far as Ma was concerned, even technological knowledge was not necessary as he strived to achieve exceptional success as an internet entrepreneur: "I'm not good at technology," he declared in 2014. "I was trained to be a high school teacher. It's a funny thing. I'm running one of the biggest e-commerce companies in China, maybe in the world, but I know nothing about computers. All I know about computers is how to send and receive email and browse."[292]

Jack Ma, who first started as a website designer and then went into business-to-business e-commerce, continued to develop his business in new directions.

In 2003, he founded Taobao, the largest Chinese business-to-consumer shopping website. He was met with skepticism when he unveiled his plans for Taobao, both within his company and from investors. After all, Alibaba's business-to-business operations were not yet profitable. Plus, at this time, it was also difficult to raise new funds from venture capital companies. Should the company really open a new front where it had not yet won the business-to-business battle? Many of the people he spoke to were wary. But Jack Ma was right. In 2007, he even managed to beat his fiercest competitor, eBay, which had far greater financial muscle than Ma's company. eBay was forced to wind up its business in China because it never managed to understand the Chinese market, including the mentality of the large numbers of small retailers who use Taobao. In 2004, Ma went on to found Alipay, the world's largest internet payment service.

Jack Ma was and is always open to new ideas. "From day one," he explained in 2004, "all entrepreneurs know that their day is about dealing with difficulty and failure rather than defined by 'success.' My most difficult time hasn't come yet, but it surely will. Nearly a decade of entrepreneurial experience tells me these difficult times can't be evaded or shouldered by others – the entrepreneur must be able to face failure and never give up."[293]

Larry Page and Sergey Brin, the founders of Google, have some things in common with Jack Ma – they also started out without a fully fleshed-out business plan and changed their business model again and again.

The two creators of Google, both born in 1973, had a bright idea – they wanted to build the best search engine in the world. They weren't happy with the performance of existing search engines such as Alta Vista, and were convinced they could do better. While using Alta Vista, they had discovered that search results showed not only a list of websites but also apparently meaningless information on links. By integrating the link popularity factor into the algorithms used for searching the web, the engine's performance could be improved considerably, they found.

The two college students were obsessed with the idea of creating the best and most advanced search engine in the world. At first, they weren't even planning to start their own company, but they needed money to buy hundreds of PCs, which they connected to each other to search the internet.

They did succeed in finding venture capital investors. But they still didn't have a definite business plan. In *The Google Story*, David A. Vise and

Mark Malseed comment: "Neither of the guys had a clear idea of how the company would make money, though it seemed to them that if they had the best search engine, others would want to use it in their organizations."[294] Contrary to the advice regularly given to business students, they didn't bother drafting a business plan either. The question of how Google was going to make money remained unanswered.

Page's and Brin's original idea was to sell licenses for their search engine technology to other internet companies. This proved to be very hard to put into practice. Michael Moritz of Sequoia, one of the two original venture capital investors in Google, remembers: "During the first year, we collectively had concern that the market we were pursuing was more difficult and more intractable than we had originally anticipated. The conversations with potential customers and negotiations with potential customers were protracted. There was a fair amount of competition, and we didn't have a direct sales force."[295]

Page and Brin didn't let this stop them. At first, they were opposed to selling advertising space because they thought the objectivity of the search results might be compromised. They pointed to the negative example set by other companies who had gone down that route. In any case, the banner advertising used at the time hadn't proved very efficient.

Eventually, they discovered a company which seemed to manage combining advertising with search results quite successfully. It looked as if the concept might work after all. Page and Brin decided to modify it and use it as the basis for their business model. It was a simple strategy: their search engine would be free for users; the money would come from advertising sales.

In the early years, Google incurred losses. In 2000, the company operated with a deficit of $14.7 million. But only a year later, it made a profit of $7 million. Over the next few years, that sum would rise steadily, from $100 million in 2002 to $400 million in 2004 and $1.5 billion in 2005. In 2018, Google achieved a turnover of $136 billion and a profit of $26.3 billion. Today, the Google brand is worth more than Coca-Cola or McDonald's – with a net worth more than $300 billion, it was the most valuable brand in the world in 2018.

In 1998, when they had created the technological basis for what was to become the Google search engine and were trying to sell the license to companies such as Yahoo!, Page and Brin had been given short shrift everywhere. They were asking for a million dollars for their system, which everybody they offered it to thought was way too much. It was a 'defeat' that would prove to be a lucky escape for the creators of Google – if they had found any takers for their offer, they would probably never have founded their company. Once again, an apparent setback proved to be the seedbed for an even larger success.

As the story of Google demonstrates, the key factor for a successful business start-up is not perfect planning, but the ability to learn and adapt quickly. Many people might be inclined to laugh at a couple of would-be entrepreneurs with no business plan and no clear idea of how they are going to make money. No bank in the world would have given them a loan to finance their business idea. But a great vision combined with pragmatism, the willingness to experiment and the ability to learn is worth far more than a piece of paper with an elaborate business plan, which only a professor of economics would get excited about.

The pragmatic and experimental attitude that served them so well in their early days remains a hallmark of the Google creators' success even to this day. New services are frequently launched as beta versions to indicate that they are still in development. Google owes its existence to its founders' willingness to experiment.

Successful athletes need great stamina. But at various stages of their careers, all successful athletes will come to a point where their performance stagnates. Attempting to fight back by sticking to the same training routine but training more and longer bears the risk of over-training, which is harmful to the body and results in even worse performance. In order to overcome these periods of stagnation, which inevitably occur in every athlete's career, and to keep improving and developing, he or she has to be open to new training routines.

Oliver Kahn, the soccer player, quotes Albert Einstein, who once said: "Repeating the same experiment over and over again without changing the set-up is a kind of madness."[296] Kahn advises top athletes and anyone else who is aiming for success to be open to "goal-oriented experimentation in the area ... in which you want to succeed ... Never senseless or nonsensical, but wild, extreme, just: open to experiments."[297] He also warns against misguided perfectionism: "The art is not in being perfect, that might even result in pure time-wasting. 'Perfection is the enemy of getting started.'"[298] We might add: perfection is frequently little more than a convenient excuse for not getting started because conditions are not perfect.

Willingness to experiment requires the courage to make mistakes. "Try to focus on doing it right; not on not doing it wrong," Kahn emphasizes.[299]

That's good advice, which you should commit to memory: "Try to focus on doing things right; not on not doing anything wrong." What distinguishes successful people from those who spend their whole lives dodging potential failure is their single-minded focus on success, on wanting to do things right. Unfortunately, those who merely try to avoid doing anything wrong tend to fit in well in a lot of large companies as well as in government institutions, where success counts for very little, whereas failure carries severe penalties. In the worst-case scenario, this leads to an attitude along the lines of: "If I work a lot and risk a lot, I will make a lot of mistakes, if I work less and risk less, I will make fewer mistakes, and if I don't work at all, I won't make any mistakes." In any case, an exaggerated fear of making mistakes will stop you from experimenting and make you stick to tried and tested procedures instead.

Even if you fail with a business model, that doesn't make you a loser – quite the contrary. Many people are so scared of failing with their business idea that they won't even try to put it into practice. In fact, many successful entrepreneurs failed with one business idea or another – but they learned from their failure and in many cases turned it into the basis for even larger successes.

"If everything you try works, then you are not trying hard enough," said the American computer pioneer and co-founder of Intel, Gordon Moore. And how right he is! Winners are not winners because they succeed in everything. On the contrary, winners set big goals and experiment on the way to achieving them. They do not need a guarantee that something will succeed before they tackle it. They know and accept that much of what they try will fail. "If you don't fail now and again, it's a sign you're playing it safe," the American actor Woody Allen aptly said. And the founder of Nike, Phil Knight, said, "If we're not making mistakes, we're not trying enough new things." Even a brilliant investor like Warren Buffett has to report every year on investments he's been totally wrong about. It is neither possible nor necessary to be right all the time. You just need to make sure that you are right more often than you are wrong. If you dare to do something new and are not afraid of the next step, then it may well be that this step is too small for you.

It doesn't matter whether you are an entrepreneur, employee, freelance professional, academic, artist, or athlete: you will not succeed unless you are willing to experiment and to make mistakes. Saying that you've "already tried everything" is an easy option. If you review your life with a self-critical eye, you will probably see that it's not true. In sports as in business, there is an infinite number of ways to approach things and to proceed – nobody can seriously claim that they have "tried them all." Usually, this is nothing but an excuse to explain to yourself and others why you're not making any progress.

McDonald's restaurants are famous for their elaborate system of operation in which every detail has been optimized for maximum efficiency. This system was not born out of a sudden flash of inspiration but perfected over time with a combination of experimentation and stamina. The fact that none of the executives who ran the company in the 1950s had a background in the catering industry proved to be an advantage. "Because we lacked prior restaurant experience, nothing was taken for granted," says Ray Kroc's contemporary and eventual successor Fred Turner. "We had to learn everything on our own ... We were continuously looking for a better way to do things, and then a revised better way to do things, and then a revised, revised better way."[300]

Ray Kroc himself always encouraged his restaurant managers to voice any differences of opinion and to be experimental and open to new ideas. "I had no previous experience in the hamburger business," he says. "In fact, none of us had dyed-in-the-wool reasons for saying anything. So, if they [his managers] had a different idea than my idea, I'd let them run with it for six months and see what it did." He freely admits to having made as many mistakes as his colleagues – "but we grew together."[301] James Kuhn, another McDonald's veteran from the early days, sums up the secret of their success as follows: "In fact, we are a bunch of motivated people who shoot off a lot of cannon, and they don't all land on target. We've made a lot of mistakes, but it is the mistakes that make our success, because we have learned from them."[302]

John F. Love says in *Behind the Arches*: "Everything was done on a tri-al-and-error basis. No idea was unworthy of discussion ... In short, McDonald's business evolved as a result of thousands of operating experiments made in the real world of store operations."[303]

Experimentation requires a willingness to admit mistakes and to learn from criticism. While people who are dogmatic and opinionated find this more difficult than others, self-confidence is actually an asset in this regard. The more self-confident you are, the less you will feel threatened by criticism. Bill Gates for example was always willing to change his mind if somebody else had better arguments on their side. "Bill is not dogmatic about things. He's very pragmatic," says one of the original Microsoft programmers. "He can be extremely vocal and persuasive in arguing one side of an issue, and a day or two later he will say he was wrong and let's get on with it. There are not many people who have the drive and the intensity and the entrepreneurial qualities to be that successful who also have the ability to put their ego aside."[304]

Another member of Gates' staff remembers: "If he really believed in something, he would have this intense zeal and support it and push it through the organization and talk it up and whenever he met with people talk about how great it was. But if that particular thing was no longer great, he'd walk away from it and it was forgotten ... It made him incredibly agile in a business sense."[305]

In the 20 years Garry Kasparov spent at the top of his profession as a world-class chess player, he had to cope with "a constant barrage of both condemnation and praise." He warns against the temptation "to ignore the former and embrace the latter. We must fight our own egos and defensive instincts to appreciate that some criticism is deserved and constructive and that we can use it as a tool."[306] Kasparov insists on the importance of self-criticism. He urges fellow players to learn not only from defeat but also from victory, "to look for mistakes in our successes." Winning a game does not necessarily mean that a player has done everything right, he argues – the winner might just have been lucky.[307] "Success is seldom analyzed as closely as failure and we are always quick to attribute our victories to superiority rather than circumstance. When things are going well it is even more important to question. Over-confidence leads to mistakes, a feeling that anything is good enough."[308]

If you are a manager, executive or entrepreneur, you must learn to allow your employees to make mistakes. Of course, it is not acceptable for somebody to keep making the same mistake over and over again because they are unwilling or unable to learn. But if a mistake happens because somebody has taken a risk and tried something new, they should not be sanctioned for that.

By punishing every mistake, you will suppress any willingness to experiment in your employees. When Jack Welch was working for General Electric at the start of his career, he was lucky to have a boss who would allow him to make mistakes. His department was testing a new chemical process when an accident occurred. "I was sitting in my office in Pittsfield, just across the street from the pilot plant, when the explosion occurred. It was a huge blast that blew off the roof of the building and knocked out all the windows on the top floor. It shook everyone, especially me, to their very toes."[309]

Because Welch was in charge of the project, the buck stopped with him. The next day, he had to drive 100 miles to Bridgeport in Connecticut to report the accident to his superior. "I knew I could explain why the blast went off, and I had some ideas on how to fix the problem. But I was a nervous wreck. My confidence was shaken almost as much as the building I had destroyed," Welch remembers.[310]

Welch did not know his boss very well and had no idea how he would react. In the event, his boss showed a lot of understanding and asked all the right questions: how had the accident happened, what had Welch learned from it? Rather than getting angry and attributing blame, he took a rational approach. "It's better that we learned about this problem now rather than later when we had a large-scale operation going. Thank God no one was hurt."[311] Welch was very impressed by his reaction.

Welch thinks that you have to develop an instinct for the appropriate reaction to an employee's mistake: "When to hug and when to kick. Of course, arrogant people who refuse to learn from their mistakes have to go. If we're managing good people who are clearly eating themselves up over an error, our job is to help them through it."[312]

You might want to remember this story the next time one of your employees makes a serious mistake! If you can't learn to accept mistakes – your own and those of others – you will not be successful because success is based on the combination of stamina and experimentation. And the willingness to experiment includes making mistakes. British billionaire Richard Branson has achieved a lot of success in the course of his career – but because he has always been willing to try out new things, he has also experienced his share of failure and defeat. "But what is worse," Branson asks, "making the occasional mistake, or having a closed mind and missing opportunities?"[313]

Take a critical look at your own weaknesses: do you suffer from a lack of stamina; do you tend to give up too easily? Or do you lack the willingness to experiment? For somebody who is aiming high, being moderately successful can often be more harmful than failing altogether. After a real failure, anybody in their right mind will start thinking about what lessons they can learn from it, and about how to do better next time. Moderate success on the other hand will often stop you from experimenting. Once they have achieved a certain degree of success, people tend to stick to what they consider to be their tried and true way of doing things, without even asking themselves whether they might not have been even more successful if they had gone about it differently.

In order not to fall into the moderate-success trap, you deliberately have to set your goals far higher so that you will not be able to achieve them unless you try a new way of doing things. You have to force yourself to experiment and to try out things you have never tried before.

Do you tend to spend too much time making plans? Do you use planning as an excuse for not acting? I have got news for you: the planned economy has been refuted by history once and for all. The free-market economy based on competition, spontaneity and experimentation has won the day. Never mind whatever you may have read about the importance of detailed planning in other self-help guides to success! Of course, a certain amount of planning is necessary, but please do not overdo it. It's much more important that you dare to dream, to set yourself some really high goals. Don't be too afraid of making mistakes – just get going and start experimenting!

CHAPTER 10

Dissatisfaction as a Driving Force

"Raise your sights. Blaze new trails. Compete with the immortals"[314] – this was David Ogilvy's motto. The legendary ad man who started one of the largest agencies in the world "had a near-psychopathic hatred of laziness" and mediocrity, a former employee remembers. "No matter how good, everything had to be better."[315] One of the most important maxims he picked up in the course of his life, says Ogilvy, was "to have exorbitant standards, to try and do everything you did better than anybody's ever done it or will ever do it again."[316]

Successful people exude a specific combination of satisfaction and dissatisfaction. They derive a basic confidence – call it satisfaction – from the successes they have already achieved. At the same time, they are never satisfied with what they have achieved. They are always striving for more and they firmly believe that anything good can still be improved. Many successful people are perfectionists in the positive sense of the word.

Finding the right balance of perfectionism is not an easy task. Ray Kroc, the creator of McDonald's, whose story has already featured elsewhere in this book, did manage it. He had such high standards that – as one of his closest business associates put it – "when he saw a bad McDonald's, he went berserk."[317] Kroc had invented the formula QSC (Quality, Service, Cleanliness) and that formula had become a kind of gospel for him.

The art of turning potatoes into French fries was not something anybody had ever spent a lot of time thinking about. Kroc turned it into a science project. In the first 30 years of its existence, the McDonald's company invested over $3 million in research and development on how to make the perfect French fry.

In the course of the research, it was discovered that the quality of the fries depended to a large extent on the type of potato used, which for best results had to have a solids content of at least 21%. Ray Kroc sent experts out to his suppliers to measure their potatoes' solid contents with a strange-looking appliance called a hydrometer. The sight of the McDonald's experts with their hydrometers rendered some of the potato farmers speechless. It was the first time anybody had ever showed up to test their potatoes with scientific methods.

Kroc still was not satisfied. He started investigating storage conditions and was shocked to hear that most suppliers stored their potatoes in man-made caves lined with sods of peat. He then looked for processing plants prepared to invest in a state-of-the-art storage system with automated temperature control.

This still wasn't good enough for him. He had the deep-frying process in the restaurants analyzed with scientific precision in order to work out how to improve it. His secretary's husband, who used to work as an electrical engineer for Motorola before he started running a McDonald's restaurant with his wife, spent several months studying the deep-frying process in the basement of his restaurant. He came to the conclusion that the company needed its own research laboratory because the quality of the French fries was still uneven in spite of all the improvements they had made – something Kroc would not tolerate. He agreed to establish a small research lab.

Some people ridiculed him for his perfectionism – but he wanted the French fries to taste exactly the same in all of his branches. This would give him an advantage over his competitors who did not invest as much time and money in selecting the right kind of potato and perfecting the deep-frying process.

Fred Turner, Kroc's closest associate, was another perfectionist. He literally wrote the book on standardizing the quality of service and food in all McDonald's franchises. Shortly after he had started working for the company, he issued a 15-page manual, soon to be replaced by a 38-page guide. After he had talked to hundreds of employees and franchisees, Turner had the next edition printed and bound. He kept adding to it over the years, and the volume grew from 75 in 1958 to 200 and eventually over 600 pages.

Turner had turned the art of running a fast food restaurant into a science. His book exhorts anyone involved in the McDonald's operations: "YOU MUST BE A PERFECTIONIST! There are hundreds and hundreds of details to be watched. There isn't any compromising."[318] Both Kroc and Turner were convinced that there was only one right way to run a McDonald's. They could not stand franchisees who deviated from their rules and did things their own way. "Either, (A) the details are watched and your volume grows, or (B) you are not particular, not fussy, and do not have a pride or liking for the business, in which case you will be an also-ran. If you fall into the 'B' category, this is not the business for you!"[319]

The manual contained elaborate instructions on how to mix a milkshake, how to flip a burger, and how to make French fries. In order to maintain quality standards, there was detailed information on the exact cooking times and temperatures for each product. There were precise instructions for every step of the process, down to individual hand movements and exact guidelines on how much onion and how many grams of cheese had to go on a burger. Even the size of the French fries was standardized.

If you are striving for this degree of perfection, you have to be careful not to lose sight of the woods for the trees, otherwise you may well end up being your own worst enemy. An excess of perfectionism can do more damage than good by paralyzing, rather than motivating you. In the case of McDonald's, the perfectionist approach worked only because of the restrictions Kroc and Turner had imposed on themselves concerning the range of dishes on offer, and the choice of suppliers. "It wasn't because we were smarter," says Fred Turner. "The fact that we were selling just ten items, had a facility that was small, and used a limited number of suppliers created an ideal environment for really digging in on everything."[320]

Kroc was unrelenting in the implementation of standards he considered necessary. What was the point of having a few exemplary restaurants that adhered religiously to his quality standards, if all the rest failed to live up to them?

"We have found out as you have that we cannot trust some people who are nonconformists," he advised the McDonald brothers in 1958. "We will make conformists out of them in a hurry ... So, from the standpoint of growth on the firmest kind of foundation, the only way that we can positively know that these units are doing what they are supposed to do ... is to make it so that they can have no alternative whatsoever ... The organization cannot trust the individual; the individual must trust the organization [or] he shouldn't go into this kind of business."[321]

For all his obsession with standards and norms, Kroc still urged his employees to experiment and to be creative. Because he realized that franchisees were closer to the market, he welcomed any suggestions for continuous improvement, which would then be systematically tested. What he did not want was for franchisees to deviate from his standards and try out new things on their own accord. Kroc was unwavering when it came to enforcing his standards. He insisted that wearing a beard was a breach of basic hygiene regulations. His friend Bob Dondanville, who was a fellow Rolling Green Club member and one of the first McDonald's licensees, enjoyed annoying Kroc. He completely ignored the latter's constant admonitions to shave off his beard. The very idea of the bearded Dondanville slicing roast beef in the display window of a McDonald's drive-in filled Kroc with despair. Dondanville had started growing a beard while he was waiting for his restaurant to be built, and he had originally promised to shave it off for the grand opening. But then he decided to keep his beard just because it upset Kroc so much.

But these were comparatively minor infractions against Kroc's perfectionist regime. In the beginning, he was engaged in a constant war of attrition with franchisees who refused to implement his QSC standards. His stamina, stubbornness and steadfastness, which enabled him to impose them on reluctant franchisees, was the key to his success.

Some people considered Kroc a dictator – but if he was, at least he was able and willing to listen to, and to respect, the opinions of others. "We knew he had a temper and was capable of blowing up at any moment," Turner says, "but he would listen to me, give me my day in court, and let me know what he thought. And if I was arguing my point with conviction, he usually let me have my way."[322] Kroc was not concerned with showing others who was boss, or with winning every argument at any cost. He was fighting for a cause, and he welcomed any suggestion that might help him to achieve his goal of perfecting the production process and service in every McDonald's restaurant.

All extraordinarily successful people strive for perfectionism. While Kroc turned the quest for the perfect French fry into a science, only the best was good enough for Boris Becker when it came to stringing his tennis racket. His racket, he said, was to him what violin prodigy Anne-Sophie Mutter's instrument was for her. Every string had to be exactly 0.8 millimeters thick. His racket weighed exactly 367 grams. He regularly returned eight out of ten rackets to the factory, claiming that they were unsuitable for use in professional tennis.

"Agassi, Sampras and I, professionals who could afford it, worked with our own racket experts. Mine followed me, together with his machinery, as far as Australia. This investment paid off. My near perfection was partly thanks to the materials I had access to."[323]

Becker was extremely sensitive to the most minute changes to his racket. When he moved from Puma to the Taiwanese manufacturer Estusa, he requested countless modifications and adjustments of the newly developed model. "My demands got my business partners so worked up that they flew in one of the top racket experts from the USA. They spray-painted both their Estusa and my old Puma black and asked me to tell them which one was the Puma. It took me just two hits of a ball – so that settled that."[324]

After Becker's contract with Estusa had expired, his Romanian manager Ion Tiriac bought up the remaining stocks of Estusa rackets worldwide. When they had been used up, Becker found another company which was "prepared to 'bake' a few hundred rackets to my specific requirements. I finally bought the racket machine from them to secure my supply."[325]

The constant striving for improvement, which I like to call 'dissatisfaction as a driving force,' is an essential requirement for success. It was certainly what drove Werner Otto, the founder of the Otto mail-order company. The business he started with a seed capital of 6,000 deutsche marks in 1949 grew to be the largest mail-order company in the world, long before the emergence of online retail giants such as Amazon. With an estimated fortune of around €10 billion, the Otto family ranked among the 12 richest families in Germany in 2018.

After Werner Otto had returned from fighting in the war, he started a shoe factory in 1948, but was unable to make a go of it against stiff competition. But Otto did not let this setback bother him. At age 40, he formed the Werner Otto Versandhandel company. He started his mail-order business with three employees working out of two small shacks. The first catalog, which was issued in 1950, consisted of 14 pages featuring 28 pairs of shoes. A total of 300 copies were printed. Otto had glued the pictures to the pages himself.

The following year, Otto printed 1,500 copies and turned over a million deutsche marks. He kept coming up with new ideas on how to stimulate interest and boost his sales. In 1952, he introduced so-called group orders, which meant that customers who ordered jointly with friends, neighbors or relatives, received a discount. In 1958, the business turned over 100 million deutsche marks and 250,000 copies of the 168-page catalog were printed.

Otto was constantly striving for growth and improvement. In April 1954, he wrote a memo to all department managers in his company asking them for an "account of their personal productive performance." As for the information to be itemized in these accounts, which were to help him evaluate the 'mental elasticity' of his staff, he specified: "I will mark with a zero any monthly report which concerns itself with the listing of trivialities, which indicate no further development whatsoever." Managers, he added, should "put nothing else into the report except for their own strokes of genius, which have led to progress within the department in some way. If there is nothing to report, the lack of progress must be indicated by stating: 'No development has taken place in the department.'"[326]

Some department managers obviously assumed that reiterating ideas Otto himself had expressed in their own words would be enough to impress him. That's why his instructions included the warning: "Any department manager's idea for further development which has previously or at the same time been expressed by me will not count. I expect my department managers to think one minute faster than I myself can think. Thus, I do not wish to be presented with my own work by any department manager."[327]

Otto would constantly lecture his staff on the importance of not "going round in circles." He championed a certain managerial type, whom he called a "company builder ... the man who senses the future, who pushes developments forward, who drives his department towards something new."[328] Otto was afraid the success his company and its employees had already achieved would make them complacent and stop them from reacting to changes in society and calculating their implications for the future of the business.

The following quote from Werner Otto will illustrate what I mean by calling dissatisfaction a driving force: "The next thing is newer and better than the previous stage of development which we have left behind. The next thing is always genuine progress. Those who stay in one place, performing the same task over and over again, those who stick with the acquired routine of what they have already achieved, those who are not burning with the desire to take things further, won't get far here because we are always working on building the future."[329]

There was nothing Otto despised more than employees with the mentality of civil servants, who would above all try to avoid mistakes, and would never risk anything or experiment. At the company's Christmas party, he even praised employees who had made mistakes during the last financial year. He was grateful to those who made mistakes because they had dared to go off the trodden path, he told his staff.

True to his word, the first of his own business principles was 'know yourself.' He elaborates: "Try to look your mistakes square in the eye, which means looking yourself in the eye! We can only improve our performance by taking a long, hard look at our weaknesses."[330] This really is one of the most vital factors for success – whether personal success or the success of a business. Of course, confronting our weaknesses and mistakes feels uncomfortable at first. So does constantly being on the lookout for things that aren't working as well as they ought to. But it's the only way forward.

It's the most hard-working, capable and active people, Otto said, who make the most mistakes. But the difference between them and those who are simply incompetent is that they are self-critical and willing to confront their mistakes. Only those who lack self-confidence feel the need to defend their mistakes, rather than asking themselves what has caused the mistake and what they can do to prevent it from happening again.

Within his company, Otto promoted a culture of what he called "deficiency analysis." He was convinced that his business would not progress unless processes that didn't work as well as expected were constantly monitored and analyzed. He was surprised to see that other companies, his suppliers for example, tended to be less than pleased to have any deficiencies pointed out to them. He himself was always grateful for criticism, especially from outsiders. "People outside the company may lack the insider's knowledge, but from the distance they can sometimes see scope for improvement within the company which the expert has become blind to through familiarity."[331]

Otto had very high standards when it came to personnel decisions. That didn't always make it easy for his leading executives – on the contrary. In seven years, he fired 12 heads of marketing who failed to live up to his expectations. "Most people," he said, "would have given up after the third or fourth time. I stuck to my guns."[332] Number 13 proved to be so good at his job that he ended up running the marketing department for more than 20 years.

Don't confuse 'dissatisfaction as a driving force' with an excessive perfectionism, which does more harm than good. Superficially, those who are constantly striving to do even better may resemble the perfectionist type. Werner Otto highlights the difference between the two when he points out that an entrepreneur must not be too preoccupied with current problems. "He must never try to fulfill anything 100%. That would mean constantly dwelling on things of the past." This attitude, Otto says, is a waste of energy, time and money. "The entrepreneur needs enough time to recognize any changes which must be implemented in his company in order to gain the future."[333]

Perfectionists in the negative sense of the word are perfect at hesitating when they ought just to get started and learn by doing. They always have the perfect excuse for why they aren't quite ready to do what they keep talking about doing. Otto was never like that. When he started his shoe factory after the war, he didn't know anything about the business. He thought his naivety worked in his favor. "As a novice shoe manufacturer, I did have one advantage on my side: I knew nothing about shoes and had never seen a shoe factory before." Therefore, his optimism had not been "affected by any expert knowledge."[334]

Like other successful entrepreneurs, Otto was never too proud to ask for advice. When he traveled to the United States in 1955 in the company of other mail-order retailers, he asked his American business partners a lot of questions – much more so than his colleagues did. "They acted as if they already knew everything, which I thought was completely the wrong attitude." He spent entire nights 'pestering' the American mail-order specialists in order to come up with new ideas on how to improve his own business.[335]

Ted Turner was never satisfied with the extraordinary successes he achieved in various areas throughout his life. Among other things, he created the news channel CNN. When CNN was launched on June 1, 1980, it was watched by 1.7 million American households. Today, CNN is the second-most watched U.S. news broadcaster behind Fox News and can be viewed in more than 200 countries. Turner is also the second-biggest private landowner in the United States, with land holdings of 8,000 square kilometers (almost 3,100 square miles). The largest breeder of buffalo in the world, he owns around 15% of the global buffalo population. He also used to be one of the top competitive sailors in the world, a sport he found time for even while building his media empire. He won the legendary America's Cup in 1974 and was inducted as an honorary member into the America's Cup Hall of Fame in 1993. He also earned himself a reputation as a notorious playboy until he married his third wife, actress Jane Fonda, in 1991 and stayed with her for the next ten years.

Turner, his biographer Porter Bibb says, "has carefully arranged his own life to avoid any possibility that he might ever have to rest on his own laurels."[336] Even as a youth, he set himself very high goals. To quote his former math teacher: "When he set his mind to something, he always stuck to it until he eventually achieved it or got struck down trying."[337] Turner's father had been very successful himself and was a millionaire. But by his son's standards, he was a loser because he hadn't set his sights high enough. "My father always said to never set goals you can reach in your lifetime. After you accomplish them, there's nothing left."[338] Ed Turner taught his son to aim high and to keep redefining his goals as he climbed higher and higher on the ladder of success.[339]

As a teenager, Ted Turner devoured tales of heroism. "I was interested in one thing, and that was finding out what you could accomplish if you really tried," Turner says: "My interest was always in why people did the things they did, and what causes people to rise to glorious heights."[340]

Turner was born on November 19, 1930 in Cincinnati, and grew up in Savannah, Georgia. His father, a manic-depressive like Ted himself, committed suicide in 1963 and Ted took over the management of the Turner Advertising Company. He saw the potential of cable TV early on – at a time when it was still a niche market. Turner always thought one step further than his competitors. For him, business was "like a chess game and you have to look several moves ahead. Most people don't. They only think one move at a time. But any good chess player knows when you're playing against a one-move opponent, you'll beat him every time."[341]

In 1980, Turner came up with the idea of creating a round-the-clock news channel, a concept which didn't exist at the time. When he presented his idea to the cable network executives, they turned him down. But Turner was so confident that he risked everything for it. Reese Schonfeld, the journalist he hired to run the news channel, remembers: "It wasn't just the money. It wasn't even his conviction ... It was also the fact that he was willing to lose everything – his television stations, his sports teams, his plantation, his yachts, everything – if Cable News Network didn't work."[342] Turner was forced to put up his real estate holdings, gold and other private assets as collateral for a credit line to finance his plans. "There is risk in everything you do," Turner says. "The sky could fall, the roof cave in. Who knows what's going to happen? I'm going to do news like the world has never seen news done before."[343]

Turner had to fight against massive resistance from the large American television channels. In front of his staff, he brandished a huge broadsword he kept in his office, waving it above his head and shouting: "We will not be stopped! No matter what it costs, we're going on!" Using legal and any other means at their disposal, his competitors tried everything to stop the launch of the channel but Turner persisted: "I said we'll sign on June first, and we will sign on June first ... We won't sign off until the end of the world – and we'll cover that live!"[344]

The new channel incurred huge losses at first and the investments that were needed to keep it going far exceeded the $20 million that Turner had calculated. It was its live coverage of the Gulf War that proved to be the making of the channel. Prior to the invasion, CNN had already negotiated with the Iraqis and obtained permission to report from Baghdad using new portable satellite transmitters. A private jet CNN had chartered for $10,000 a day was ready and waiting in Amman to evacuate the CNN team, if necessary. President George W. Bush made a personal appeal to Ted Turner to get his team out of Baghdad before any fatalities occurred. But the journalists stayed and CNN was the only channel to report live from the war zone. On the very first day of the war, 10.8 million households tuned their televisions to CNN, more than ever before. Before the war started, the channel had rarely been watched by more than a million people; now that number rose to 50 to 60 million.

In 1996, Ted Turner sold the news channel to the media corporation Time Warner for $7.4 billion. He stayed on as vice-president in charge of television. In June 2003, after Time Warner's merger with AOL, he retired from his position. In 2010, Turner joined forces with Bill Gates, Warren Buffett, Larry Ellison, Michael Bloomberg and other billionaires to launch an initiative with the commitment to donate over half of their wealth to charity.

If you want an illustration of how powerful a driving force dissatisfaction can be, look no further than the remarkable career of the American cosmetics tycoon Estée Lauder. A woman who started out mixing moisturizing lotions in her parents' kitchen became a billionaire, the only female to make *Time* magazine's list: "Top Twenty most influential business people of the 20th century".

Estée Lauder's uncle Johann Schotz, a chemist who had emigrated to the United States from Hungary, had built a laboratory in a stable behind his house where he mixed moisturizing lotions. Lauder, who was born Estelle Mentzer, helped him sell his lotions and realized she had a phenomenal talent for sales. In her autobiography, she says: "I have never worked a day in my life without selling."[345] Her uncle suggested she should go to Miami. Palm Beach was full of rich women, a promising location for a high-end cosmetics business. Lauder wasn't shy. She would approach strangers on the street, suggest they change their make-up, hand out samples or even sell her lotions directly to them. A friend of hers ran a beauty parlor where she applied make-up to customers' faces while they were getting their hair done. "Touch your customer and you're halfway there," she soon discovered.[346]

She eventually got the Bonwit Teller department store on Fifth Avenue in New York to stock her products. Her big dream was a display counter in the famous Saks Fifth Avenue department store. If Saks sold her products, she was sure to get nationwide attention. She kept trying to persuade Saks' buyer to stock her cosmetics. But he would not do it. First of all, Saks insisted on being the exclusive stockist and her products were already being sold at Bonwit. And secondly, the buyer said, so far they hadn't had any customers asking for Lauder's products. Saks had a very customer-oriented policy: if a customer asked for a product that they didn't stock, the sales staff would get that product from another shop and sell it on for the same price. But if customers kept asking for a product, Saks would add a new line to their range.

This is where Lauder saw her chance. She had to create a demand. When she was asked to give a speech at a charity event, she handed out stylish lipsticks that cost $3 apiece. The women in the audience loved them – as soon as the speech was over, long queues of customers wanting to buy the same lipstick started forming outside Saks. The buyer had no choice but to start stocking her products. Shortly after, she formed Estée Lauder Companies together with her husband, who became financial director.

After she had made her first $50,000 to $60,000, she decided to hire an advertising agency. She approached BBD&O, a company which had made a name for itself with successful campaigns for Lauder's competitor Revlon, among others. But the agency's director told her she didn't have enough money to afford a successful campaign.

As we have seen before, successful people rarely accept 'no' for an answer. For Lauder, it was all the incentive she needed to come up with an innovative idea that would give her a vital edge over her competition. Handing out free samples in shops is standard practice in the cosmetics industry today – at the time, it was a novel approach. It was Lauder who came up with the idea. She asked Saks whether it would be all right for her to launch a direct marketing campaign and send out vouchers for free samples which customers could then redeem in the Saks store.

Her biggest break came a few years later when she launched a bath oil made from flower and herb extracts that she called *Youth Dew*. Lauder's secret was that she wasn't selling products but promises – in this case the promise of eternal youth and beauty magically encapsulated in a bath oil. *Youth Dew* sold phenomenally well, counting for 80% of her turnover at Saks in the mid-1950s. Its turnover skyrocketed from $50,000 in the very first year to $150 million 30 years later. For decades to come, the magic scent in the dark blue tub remained the company's trademark.

Previously, cosmetics had retailed at around $2 to $5. Lauder had the courage to charge a lot more for her lotions and scents. Her intuition was that her customers would value a product more if they had to pay more for it. The advertising slogan for her Re-Nutriv lotion was: "What Makes a Cream Worth $115.00?" Lauder's competitor, Helena Rubinstein, soon realized the value of charging high prices. Asked why her latest lotion wasn't selling as well as she had expected, she replied: "Not expensive enough." It only cost $5.50.[347]

Lauder marketed her high-end products by appealing to the tastes of members of the jet set, celebrities and other similar disseminators. To this purpose, she returned to Palm Beach, where the beautiful people gathered. "You see, the whole world comes to Palm Beach. And you have them right here in a nutshell all at once in a season. And when you entertain those people here, they're going to reciprocate when they're back where they came from: Europe, the south of France."[348] She also thought this would be the best way to make it into the tabloids, which many women read.

Lauder targeted celebrities such as the Duke and Duchess of Windsor, at the time the most famous visitors to Palm Beach. She went to a lot of trouble to find out which train they were planning to take, then got on the same train and waylaid them ("Oh, are you taking the train, also?"[349]). A newspaper photographer she had tipped off captured their meeting for posterity. In due course, the aristocratic couple would become Lauder's friends, as were many other prominent figures of society. It was the best possible advertising for her company.

A lot of competitors started copying Lauder's products. Charles Revson, the creator of the successful Revlon brand, was especially guilty of this, as one of his employees reports, quoting Revson's motto as follows: "Copy everything and you can't go wrong. That way you let the competitors do the groundwork and make the mistakes. And when they hit with something good, make it better, package it better, advertise it better and bury them."[350]

Lauder tried to figure out how to react to the increasingly competitive market. Finally, she simply founded another business, which she positioned differently in order to compete with her own company. She called the new enterprise Clinique. "The reason we launched Clinique is that I felt that if I were going to go into business against Estée Lauder this is exactly how I would do it," Lauder stated.[351]

But she was also committed to the constant improvement of her own products, and proved to be something of a perfectionist. Saks' sales staff were surprised when she recalled a new product, which had only just been delivered to the store because a single ingredient was missing. They didn't understand why the product had to be taken off the shelves – nobody would notice the difference anyway, they argued. "But I'll know the difference!" she replied and stuck with her decision to recall the product.

"Creating a fragrance," Lauder affirms, "is something like composing a symphony." Her most essential maxim: a new scent had to trigger a strong emotional reaction. People either had to love it or hate it. "Then I know, I'm on the right track. If the scent evokes only a lukewarm reaction, I throw the formula away."[352]

Dissatisfaction means completely different things to successful and unsuccessful people. Unsuccessful people associate dissatisfaction with a negative experience of paralysis. For successful people on the other hand, it is a powerful driving force. Perfectionism also has different meanings for the two groups. Losers wait passively for perfect conditions and look for excuses not to start acting or not to finish what they've started. Winners act despite imperfect conditions and constantly strive to improve them.

Arnold Schwarzenegger once confessed to *Newsweek* magazine that he'd always felt driven by the fear of failure, by a sense that nothing he'd ever done had been quite good enough.[353] Madonna, too, attributes her near-obsessive desire to become famous to fighting a feeling of inadequacy. "I have an iron will, and all of my will has always been to conquer some horrible feeling of inadequacy. I'm always struggling with that fear. I push past one spell of it and discover myself as a special human being and then I get to another stage of it and think I'm mediocre ..."[354]

These self-analyses suggest that dissatisfaction as a driving force is in itself driven by a deep-seated feeling of inadequacy. Whether this is really true or not is hard to say. Madonna and Schwarzenegger may simply have repeated favorite phrases of popular psychology, which on the surface sound plausible enough.

What is certainly true is that a lack of ambition is one of the hardest obstacles for success to overcome. However, it seems unlikely that this is something you are suffering from – if you were, you would hardly have bought a book that is all about setting yourself goals and aiming higher, let alone read to the end of Chapter 10.

How can you harness your own dissatisfaction as a driving force on the road to success? Above all by programming higher and more ambitious goals into your inner GPS – as I have suggested in Chapter 8. Once you have planted a higher goal in your subconscious, you will feel a constant tension resulting from the discrepancy between your actual situation and your projected target. This tension will generate the necessary energy to fuel your dissatisfaction and to drive you forward.

The gap between what you are today and what you have today on the one hand, and your high goals on the other hand, can be closed only by developing completely new ideas. You will not achieve your financial or any other goals merely by working hard and 'trying hard.' Ideas are the key to your success. The tension that results from the difference between what you have and what you want, between your current situation and the goals you have programmed into your inner GPS – that tension can only be resolved by new ideas that your subconscious will put at your disposal to help you achieve your goals.

CHAPTER 11

Ideas Will Make You Rich

Mid-19th century America was gripped by the gold rush. Tens of thousands quit their jobs and moved to California after rumors had spread that gold had been found there and anyone could get rich quickly. Of course, most people didn't grow rich but ended up bankrupting themselves and having to go back to where they had come from. Among the winners was Levi Strauss, who had emigrated from Germany to America with his mother and sisters when he was 18. It wasn't gold that made him rich, though, but a pair of workman's trousers.

Strauss was living in New York when he heard about the boom in California. He had no ambitions of becoming a prospector – instead, he was hoping to sell useful products to the many thousands who had followed the lure of gold all the way to California. Back in Germany and after his move to the United States, he had made a living as a door-to-door salesman for all sorts of items.

One day he had trouble with unhappy customers who were complaining about the poor quality of the canvas material he had sold them. They asked for their money back because, contrary to what they had been led to believe, the material wasn't waterproof. Strauss didn't have the money to reimburse them. He offered to use the remaining materials to make trousers that would be tougher than anything they could buy anywhere else. The men agreed – and the rest is history.

Strauss soon realized that prospectors needed trousers that could stand a lot of wear and tear. After he had sold the first pairs for $6 each, his trousers started selling like hotcakes. The original pairs were brown because they were made from hemp. Later, Strauss started using a blue cotton fabric called denim.

Soon, his family could no longer keep up with the demand. Strauss took the fabric to various tailors in San Francisco and got them to make trousers according to his specifications. The only problem was with the pockets in which prospectors carried their tools – they had a tendency to rip.

Jacob Davis, a tailor from Riga, came up with a solution: after a customer had complained to him about her husband's trousers, which kept ripping, he tried using copper rivets, which were normally used to reinforce the harness horses wore. He attached the small metal parts to reinforce the front and back pockets, as well as the seams running along the upper leg. What started as an improvisation soon turned into a lucrative business idea. Customers loved his denim trousers – within 18 months, he sold 200 pairs for three times as much as he had charged without the rivets.[355]

Davis came up with the idea of patenting his invention. But he didn't have enough money, nor could he write. With the help of a friend, he painstakingly composed a letter to Levi Strauss, hoping that he would understand the significance of Davis' invention and help him to register the patent. And that's exactly how it happened: Strauss got the idea as soon as he opened the parcel containing the letter and a sample pair, and he did apply for a patent in both their names.

The patent office turned them down at first because the rivets had already been used to reinforce the boots of the Northern troops during the Civil War. Not one to give up so easily, Strauss modified his application – and was refused again. "For ten months, he polished and revised the claims on the forms, paying fee after fee, until on May 20, 1873, he finally held Patent No. 139,121 in his hands."[356] He sold his first patented pair two weeks later on June 2, 1873. Strauss subsequently bought Davis' share of the patent off him and promised to build him a nice house. It was definitely an investment worth making!

The trousers were such a huge success that Strauss decided to build a factory which would produce nothing else. In the very first year, he shifted a total of 5,800 pairs of trousers and other items with rivets, a year later that number rose to 20,000 with a total value of almost $150,000.

Of course, the competition soon caught on and tried to copy the product. Strauss fought and won many lawsuits against plagiarists. His company remained the market leader for the new trousers, which he decided to call 'jeans.' Not many companies founded 150 years ago still exist. And not many products invented 150 years ago are still going strong and selling worldwide. Jeans are one of those few products. And today, the company Levi Strauss founded is a global corporation with around 17,000 employees, which sells its products to 110 countries.

Another man who, with the right ideas, went on to become the richest man in the United States was Henry Ford. He is widely regarded as the inventor of industrial mass production and turned the car into a mass-produced commodity in the United States. In particular, his legendary Model T, of which over 15 million units were sold, made history and changed the face of America forever.

Ford started his career by inventing things in his spare time. His main job was as an employee in the Edison Company. Outside his regular job, he started to try to invent a car. In 1899, in response to being informed that he was about to be promoted, he quit his main job and founded his first company. Otherwise, he realized, he would not have had time to continue working on his car. However, his first company was a failure and folded after selling fewer than a dozen cars.

Ford first became famous as the driver of the Model A, with which he won a major car race in 1903. Unlike other inventors, Ford himself was not so much the craftsman as the inspiring ideas man who knew how to delegate. He understood that only ideas mattered – he left it to others to implement them. "I never saw Mr. Ford make anything," said one of his early assistants. "He was always doing the directing."[357] If Ford had thought like many other inventors, he would never have become nearly so rich.

From the very beginning, Ford concentrated on building cars with a very light weight. And above all, he wanted to build a car that was far cheaper than any being manufactured by his competitors. At that time, the motor car was still a luxury article for extremely rich people. Cars cost far more than single-family houses: in today's prices they would cost as much as several million dollars. At that time (1906), more than half of the cars in the United States cost between $3,000 and $5,000. Ford frequently butted heads with investors in the automobile segment because he wanted to build a car that would cost only a tenth of that. But he was right: a decade later, only 2% of the cars sold cost in the $3,000–$5,000 range.

With the car he built, Ford opened up a whole new group of buyers – the largest there was in the United States at the time, namely regular farmers. He sold two-thirds of his cars to farmers. His biographer stresses the social consequences this had for the United States: "In a decade, the Model T broke the age-old isolation of the farm."[358] Many farmers began to borrow money against their farms just to be able to afford a car.

The Model T was more than a car brand: it became a myth in the United States. Ford constantly refined the Model T, making regular small improvements, but the car basically remained mostly unchanged. The biggest changes were in terms of price, which Ford constantly reduced. In October 1910, Ford lowered the price from $950 to $780, a year later to $690 and again a year later to $600. In 1913, it cost only $550, followed by $490 in 1914, $440 in 1915, $360 in 1916 and $290 in 1924.

At the same time as the price cuts, he significantly increased the wages of his workers and gave them a minimum wage of $5 a day, which in many cases meant their previous salaries doubled. This led to a veritable rush of workers who all wanted to work for Ford. The investors, who owned most of Ford Motor Company, didn't like the fact that Ford was constantly lowering prices and raising wages, a situation that meant that, after capital investments, there was almost nothing left for shareholders' dividends. They took him to court, where they won and forced Ford to pay higher dividends.

Ford then succeeded with a big bluff: he announced he was leaving to start a new company that would have four or five times as many employees as the 50,000 at Ford. He announced that he already had the plans for a car that would cost only $250 ready and waiting. That scared the shareholders and they were willing to sell their shares to Ford. His biographer writes: "But by the end of 1919 Henry Ford held the largest company ever in the hands of one person. His operation was worth a billion dollars, and he owned it as completely as he did his piano and his birdhouses."[359]

Everything man-made started as an idea, as an image in somebody's head. Today, ideas are more valuable than ever before. And turning an idea into a giant fortune doesn't necessarily take decades anymore – sometimes it can happen over the course of just a few years. The invention of the internet has done much to accelerate these processes, as we've already seen with the success story of the creators of Google. Or take Mark Zuckerberg, who became a billionaire in just a few years with his invention, Facebook. According to *Forbes*, he was one of the richest people in the world in 2019 with assets of around $62 billion.

The story of Facebook, which today is the most successful social network in the world by far, started at Harvard University. The site takes its name from the so-called 'facebooks' given to students at many American universities, which contain pictures of every student enrolled at the institution. Harvard didn't have a facebook for the whole of the university, but only for each individual dorm on campus.

Mark Zuckerberg was a psychology major at Harvard. By accident more than anything else, he discovered the attraction of social networks and the speed with which they can spread. In late October 2003, he illegally logged onto the Harvard server to download pictures of his fellow students. It all started as a bit of fun – he was planning to ask other students to grade female students by their looks.

He called his site Facemash.com and emailed the link to some friends. When he came back to his room after a class, his laptop had crashed because the site had had so many hits. One of his fellow students had forwarded his email to the Politics Department. Women's groups such as the Latina Women's Issues Organization or the Association of Black Women at Harvard had also got hold of the link and were not amused. By trying to drum up support for their campaign against the site, they inadvertently stirred up more interest.

Suddenly, Facemash was everywhere: "A Website where you compared two pictures of undergraduate girls, voted on which one was hotter – then watched as some complex algorithms calculated who were the hottest chicks on campus – had gone viral throughout the campus. In under two hours, the site had already logged 22,000 votes. Four hundred kids had gone onto the site in the past 30 minutes," as Mezrich says in *The Accidental Billionaires*.[360]

Many other students would have stopped at that but Zuckerberg started thinking about what the instant popularity of Facemash might mean. It wasn't just that he had posted pictures of pretty girls online – there were lots of websites like that. What made Facemash unique was that it featured pictures of Harvard students whom most other students knew by sight or even personally.

In the following months, he worked on the idea of creating a website that would represent real-world social networks and that would feature not just images, but written profiles and a variety of applications. Every user was to have his or her own profile which they could use to introduce themselves or to upload photographs or videos. There would be a notice board where users could leave messages which would be publicly accessible, or publish notes and blog posts. Users would be alerted to new posts on their friends' profiles.

Zuckerberg called his project Facebook. His friend Eduardo Saverin loved the idea when Zuckerberg told him about it. In return for the $1,000 he needed to finance his project, he gave Eduardo a 30% share. Soon after, they were joined by two other students, Dustin Moskovitz and Chris Hughes.

The original Facebook site promised its users: "Thefacebook is an online directory that connects people through social networks at colleges. We have opened up Thefacebook for popular consumption at Harvard University. You can use Thefacebook to search for people at your school, find out who are in your classes, look up your friends' friends, see a visualization of your social network."[361]

Thefacebook was registered as a domain on January 12, 2004. Shortly after, some other students caused trouble for Zuckerberg by claiming that he had stolen their idea. After his Facemash prank, they had approached him to ask him for help with the programming of their own website. To this purpose, they had given him a source code which they now said was the real beginning of Facebook. Zuckerberg, they maintained, had broken an oral contract between themselves. The students took their complaint all the way up to the president of Harvard, who told them to settle the argument between themselves. In 2004, the year Facebook went live, the students sued Zuckerberg for alleged plagiarism on behalf of their company ConnectU. Facebook told the public that they had settled out of court and paid $65 million in compensation.

In spite of all this trouble, Facebook spread like wildfire. At first, the site was only open to Harvard students. Then Zuckerberg allowed students from other universities in the U.S. to join and finally it was opened to high schools and companies. In September 2006, university students from other countries were allowed to join, and soon after that any remaining restrictions were lifted. In the spring of 2008, German, Spanish and French versions were launched and many other languages soon followed.

In the summer of 2010, Facebook passed the magic threshold of 500 million users worldwide and it took just another three years to pass the one-billion-user threshold for the first time. In 2019, Facebook registered more than 2.7 billion active users across its many platforms, which, since 2014, have also included the WhatsApp messaging service. Zuckerberg would often emphasize the fact that he had yet to develop a fully formed business model. This was something he had in common with the creators of Google. Like Larry Page and Sergey Brin, Zuckerberg was convinced that ample opportunities to make money would present themselves as soon as his site had enough users to dominate the market. Like them, he was right. Facebook's profits in 2018 totaled $22.1 billion, while its revenues reached $55.8 billion.

Very early on, Zuckerberg was able to convince a number of financial backers that there was a lot of money to be made from his idea, although it took until 2009 for the site to turn a profit. In 2004, Facebook was launched with the modest sum of $18,000 which Zuckerberg's friend Eduardo Saverin had put up. When Facebook went public in May 2012, the company made a profit of around $16 billion, the largest ever IPO of an internet start-up. Based on the issue price of $38 per share, the company was worth $104 billion. Although the company's share price dropped significantly over the following weeks, plummeting to half the original value by August 2012, it subsequently recovered and stood at $170 in September 2019.

Like Larry Page and Sergey Brin, Zuckerberg is part of a new generation of entrepreneurs. In the company's early days, the way he dressed was a calculated attempt to distinguish himself from the norms and conventions of the business world. His favorite outfit consisted of flip-flops, jeans and a fleece worn over a gray T-shirt. He once showed up at the offices of the venture capital company Sequoia in pajamas. Zuckerberg's comment was: "I am no exception. Steve Jobs even walked in without shoes."[362] Today, however, he is just as frequently seen in a fine suit and tie combo, as was the case during U.S. Senate hearings.

The history of Facebook demonstrates the power of ideas, which nowadays spread faster than ever thanks to the internet. However, having the right idea isn't enough: you also have to think big enough in order to be financially successful. At the time Facebook was founded, a number of social networks already existed. Zuckerberg not only had a number of ideas his competitors didn't have, he also had a catchy name for his project. Within a short period of time he was able to find investors willing to back a project with hundreds of millions of dollars, without any business plan at all.

One of the most inventive and resourceful people I have ever met is Hans Wall. I got to know him by coincidence when I was buying his house in Berlin. You can see his name on every bus stop in the German capital – Wall AG, the public limited company he built, is active in more than 50 European cities. In 2009, he sold it to his competitor, the French JCDecaux group, the global leader in the 'street furniture' market which operates in 55 countries.

After finishing his compulsory basic education, Wall had left school to start an apprenticeship as a mechanic. In the early 1970s, he came up with an ingenious idea. He made German cities an offer they could hardly refuse: he was going to build bus shelters and other street furniture, and take charge of all cleaning and maintenance work – completely free of charge. His only condition: his company would get to keep any income generated by advertising.

Wall had seen something others had also 'seen' but not thought about: most bus stops were sorry affairs. Passengers waiting for a bus had to stand in bus shelters that were both draughty and ugly. Most of them had been put together from sheet metal, wood and corrugated plastic – not exactly an attractive proposition for prospective advertising clients.

Wall replaced the ugly bus shelters and their cardboard ads with illuminated glass display cases. He was able to attract new clients who were willing to pay far more for a quality display of their ads than for posters stuck to the walls of cheap, and frequently vandalized, bus shelters.

Wall approached one mayor after another and explained his idea. Within three years, he had built a total of 1,300 bus shelters in more than 40 German cities. However, he had underestimated the logistical problems involved in their regular cleaning and maintenance. He soon realized that his plan was not economically viable. He was lucky enough to find a buyer for his bus shelters.

His idea was good – but it would only work in large cities with a lot of bus shelters in close vicinity to each other. Conquering the German capital with his idea became a kind of obsession for Wall. At the time, the municipal public transport services were inviting tenders for a project which included designing public conveniences that had to be accessible for people in wheelchairs.

Wall's competitors claimed this was an impossible challenge. They did seem to have a point at first glance – the disabled toilets that were on the market at the time were far too large to be put up in the middle of the city. "I knew," Wall says, "that if I told the city of Berlin the same thing, namely that they were asking the impossible, I didn't stand a chance against large companies of international renown – I had to find a way of making it possible."

For Wall, defeat was not an option. "In an era where it's possible to send men to the moon, and to build nuclear missiles, it has to be possible to build a toilet suitable for the disabled – all it takes is the will to do it," he told himself. His training as a mechanic stood him in good stead – he spent many nights tinkering with different ideas, hired competent engineers and finally invented a toilet suitable for the disabled, which used minimal space. Today, his design is patented globally. His solution: a toilet bowl which swiveled 72 degrees to the left or to the right, with a total width of only six feet. Thus, the smallest disabled toilet in the world had been created, for which Wall received the European Commission's Breaking Barriers Award in 2001. "If it hadn't been for that toilet, I could never have beaten my fiercest competitor, a much larger company," Wall maintains.

Today, Wall is an inspiration to company founders: "Even as a small company, you still stand a chance against competitors with far more capital. It doesn't matter if you have no money – you can make up for it with good ideas, speed and commitment." His favorite example is the fight for the American metropolis Boston, which he won in 2001.

Like Berlin many years previously, Boston had invited tenders for a 'street furniture' project. Some of the applicants had over 100 times more capital and clout than Wall, among them companies like Viacom and his old rival JCDecaux from France. In order to come up with a more visually attractive design than the competition, Wall hired world-famous designer Josef Paul Kleihues, whose brief was simply to come up with something very special, as befitted the city's distinguished history and tradition.

However, Wall realized that even that would not be enough to beat his powerful competitors. "I staked everything on a single bet. Instead of show-casing small-scale models like my competitors, I had my team build 20 actual life-size pieces. By putting them up in the streets of Boston, we demonstrated far more commitment than our competitors." The mayor of Boston was full of praise for their gift to his city. The German entrepreneur had every reason to be proud when the mayor announced that Wall's tender had been chosen for its faithfulness to the city's historical legacy, which made the entrepreneur especially proud.

"I have always considered it an advantage that my company was smaller than many competitors. Large companies often become hampered by bureaucracy, that's why they are too slow. This problem is compounded by arrogance because they underestimate smaller competitors such as our company, which meant that I knew I had a real chance. Especially because I was far more hungry for success than the large established companies." Wall himself never became arrogant, not even when he beat far larger competitors. "At first, I often had to acknowledge without envy that my competitors were better and more professional. Rather than casting aspersions on the competition, I learned from those who beat me and saw it as a challenge to become even better than we already were." He does not regard fierce competition as a disadvantage. "On the contrary. We would never have grown as much as we did if we hadn't had a competitor as high-quality and powerful as Decaux whom we were constantly forced to compete against, and to compare ourselves with. The fierce competition hasn't done us any harm whatsoever, instead it has helped us by forcing us to keep improving our quality and our speed, and to keep developing new ideas."

Many people have doubts about whether they are creative enough. However, this book features examples which show that being successful does not necessarily require inventing anything new. All it takes is a good idea on how to make money from somebody else's inventions. From Levi Strauss to Sam Walton of Walmart fame to Bill Gates, successful entrepreneurs have always taken their key ideas from others. Most inventions, be it the recipe for Coca-Cola or the disc operating system which would become famous under the abbreviation MS-DOS, did not make their original creators rich. The people who did get rich were the ones who knew how to turn a good idea into a viable business model.

"It's not just about having good ideas, it's about putting those ideas into practice," says Ekkehard Streletzki. "So many great new ideas are conceived every day, but most of them never see the light of day." Among other businesses, Streletzki owns Europe's largest conference, entertainment and hotel complex, the Estrel Hotel and Conference Center in Berlin. Its 1,125 rooms make it Germany's largest as well as most commercially successful hotel, which is profitable even at an occupancy rate of only 35%.

Streletzki came up with the idea when he saw hotel prices shoot up from 100 to 400 or even 500 deutsche marks per night in the aftermath of German reunification. Streletzki had never taken an interest in hotels before and knew little about them, as he freely admits. But he decided to build a 4-star hotel and charge no more than 100 deutsche marks per night for a basic room. However, his choice of location was controversial to say the least. He bought a plot of land in Neukölln, which was considered the most unsafe part of Berlin at the time. Right next to an old junkyard, miles away from the city center – that's where he was planning to build the largest hotel in Germany.

Few people openly admitted just how crazy they considered his idea – after all, Streletzki had already made a fortune as a successful entrepreneur and real estate investor. "But you could tell by the looks people gave me and by reading between the lines of what was said – you could tell that people thought building Germany's largest hotel in Neukölln was a crackpot idea. The truth is, I was the only one who thought it was a great idea." But even he admits to having felt plagued by doubts late one night when he looked at the construction site with its 17 large cranes and thought to himself: "I must be crazy to do this."

Streletzki's ambition didn't end there, however – once he had built the hotel, the wanted to run it himself too. Rather than finding a large chain to operate it for him, he recruited a manager who had previously run a Ramada hotel and hired 220 members of staff months before the hotel even opened, which meant that it was fully staffed from day one. "The pre-opening stage cost me twelve million deutsche marks," Streletzki remembers. In total, the initial stage of the project cost 240 million deutsche marks, a third of which was Streletzki's own money that he had made in a smart real estate deal.

Rather than spending lots of money on commissioning a marketing agency to come up with a catchy slogan, Streletzki centered his marketing campaign around his own concept: "Four stars at two-star prices." The Estrel Hotel proved to be a resounding success as soon as it opened. "We started turning a profit in the very first year, which meant that we were able to repay interest and loans," Streletzki says. Five years later he added a conference center that cost another 100 million deutsche marks. Large German and international corporations now regularly hold conferences here.

Originally, Streletzki had decided to build the hotel because the then mayor of Berlin, Eberhard Diepgen, had promised him that the capital's new international airport would be operational by 1996/1997 at the latest. "Nobody could predict that it would take another 25 years," as Streletzki says. In 2013, when those responsible kept postponing the inauguration of the new airport again and again and the media started speculating that it might never be operational, Streletzki launched an architectural design competition for another building with an additional 800 rooms and a new annex to the conference center.

Unconventional ideas have always been Streletzki's forte. After qualifying as an engineer, he owned a small structural engineering company with a staff of ten in Munich in the 1970s. "In the run-up to the Olympic Games in 1972, we had plenty of work, but afterwards construction work dried up almost overnight."

"Necessity is the mother of invention," as the saying goes, and the British writer John Fowles coined the aphorism: "A drowning man soon learns to swim." An acquaintance told Streletzki about an architect from Munich who was working in Saudi Arabia. His interest was piqued and he thought: "If architects are needed in the Middle East, surely they'll need structural engineers too." His instinct proved to be on the mark. "I did some research, put some documents together and a few weeks after I'd been told about the architect who was working in Saudi Arabia, I boarded a plane to Tehran." His first stop was the German embassy. He simply introduced himself and asked whether they knew of any local companies who needed structural engineers. Ten minutes later, a member of the embassy gave him a ride to a firm of architects in the immediate vicinity.

In the following years, Streletzki's company worked on a gigantic construction project to build new high-rises and a shopping mall in Tehran. "My company had so much work that I was able to hire new staff at a time when other structural engineering companies in Munich had to let go of their staff or give up altogether."

What are the lessons to be learned from Ekkehard Streletzki's story? Don't just have the courage to think big and outside the box – above all, you'll need the courage to put your ideas into practice! Or would you rather be one of those people who sit at the bar year after year telling their fellow barflies how they once had a great idea and a great opportunity – adding, "I could've if I'd wanted to"?

Theo Müller, who became a billionaire by making buttermilk, kefir and yogurt staples of the German diet, is another case in point. When Müller took over his father's dairy in 1971, he had five people working for him. Today his group, which owns Müllermilch, Weihenstephan and Sachsenmilch among other brands, has 24,000 employees and in 2019, posted revenues of just under €6 billion. With a fortune of €5 billion, Müller ranked 31st in a list of the 1,000 richest Germans in the magazine *Bilanz* in 2019. Incidentally, he was also one of the people I interviewed for my book *The Wealth Elite*. The interviews were meant to be anonymous, but as magazine *Der Spiegel* wanted a face to attach to a major article about the book, he agreed to have his name mentioned.

"It all started with soured milk," Müller says. In 1970, he launched a new product called 'Kneipp Dickmilch' ('Kneipp soured milk'), of which he sold three million units in the first year. Müller was one of the first entrepreneurs to understand that staples such as long-life milk were nowhere near as profitable as branded products. In 1971, he discovered a process to render buttermilk – which had previously been a mere by-product of making butter – much thicker and creamier. "By using evaporation to remove the water, we were able to create a thick and creamy product which we called 'Müller's pure buttermilk.'"

Another thing Müller understood from the start was the power of marketing and advertising to position his products. In 1974 he launched an advertising campaign on Bavarian TV. His message was as simple as it was effective: "Now there's a buttermilk that tastes like no other." Müller stresses that this was "important not just to grab the attention of the end-users, but also to register with retailers." The new buttermilk proved a hit, selling over 100 million units by 1975. By then, Müller had succeeded in transforming his five-staff dairy into a large-scale operation that turned a profit of five million deutsche marks a year.

In the mid-seventies, he added other brand products such as kefir and hired a marketing and sales expert who kept coming up with ideas for new products. "Another great idea was our rice pudding, of which we sold 60 million units in the very first year," he says. In the next ten years, the company kept launching new innovative products such as the 'Müller corners', which today sell over a billion units a year in Germany and the UK.

In the late 1980s, Müller expanded into the UK market. He also bought up one small dairy after another in Germany. "In total I bought about 200 dairy farmers out of their cooperatives in the seventies and eighties. I did that by offering them one pfennig more per liter of milk." In 1994, he bought up the bankrupt Sachsenmilch company for €15 million. "Nobody else wanted them, although €170 million had been invested into a new dairy facility, buildings and other machines alone." Since the supply contracts with the dairy farmers were worth about as much as the purchase price, everything else came as a bonus. Müller subsequently turned Sachsenmilch into a leading brand, investing almost a billion euros into this company alone.

What's the secret of Theo Müller's success? "It's an entrepreneur's job to create value," he says. He succeeded in creating value by launching new products that immediately became popular with consumers. Above all, he turned a staple into a range of branded products. "A branded product such as the 'Müller corner' is about six or seven times more profitable than a staple such as long-life milk, which any manufacturer can produce." Across the industry, Müller says, only 15%

of dairy products have a brand identity. For the products sold by his group, that number stands at 50%. This is what has allowed Müller to achieve huge profit margins, which he then uses for new investments to build his corporate empire.

"Advertising has played an important role," he says, "but it's been even more important for us to develop truly innovative products. On the other hand, those innovations certainly wouldn't have been nearly as successful if it hadn't been for our investments into advertising, which have always been far more substantial than our competitors."

Ideas are the basis of success. This doesn't just apply to entrepreneurs. Any employee stands a better chance of promotion the more ideas he or she contributes to the company. Of course, every company needs employees who simply implement and process the ideas of others. But, important though these employees may be, they will only very rarely be promoted to the very top ranks of a well-run company. What is of paramount importance to any company is recognizing new market opportunities, creating new products, or adapting existing products to changing customer expectations and developing new ideas on how to optimize services and solutions. By making major contributions to these processes, and by positioning themselves as ideas people, employees can create an important basis for their future careers.

Jack Welch, one of the most successful executives of recent history, saw his key task as CEO of General Electric (GE), which at the time employed a workforce of 300,000 people worldwide, as creating a culture in which new ideas were continuously being developed. Every year in early January, 500 leading GE managers came together for a two-day meeting, where speakers from all levels of the company would give ten-minute speeches on the progress they had made over the past 12 months. "No long, boring speeches, no travelogues, just the transfer of great ideas."[363] The event was held to celebrate the best people with the best ideas.

In March, the global corporation's 35 leading executives would meet. Each of them was expected to "put forth one new outside-the-box idea that can apply to other units."[364] Welch even launched a corporate initiatives group made up of 20 MBAs whose only job was to develop and promote the exchange of ideas. "Every time we got an idea, we flogged it."[365] Throughout the company, Welch tried to install a culture which encouraged new ideas that would flourish and spread.

Whether you are an entrepreneur or an employee, and whatever goals you have set for yourself, you will not be successful until you have discovered the importance and the power of ideas. Unfortunately, a common misconception holds that creativity is an innate quality. The truth is that creativity is something you can train.

Here's a list of steps on how to do that:

1. To increase your creativity, the very first thing you have to do is stop thinking of yourself as somebody who is 'not very creative.' Instead, you have to realize that creativity can be trained and exercised like a muscle.

2. Surround yourself with people who are creative and successful – preferably far more successful than you are! This will help you increase your creativity.

3. Read as much as you can – especially the life stories of successful and creative people. New ideas often develop by transferring concepts from other areas of life to your own area. After finishing this book, start rereading it from the beginning, and at the end of each chapter, jot down the ideas it has inspired for your own life.

4. Start keeping an 'ideas log' in which you write down any idea that comes to you. Train yourself to write down your ideas as soon as they enter your head – even and especially if you are not quite sure whether and how to turn them into reality.

5. Learn to escape from the rat race by delegating routine tasks to your staff whenever possible in order to devote more time and energy to developing ideas. You will find more advice and information on this in Chapter 14 ('Efficiency').

6. Use your time on vacation to develop new ideas. This will only work if you leave your day-to-day business behind when you go on vacation.

7. Take a blank sheet of paper, sit down for 45 minutes in a room where there is nothing to distract your attention. Write down any ideas that come to you on a given subject. As you do in brainstorming sessions with others, collect ideas without examining them critically. Sometimes it only takes a little bit of tweaking to turn a 'bad' idea into an ingenious one! And when it comes to reviewing a new idea, you should get into the habit of writing down at least five arguments in favor of that idea before considering the various arguments against it.

CHAPTER 12

The Art of Promoting Yourself

Inventors and explorers often have ingenious ideas without ever reaping the material benefits. Those who do benefit from their inventions are the people who come up with ingenious marketing strategies to sell them. Entrepreneurs, freelance professionals and employees all need to master the art of advertising themselves. If you want to achieve extraordinary goals, this is one of the most vital and fundamental requirements.

Take the inventors of Coca-Cola, or of the drink which is today universally known as Red Bull, or of baking powder – none of them got rich. Those who did were the marketing geniuses such as Dietrich Mateschitz, the man behind the commercial success of Red Bull, the investors who very early on bought the recipe for Coca-Cola. Another example is August Oetker, the German entrepreneur who more than a hundred years ago became the leading manufacturer of baking powder, thus laying the foundations for one of the most successful family businesses of the last century.

Let's start with the story of the Austrian entrepreneur Dietrich Mateschitz, who is today one of the richest men in Europe thanks to the success of the Red Bull brand. In 2018, 6.8 billion cans of Red Bull were sold worldwide, cementing the company's position as one of the most valuable brands in Europe.

In the early 1980s, Dietrich Mateschitz was working for the Anglo-Dutch conglomerate Unilever. By pure chance, he noticed that Taisho Pharmaceuticals, which made a drink containing an ingredient called taurine, was topping a list of the largest taxpayers in Japan. Metschitz's interest was piqued. On his next business trip to the region, he approached one of Unilever's Thai franchising partners, the manufacturer of a drink called Krating Daeng – Thai for 'Red Bull'. So intrigued was Mateschitz by the energy drink, which was unknown in Europe and the U.S. at that time, he bought the distribution rights to sell the drink outside of Asia. A year later, at the age of 41, he quit his job with Unilever.

An experienced marketing professional, Mateschitz knew about the importance of advertising. For him, this was more than just one factor among many upon which the success of his company was built – it was the single most important component. No other entrepreneur had ever applied marketing strategies quite as zealously as Mateschitz did. He invested his life savings of five million Austrian shillings (just over $500,000) into his new company. Most of it was spent on developing a marketing concept which was to be the essential ingredient in Red Bull's recipe for global success.

Mateschitz had originally intended to start his company in Germany, but increasingly despaired of the slowness and complexity of German bureaucracy, which refused to fast-track his permit. He gave up after a year and formed a company in Austria instead. Incidentally, it would take almost ten years for the drink to be licensed in Germany.

In Austria, the new drink hit the shops on April 1, 1987. It did not get off to a good start. According to Wolfgang Fürweger, the author of a comprehensive company history, "the story of Red Bull was very nearly cut short before it had really started. In the beginning, sales didn't really get off the ground. The company and its founder were in bad financial shape."[366]

However, Mateschitz believed in his idea. The fact that several hundred thousand cans were sold in the first year he saw as confirmation that he was on the right track. In 1988, that number rose to 1.2 million, and in its third year on the European market, with sales of 1.7 million cans, the company started turning a profit.

Mateschitz was firmly convinced that the success or failure of his product would depend not only on its taste and quality, but also on the right marketing and advertising strategy. He had asked Johann Kastner, an old friend of his from university, to devise a strategy, but none of Kastner's proposals were good enough for Mateschitz. For 18 months, he rejected one idea after another. Around 50 different proposals were binned during that time. Seemingly unable to meet his friend's exacting standards, Kastner almost gave up more than once.

But good ideas have a tendency to hit you when you least expect it, often in the middle of the night. That's exactly what happened with Red Bull. One night, Mateschitz got a surprise phone call from Kastner, who had finally come up with the perfect advertising claim: "Red Bull verleiht Flüüügel," which worked almost equally well in English ("Red Bull gives you wiiings"). It proved to be a stroke of pure marketing genius and hit exactly the right note with the target group.

As it turned out, the official authorities unwittingly gave Red Bull a massive push on the road to success. Germany and some other countries initially banned the drink due to concerns about potential health risks, which have since been disproved in a number of studies. Its cachet as illegal contraband which had to be smuggled into the country made the drink and the Red Bull brand even more popular with teenagers and young people.

In Austria, the home of Red Bull, the Social Democratic Party (SPÖ) wanted to ban the drink. In France, it was classed as a drug and licensed for medicinal use only. In Scandinavia and Canada, the company faced similar problems as well. But instead of scaring consumers off, the huge health warnings printed on the cans which the Canadian government enforced only added to the appeal of the drink.

What makes Red Bull special is that the company neither produces nor distributes the drink. Other companies in the beverage industry use marketing and advertising to support their core operations, which are production and distribution. But like other successful entrepreneurs, Mateschitz cared little about the 'normal' way of doing things. His company has no production plants and warehouses because Mateschitz has opted to outsource those parts of the operation. His company's core business is marketing. According to industry sources, Red Bull invests a third of its total revenue into strengthening and advertising the brand.

From the very beginning, Mateschitz found unusual ways of doing this. If the story of Red Bull can teach us anything, it's that good ideas are worth more than a large budget. Most of the company's marketing budget was spent on sponsoring unconventional extreme sports to raise Red Bull's profile as the beverage of choice for trendy young daredevils who liked to live on the wild side. "These events may not have drawn huge crowds, after all they were usually held in out-of-the-way places, but because they were so extravagant, they did attract a lot of media attention, which made them popular with wider audiences. Among the better-known of these events are air races – a kind of Formula One for planes – or the Dolomites Man contest, one of the toughest relay races in the world for mountain runners, paragliders, canoeists, and mountain bikers."[367]

Mateschitz came up with the ingenious idea of positioning the Red Bull brand in the context of these outdoor challenges. He had the races filmed and offered the footage to the media. "If they went about it in the 'usual way,' i.e., by booking advertising space, a marketing budget of a billion euros would not be enough to buy Red Bull the kind of prime-time exposure, newspaper and magazine coverage the brand has been able to garner."[368]

The example of Red Bull shows that you don't necessarily have to spend a lot of capital to achieve a huge impact. Creative thinking can be far more effective. Rather than sponsoring more expensive established sports, Mateschitz preferred to invest in long-term partnership deals with athletes who were involved in extreme sports such as paragliding, freeclimbing, snowboarding and 'tombstoning' (jumping off high cliffs), as well as with stuntmen and other thrill-seekers, thus positioning Red Bull as a young and dynamic brand.

It was only later that Mateschitz invested in mainstream sports like soccer or Formula One, which required far more capital. In 2010, the sixth year of the Red Bull Formula One team's existence, they became World Champions for the first time, winning both the Constructors' World Championship and the Drivers' World Championship with Sebastian Vettel. The team was able to repeat this success in 2011, 2012 and 2013. In addition, the Red Bull team has held the record of 18 pole positions in 19 races since the 2011 season.

There are some remarkable parallels between the stories of Red Bull and Coca-Cola. The latter was invented by the American pharmacist John Stith Pemberton. Among the medicines he mixed in his laboratory in Atlanta was a 'tonic,' which contained coca leaves and cola nuts. It was supposed to relieve headaches and cure chronic fatigue, impotence, feebleness and many other ills. His 'tonic,' which was first sold in 1886 and was simply called 'Cola,' was a thick syrup. Mixed with water, it tasted quite good too, as consumers soon came to realize. Unaware of the huge potential of his invention, Pemberton sold his shares in the company as well as the secret formula to several people, among them Asa Griggs Candler, who in 1892 joined forces with his brother and two other investors to found the Coca-Cola Company. His investment had cost Candler all of $500.

Only a few years after founding the company, Candler too was already spending $100,000 a year on advertising, an unprecedented amount at the time. Just like Mateschitz a century later, Candler too had to fight the public health authorities in order to get his drink licensed – although cocaine had been removed from the recipe as early as 1903. He was alternatively accused of spiking Coca-Cola with cocaine and of hoodwinking consumers by selling a drink which in spite of its name, contained no cocaine.

Shortly before his wife's death, Candler transferred all shares in the Coca-Cola company to his seven children, who sold the company to a group of investors in 1919 without telling their father. They got $25 million for it, 50,000 times the amount their father had originally paid.

Like Candler himself, the new owners focused mainly on marketing the product. Even today, Coca-Cola only sells licenses for the production of soft drinks to independent entrepreneurs. "The Coca-Cola company never saw its job in the production of the product, which after all is essentially a simple mixture of water, sugar and an aromatic essence. From the first, the company's real job was building the brand and opening up new markets."[369]

At around the same time Pemberton invented the formula for Coca-Cola, a German colleague of his was experimenting with baking powder. However, this colleague, a certain Dr. August Oetker, wasn't so much an inventor or a creative genius, but rather a marketing professional – and that's how he managed to build a fortune on baking powder. With over 32,000 employees the Oetker Group is one of the largest family-run enterprises on the European market today. The group comprises more than 400 different companies offering various products and services. These include frozen pizzas, alcoholic beverages, insurance, a bank and a shipping company (180 vessels for Hamburg Süd, another 30 for Alancia) and an annual turnover in excess of €7 billion.

It all started in 1891, when Dr. August Oetker passed his licensing exam and started running his own pharmacy in the West German city of Bielefeld. Even when he was still an apprentice, he had boasted: "For now, my main goal is to buy a pharmacy, of course; once I have succeeded with that, then I will try to achieve something special."[370] Later on, he would frequently quote the same phrase: "In most cases, a good idea is all it takes to make a man."[371] His own 'good idea' would be baking powder, which has since become a household staple in Germany and is widely used in other countries as well.

In the back room of his pharmacy, Oetker started experimenting with the manufacture of an especially high-grade baking powder. Sodium bicarbonate-based raising agents had been invented by the famous chemist Justus von Liebig a few decades earlier and one of Liebig's former students had further developed the product and started popularizing baking soda in the U.S.

Dr. Oetker's genius lay in developing an innovative marketing concept for a product others had discovered before him. He found a concise formula that succinctly summarized his product's unique selling point: "The composition of my baking powder is as good as it gets, free of any harmful additives, consistent in its quality, the discriminating housewife's choice. Its low price means it's affordable for everybody."[372]

"From the beginning," Rüdiger Jungbluth says in his history of the Oetker family and their eponymous company, "Oetker didn't sell a mundane raising agent, but rather health and quality. The company's success was based on an extremely sophisticated psychology of advertising, which we barely notice today for the simple reason that it has been copied so many times since. This strategy revealed the true greatness of the young entrepreneur August Oetker, who was neither an ingenious scientist nor a great food chemist, but rather a man with a particular gift for marketing."[373]

Baking powder was originally sold in jars, which meant that customers had to measure it out themselves. Oetker came up with the idea of packaging it in little paper bags of 20 grams each and selling them at an inflated price, which still seemed quite low to customers simply because the amount of baking powder in each bag was so small. Oetker invested heavily in marketing and advertising. In the first few years, he spent his entire profits from baking powder sales on buying advertising space in every newspaper distributed in towns with more than 3,000 inhabitants.

"How is the world supposed to know that you have something good to offer, unless you tell the world about it?" was Oetker's motto.[374] Using the song of the nightingale as an example, he explained to his staff that advertising was everywhere, even in nature. "Just like the flowers with their bright colors, which attract insects, he was going to use colorful posters and billboards to lure customers into buying his products."[375] At the time, it was highly unusual for the owner of a German medium-size company, as Dr. Oetker was then, to devour magazine articles on advertising and marketing with Oetker's alacrity.

Rather than resorting to commonplace phrases to publicize the benefits of his product, Oetker preferred to support his claims with facts and proof. His strategy anticipated an approach which 50 years later would become central to David Ogilvy's advertising philosophy. Ogilvy would have loved the copy Oetker wrote for his newspaper ads. In one of them, he reprinted a letter from the company that supplied the little paper sachets his baking powder was sold in, in which the supplier confirmed that he had ordered ten million bags. Oetker added: "Instead of undignified and unsubstantiated propaganda, I offer facts such as the ones above, which prove the extraordinary popularity of my baking powder with housewives."[376] He used the results of quality tests for advertising purposes, much like companies do today. When his baking powder came first in a comparative quality test, he made sure consumers knew about it. "He dreamt about advertising," one of his staff said.[377]

He published a best-selling recipe book as well. Of course, all the recipes in his book recommended the use of Dr. Oetker's baking powder. Millions of copies were sold, and Oetker even tried – in vain – to make it mandatory teaching material for German schools. He was a veritable fount of innovative marketing ideas. To mention just one example, he produced the first animated commercial, which showed a pound cake rising with the aid of Dr. Oetker's special baking powder.

Demand for his baking powder kept rising. Oetker was able to leave the day-to-day running of his pharmacy to others and to build a factory capable of producing 100,000 sachets of baking powder a day. After the World War II ended, August Oetker's grandson Rudolf-August, who was born in 1916, took over the company. He started investing the profits from the food business into ships in order to significantly reduce his tax burden. Within a few years, he owned 40 ocean-going vessels with an overall capacity of 370,000 tons. He also invested in the prestigious Lampe Bank, a financial institution with a 100-year-old tradition, as well as buying and founding various insurance companies, a marzipan factory and an airline. Today, the Oetker family is Germany's most famous business dynasty; 98% of Germans are familiar with the brand name Dr. Oetker.

With a personal fortune estimated at $5 billion and ownership of about 400 companies, Richard Branson is another entrepreneur who knows how to use the power of marketing. Not many people have mastered the art of advertising and presenting themselves with Branson's panache. His career in business started with a national magazine for students and a mail-order record company when he was still in school. Today, his Virgin empire consists of several airlines, cell phone providers in the UK, Australia, Canada, South Africa, the U.S. and France, broadband services, a chain of CD and DVD stores, a publishing house, a travel agency, a financial-services provider, a railway line, a wine label, a fitness chain, a radio station, a cosmetics and jewelry retailer, an events promotion agency, a soft drinks manufacturer and a company called Virgin Galactic, which is planning to organize and promote commercial space travel. All in all, the Virgin Group employs around 71,000 people and achieves annual sales of around £20 billion.

But let's start at the beginning. When Branson launched his magazine, *Student*, he had already demonstrated far more ambition than most teenagers who publish student newspapers. He was able to interview well-known personalities such as the philosopher Jean-Paul Sartre and musicians like John Lennon and Mick Jagger. "I was so full of confidence I never paused to ask myself why they were willing to let me in through their doors and talk to me face to face, and my confidence must have been catching because very few people turned me down."[378]

He used his creative skills to sell advertising space as well. Even though he didn't have a phone in his office at the school and had to use a public phone box instead, he was remarkably successful in persuading major companies to advertise in *Student*. "I'd tell the advertising manager at Lloyds Bank that Barclays were taking the inside back page – did they want the prestigious back page itself before I offered it to the Nat-West? I vied Coca-Cola against Pepsi. I honed my presentation skills, my sales pitch, and never gave a clue that I was a 15-year-old schoolboy standing in a cold callbox with a pocketful of pennies."[379]

When Branson realized that record shops didn't offer any discounts even after the retail price maintenance agreement had been abolished, he saw a business opportunity and decided to launch a mail-order business for records, which he advertised in *Student*. Virgin Mail Order became very popular with young people until a postal strike in January 1971 brought business to a halt and the company to the brink of ruin. Virgin Mail Order could neither receive cheques from customers, nor mail their records. It was the first of many crises, large and small, which Branson would have to overcome, and even then, he faced the challenge head-on, by innovating and expanding.

If he couldn't send out records to customers anymore, he would just have to open up a record shop. "We had to find a shop within a week before we ran out of money. At the time we had no idea about how a shop works. All we knew was that we had to sell records somehow or the company would collapse."[380]

Branson wanted his record shop to be a place where young people would feel encouraged to stay, listen to records and talk about music together – a novel concept at the time. His business model was simple: "We wanted the Virgin Records shop to be an enjoyable place to go at a time when record buyers were given short shrift. We wanted to relate to the customers, not patronize them; and we wanted to be cheaper than the other shops."[381] Customers were offered "headphones, sofas and beanbags to sit on, free copies of *New Musical Express* and *Melody Maker* to read, and free coffee to drink. We allowed them to stay as long as they liked and make themselves at home."[382]

By late 1972, Virgin had 14 record shops in London and in every other major city in the UK. Branson, who had left school at age 16, was still only 22 and the owner of one of the largest record-shop chains in the country.

But he soon realized that in order to make any real money in the recording industry, he would have to start his own label. He borrowed money from friends and relatives and bought a 17th century manor which he wanted to use as a recording studio. "If Virgin set up a record label," he reasoned, "we could offer artists somewhere to record (for which we could charge them); we could publish and release their records (from which we could make profit), and we had a large and growing chain of shops where we could promote and sell their records (and make the retail profit margin)."[383]

Not only did it all make sound business sense, Branson also proved to have a good ear for the record-buying public's taste. He signed the then unknown bass player with the Kevin Ayers Group, Mike Oldfield. His album *Tubular Bells* was released in 1973 and went on to sell over five million copies. Branson invested the entire profit he made from the album into new artists and into expanding the business.

But still the company was in bad financial shape, with expenditure far exceeding earnings. Branson was forced to cancel contracts with several artists, he and his partners sold their cars, closed the swimming pool they had installed and stopped paying themselves wages. The company seemed to be headed for bankruptcy. Branson knew that cutting back on costs could not save Virgin in the long run. "I have always believed that the only way to cope with a crisis is not to contract but to try to expand out of it."[384] In the midst of crisis, he still chose to take risks. "What about if we found ten more Mike Oldfields? ... How would that do?"[385]

Shortly after, he did find a provocative new act which attracted a lot of media attention and polarized the general public. "The Sex Pistols generated more newspaper clippings than anything else in 1977 apart from the Silver Jubilee itself. Their notoriety was practically a tangible asset."[386] Branson was not at all bothered by the fact that most of that publicity was negative – he saw it as free, and extremely effective, advertising.

Branson was constantly on the lookout for new challenges. When his flight was cancelled during a holiday, instead of getting annoyed like the other passengers, he came up with an idea. He chartered a plane for $2,000, which he then divided by the number of passengers. On a blackboard, he wrote: "Virgin Airways. $39 single flight to Puerto Rico."[387] This episode later convinced him to follow through with a business plan proposed to him by a young American lawyer in 1984, who suggested creating a transatlantic airline.

After his conversation with the American, Branson could hardly wait to call Boeing first thing on Monday to find out how much a jumbo jet would set him back. When he met with his business partners in Virgin Music the next day to tell them about his new project, they weren't exactly over the moon. He finally managed to bring them round – "but they weren't happy."[388]

In June 1986, British Airways reacted to the new threat from Branson by launching a promotional offer for 5,200 free tickets for flights from New York to London. Inventive and creative as always, Branson countered by running an ad which said, "It has always been Virgin's policy to encourage you to fly to London for as little as possible. So on June 10 we encourage you to fly British Airways."[389] British Airways had spent large sums on their promotion, "but most of the news coverage included a mention of our cheeky advertisement ... we reaped a large slice of publicity at a very low cost."[390]

In the early 1990s, Virgin Atlantic Airways ran into financial trouble, with severe repercussions for the entire Virgin Group. Put under increasing pressure by the banks and by BA, Branson was eventually forced to sell his record company, which had just signed the Rolling Stones. He saw no other choice but to accept EMI's offer to buy Virgin Music for a billion dollars. It was a hard decision to make after he and his partners had invested 20 years of their lives into building the company. They had signed successful artists such as Boy George, Bryan Ferry, Janet Jackson and now the Rolling Stones – and suddenly all of that was to come to an end. "It's like the death of a parent," one of his partners commented. "You think that you've prepared for it, but when it happens you realize that you're totally unable to cope." Branson himself "felt that it was more like the death of a child."[391] It took him a while to look on the bright side, and to realize what the sale meant for him. "For the first time in my life, I had enough money to fulfil my wildest dreams."[392]

In every defeat – and of course, having to sell the record company he had spent years building was a huge defeat for Branson – there is the kernel of an even larger opportunity. And Branson was never one to let an opportunity pass him by.

High achievers have to cope with defeat just like everybody else, they just react to it in a different way. Above all, they don't dwell on the past, which they can't change in any case. Rather than wasting months or even years crying over spilt milk, they look to the future and learn from their defeats. "Some you win and some you lose," Branson says. "Be glad when you win. Don't have regrets when you lose. Never look back."[393]

In the years to come, Branson tried out many more ideas and formed one company after another. Some were successful, others less so. But whenever anybody proposed a new project to him, his initial reaction would be positive. Much to his amusement, his staff nicknamed him 'Dr. Yes.' "Obviously, it had come about because my automatic response to a question, a request, or a problem is more likely to be positive than negative. I have always tried to find reasons to do something if it seems like a good idea, rather than not to do it."[394]

Branson has always been adventurous – not only as a businessman. In 1986, he broke the record for the fastest Atlantic crossing in his boat *Virgin Atlantic Challenger II*, a year later he became the first person to cross the Atlantic in a hot-air balloon. Between 1995 and 1998, he repeatedly attempted to fly around the world in a balloon. In 1998, he covered a record-breaking distance from Morocco to Hawaii before bad weather conditions forced him to give up. "If I were to think about it more carefully," Branson reflects, "I would say that I love to experience as much as I can of life. The physical adventures I have been involved in have added a special dimension to my life that has reinforced the pleasure I take in my business."[395]

All three of the entrepreneurs featured in this chapter – Dietrich Mateschitz, August Oetker and Richard Branson – have one thing in common: they positively burst with ideas. Although neither of them invented any new products, they all took the ideas and inventions of others and ran with them. By developing ingenious marketing strategies, they contributed significantly to the success of these ideas and products.

Even today, there are some entrepreneurs who still believe that having a strong product is enough, and that 'quality will out.' Of course, without a strong product the best marketing strategy in the world will not be successful in the long run. But the opposite is also true: without a strong marketing strategy, the best product in the world will not sell. The fact that consumers are bombarded with products and services makes marketing more important than ever.

On the other hand, consumers are far more critical today than they used to be. A lot of money spent on traditional advertising is in fact wasted. People do not fall for simplistic claims any more. Even if an entertaining commercial succeeds in making audiences laugh, that doesn't mean they are going to buy the product.

Well-known marketing specialists such as Al Ries believe that conventional advertising has little effect today. Instead, they recommend companies invest their resources into public relations. "You can't launch a new brand with advertising because advertising has no credibility," Ries claims. "It's the self-serving voice of a company anxious to make a sale. You can launch new brands only with publicity or public relations (PR)."[396]

Ries cites companies such as Starbucks, Google, Red Bull, Microsoft, Oracle and SAP – all of which are covered in this book – to support his claim that all "recent marketing successes have been PR successes, not advertising successes." In its first ten years, Starbucks spent less than $10 million on advertising in the United States – a 'trivial amount' compared with the company's sales figures.[397]

Traditional advertising, he argues, has become an art form rather than an effective marketing technique. Advertising professionals are far more interested in winning prizes for their novel and creative approaches than in actually promoting the product they are advertising. The essential advantage PR has over advertising is its credibility. Even if it does not unreservedly endorse the product in question, an editorial feature in a respected medium is a hundred times more effective than an expensive and clever advertising campaign. Again, this strategy will only work if the product is interesting and of a high quality. Because fortunately you cannot buy positive press coverage in quality papers. And fortunately, weak products will generate bad press in the long run.

A brand in which consumers' trust is built, not on funky advertising claims, but on credibility, transparency and communication.

However, classic press and public relations also has its limits, because young people watch far less television and read significantly less print media than older people. This is why online marketing and PR on YouTube and social media are becoming increasingly important. The *instruments* of marketing are constantly changing, but their importance has actually grown.

This is true not just of companies, but also of individuals – no matter whether you are an entrepreneur, a freelance professional, or an employee. You have to turn yourself into a brand and learn how to sell yourself. In principal, there are three types of individuals: the first group consists of those who achieve very little but are very good at presenting and selling themselves. Of course, they are bound to fail in the long run. People in the second group are very good at what they do, but far less successful when it comes to getting others to notice their achievements. Only those in the third group succeed at both: they achieve a lot and are able to sell their achievements to others.

In order to do this, you need to turn yourself into a brand. Asked about their particular strengths, many people make the mistake of mentioning too many different areas and coming across as vague and vacillating. Remember that a jack of all trades is likely to be master of none! Instead, you must learn to position yourself, to find out where your strengths really lie, and how to communicate your unique selling points to others.

If you are an entrepreneur or a freelance professional, your clients or customers are the target audience you need to reach. If you are an employee, your line manager or boss may well be the most important target for your campaign of self-promotion. There are gifted and committed individuals in every company who contribute to that company's success in important ways, but whose efforts and achievements are underrated because they are no good at promoting themselves. In that respect, they act like a company that fails to promote its products in the misguided assumption that quality will out, and that customers are bound to notice them sooner or later. In both cases – for companies as for individuals – this is a fatal mistake to make.

In order to succeed, you need to be perceived as 'standing for something,' you have to build a profile for yourself and to communicate your unique selling points. In marketing jargon, this is known as positioning and it is the core of any marketing strategy worthy of the name. This applies to companies as much as it does to lawyers, tax accountants, doctors and also to employees. Most companies, and especially most freelance professionals and employees, underestimate the importance of this kind of positioning, and of an active and professional public relations strategy.

The men and women featured in this book have all mastered the art of communication and self-promotion to perfection. Madonna and Arnold Schwarzenegger, Estée Lauder and Richard Branson, Jack Welch and Warren Buffett – all of them have achieved extraordinary successes but, just as importantly, they have all found ways of positioning themselves and of communicating those successes to others in a professional manner.

None of them owe their fame to advertising campaigns, but rather to editorial coverage in the media. Richard Branson and Jack Welch published books, made television programs or wrote regular columns in well-respected newspapers in order to promote themselves. Schwarzenegger had promoted himself as a brand from the very beginning, realizing early on in his bodybuilding career that his own inner attitude had a profound impact on the judges. He was convinced that if you sold yourself as a winner, people would see you as a winner.[398]

Even in the early days of his election campaign for the governor's office in 2003, Schwarzenegger told reporters that he would win – simply because he knew how to sell things. After all, he had already made it as a bodybuilder and, later on, as an actor by selling himself to the people in the U.S. and all over the world.[399] While others who haven't got his talent for self-promotion might pretend that selling themselves is beneath them, for men like Schwarzenegger, there is nothing indecent about self-promotion. As Schwarzenegger repeatedly stresses in his autobiography: "Same with bodybuilding, same with politics – no matter what I did in life, I was aware that you had to sell it."[400]

As we have seen in Chapter 5, high achievers typically have the courage to be different. The same courage is a prerequisite for successful self-promotion, as Schwarzenegger well knows: the courage to resist the pressure to adapt to convention, to do things the way they've always been done. He always felt that the only way to leave a lasting impression is to do something in a way it has never been done before.[401]

He was constantly advised to change his name to something Americans would find easier to pronounce. Schwarzenegger himself considered his name an advantage, precisely because it was unique. Very early on, he hired public relations experts to help him publicize the Schwarzenegger brand in the media. His biographer Cookie Lommel emphasizes how important the public's respect was for him. In order to win it, he hired one of the top PR management teams in the U.S.[402] Even as a bodybuilder, Schwarzenegger says, he was aware of the power of the press. He soon realized that the media were the best way to increase his image and marketability.[403]

Not many people are as media-savvy and as attuned to the importance of professional self-promotion as he is. "For me and my career the image has been everything," says Schwarzenegger. "More important than the reality. The most powerful thing is what people perceive and believe about me."[404] The example of Schwarzenegger shows that PR is far more effective than conventional advertising. As a person, he is one of the most famous brands in the world today – without ever having spent a single cent on advertising. He invested 100% of his marketing budget into PR instead.

Warren Buffett, too, is more than just the dispassionate investor, an image which he projects to the outside world. Every year on the first weekend in May, he celebrates the annual shareholders' meeting of his company Berkshire Hathaway with far more pomp and circumstance than most other companies in the world. Tens of thousands of people make the pilgrimage to Omaha, Nebraska, in order to see Buffett and his close friend, partner and second-in-command, Charlie Munger, perform live. He has turned the shareholders' meeting into a large trade show for the various companies owned or part-owned by Berkshire – from jewelry to furniture, carpets and televisions, or even candy, visitors can buy almost anything their hearts desire. Jeff Matthews, the author of a 300-page tome devoted entirely to the annual meeting, comments: "The contrast with most annual shareholder meetings couldn't be greater. Annual meetings of even the largest companies – and Berkshire Hathaway is among the 50 biggest private employers on Earth – are sparsely attended by shareholders and mostly ignored by the national press, except during a company crisis. Yet the Berkshire annual meeting draws shareholders, reporters, and news cameras from, quite literally, around the world."[405]

Buffett uses the company report, penned in a style that projects sincerity and a sense of humor, as a marketing tool for his company and for himself as a person, a tool which communicates the core of his brand image: competence and trust built on openness, honesty and critical self-reflection.

Buffett has successfully turned himself into a living legend. Whereas in the early days of his career he had to persuade others to invest in his business, after only a few years, "the routine had changed," as his biographer comments. "Instead of asking a favor, he was granting one; people felt indebted to him for taking their money. Making people ask put him psychologically in charge. He would come to use this technique often, in many contexts, for the rest of his life."[406]

Only those who know how to position themselves, who understand the importance of public relations and professional media communication, and who are not afraid of controversy, stand a chance of being noticed in today's marketplace. That marketplace is basically a constant hustle for pole position in the public eye.

What have you done so far to position yourself? Try to develop a marketing strategy for yourself by emphasizing and promoting your most distinctive talents, qualities and unique selling points. The more pronounced this positioning is, the better. Find a niche for yourself which has not been occupied before. Focus your attention exclusively on one single issue, as I have described in Chapter 4 of this book.

Most people – and a lot of companies too – make the mistake of wanting to excel in too many different areas at once. But in order to promote yourself effectively, you have to be truly – even more importantly, uniquely – excellent at the one thing that will make you stand out from the crowd.

CHAPTER 13

Enthusiasm and Self-Discipline

The German model Heidi Klum was one of the best-paid supermodels in the world and is now a successful businesswoman in the media industry. Her income for 2019 is estimated at €17 million, which is more than the CEOs of Germany's largest automobile companies, Daimler, VW and BMW. Was the now 46-year-old better looking than her fellow models? When Klum herself says that she is "no better-looking than lots and lots – and lots – of models out there" and that she is "shorter than most of them, and heavier,"[407] she isn't fishing for compliments but simply being realistic. In the modeling industry, good looks might get you a foot in the door – after that, whether you succeed or fail depends on other factors.

The media tend to portray supermodels in a certain light. Because of one or two successful supermodels who are said to be difficult, bitchy and unreliable, hundreds of thousands would-be successes think they don't need to be disciplined, reliable, punctual, amiable and cooperative. This is a misguided assumption which is probably the reason why so many beautiful young women who seem destined for success never make it to the big time.

There is probably no other job in the world which takes as much self-discipline as a modeling career. The schedule of a well-paid supermodel is no less crammed with appointments than that of an internationally successful top executive. The difference is that nobody expects the top executive to keep himself in shape and look great at all times, no matter how stressful his life may be.

It is no accident that out of all the tactics Klum considers essential for her own success and advises would-be models to adopt, "Be on time" is top of the list. Klum adds: "Be organized," "Watch your mood," and "Do your homework."[408] Are these natural qualities in young girls who enter the industry at 14 or 15? Of course not. But whether or not they are disciplined enough to adopt them is the decisive factor which determines their eventual success or failure.

Enthusiasm is a prerequisite for self-discipline. Nobody is going to be successful who has to keep forcing himself or herself to do things he or she doesn't really want to do (although it may sometimes be necessary to do this, of course). Self-discipline will come more easily the more enthusiastic you feel about something. "Luckily," Klum says, "I had one thing going for me besides a better-than-average face and body: I wanted it bad." Desire, she claims, is "the ultimate motivator. It makes you work like crazy and not to give up too fast or too easily."[409]

It all started in 1992, when the young German beat 30,000 competitors in a modeling contest to win a three-year contract worth over $300,000. Nineteen years old, around the same age as Arnold Schwarzenegger was when he decided that he would have to go to the United States in order to fulfill his ambitions, Heidi Klum, too, moved to New York. She lived with two other German girls in a cockroach-infested building with no hot water and leaks in the ceiling. "Every single day for three months, I went on casting calls, sometimes as many as ten a day. I was just one of thousands of new girls trying to make it as a model in New York, and every one of them looked fabulous. Typically I'd wait in line and the client would look at my book, thank me and send me packing. It sucked being such a small fish in a big pond."[410]

Her first big job was for the cover of *Mirabella*, a popular fashion magazine. After that, she got a job modeling for the *Bonne Bell* range of cosmetics, and in August 1995, she appeared on the cover of *Self* magazine. Klum's big break came three years later when she got onto the cover of the swimwear issue of *Sports Illustrated*, which reaches an audience of 55 million – every model's dream. She knew that her life would change completely from then on. Soon after, she started modeling for the lingerie line *Victoria's Secret* and appeared on the covers of magazines such as *Vogue* and *Elle*.

But Klum realized that in order to be successful in the long run, she would have to position herself and create an image for herself, otherwise she would soon fade into oblivion – just another shooting star on the horizon of the modeling industry. "I quickly realized that if you don't make yourself into a personality, more than just a face, if you don't become somebody the public knows (or wants to know), then it's over for you pretty fast in this business. It may sound crass, but you have to make yourself into somebody in order to have a longer shelf life. Otherwise you're just the flavor of the month."[411]

Not unlike Arnold Schwarzenegger, who had gone to America and made it big several decades before her, Klum was extremely ambitious and self-disciplined – and above all, she was willing to learn. Mottos such as "Never give up!" and "Try everything once!" are undeniably important, but they aren't enough to make it to the top.

The key to success, Klum says, is "acknowledging what you don't know, and seeking out trustworthy people who do."[412] This admission brings to mind something the Greek shipping tycoon Aristotle Onassis said shortly before his death, when he was asked what he would do differently if he could start all over again. He said he would change nothing except for one thing: he would find himself better advisers from the beginning – the very best ones.

Klum has achieved more than almost any other supermodel – and is worth roughly $85 million today. Her first television series was launched in the United States in 2004. She is one of 11 producers on *Project Runway,* as well as presenting the show and chairing the jury. Since 2006, she has also presented *Germany's Next Topmodel* on German television. She attributes her successes to a combination of "enthusiasm, desire, and self-discipline."

A lasting enthusiasm is one of the most essential prerequisites for achieving ambitious goals. Many people feel enthusiastic about something, but their enthusiasm doesn't last. Enthusiasm for a goal may motivate you, but in order to achieve it, you will need a lot of self-discipline.

Don't make the mistake of underestimating the importance of discipline, extreme discipline even, in meeting deadlines. People who meet deadlines are seen as reliable and trustworthy. Who would you rather give a job to? Somebody who you know from experience will probably not deliver on time, or somebody who has never disappointed you before?

Meeting deadlines is the absolute minimum. In order to make your clients or your boss enthuse about your work, you have to deliver first-rate quality before the agreed deadline. Set a rule for yourself: always try to deliver your products or services before – but never later than – the agreed deadline.

As long as that's up to you alone, it should be no problem at all. The problems start when you're running a company and some of your employees are less punctilious about meeting deadlines. Of course, you should always make sure that the people you hire are reliable and reliability should always be one of the most important values in your company culture. But the more your company grows, the more you will have to deal with unreliable employees.

A friend of mine told me about one of his employees who was intellectually superior to most of the others. He worked hard, too, and his work was of an extremely high standard. His only downfall was that he simply couldn't stick to deadlines. According to my friend, that was literally the employee's only weakness – but it was so serious that it hampered his career and, after ten years working for my friend's company, led to his dismissal.

You wouldn't want to put somebody in charge of a large department, let alone of a whole company, who is unable to organize his or her own workload. People who are notoriously disorganized and cannot meet deadlines will never be promoted to a leadership position.

The creative workers in advertising aren't exactly considered role models for good time-keeping skills. Creative people tend to be very sensitive and to be ruled by their turbulent emotions rather than by strict schedules. That's why in the advertising industry, a high degree of self-discipline combined with creativity will get you to the top. The fact that he was fanatical about punctuality was one reason for David Ogilvy's legendary success. In his best-selling memoir *Confessions of an Advertising Man*, Ogilvy writes: "Today I see red when anybody at Ogilvy, Benson & Mather tells a client that we cannot produce an advertisement or a television commercial on the day we have promised it. In the best establishments, promises are always kept, whatever it may cost in agony or overtime."[413] The code of conduct he preaches to his staff contains the following admonition: "I admire well-organized people who deliver their work on time. The Duke of Wellington never went home until he had finished all the work on his desk."[414]

Artists aren't considered paragons of self-discipline either. But the most successful of them, musicians and actors such as Madonna for example, have always been exceptional in this respect. Susan Seidelman, who directed Madonna in *Desperately Seeking Susan*, talks about her extraordinary self-control. "First call for the actors would be around 6.30 in the morning. Madonna was picked up even earlier. Before she showed up on set, she'd get up at 4 a.m. to swim laps at the YMCA health club. She had amazing self-discipline."[415]

Beate Uhse, who made her fortune as an entrepreneur in the adult-entertainment industry, describes the secret of her success as follows: "Success certainly has a lot to do with self-control. The people who deal with me say that I have enormous self-discipline – and that has definitely contributed to the company's success. There is no lift to success, you have to take the stairs."[416]

The successful investor Prince Alwaleed has a reputation for being fanatical about time-keeping. Once, when he was planning to visit six cities in four countries in the space of a single day, he even had a smaller replacement plane follow his private jet to make sure he didn't miss an important appointment due to unforeseen circumstances. "He explained that he did it as 'insurance,' in case his Boeing faced any problems, messing up his tight schedule with all those high-powered meetings. In such an instance, he would simply be able to hop onboard the smaller jet with a core team of people. At $30,000, that was expensive insurance for one day."[417]

Keeping an appointment with his friend, ex-president Jimmy Carter, in Atlanta was a bargain in comparison. Stuck in slow-moving traffic, Alwaleed promised his driver $300 – a week's wages – to get him to the Carter Center on time. The driver swung the stretch limousine toward an exit-slip road off the motorway and through the city's back-streets and got him to the meeting with minutes to spare.[418]

Alwaleed has a special travel team which is in charge of organizing and coordinating his tight schedule, making "sure that every minute is accounted for in each day, especially as the Prince is fastidious about punctuality and doesn't like to waste time."[419] If he is happy with the logistic planning of a trip, he will pay generous bonuses – sometimes the equivalent of three to six months' wages, or even an entire year.[420]

Warren Buffett also used money to discipline himself. When he felt he had to lose some weight, he would write out unsigned checks for $10,000 to his children and promise to sign them if he didn't get down to a certain weight by a certain date. His son and daughter would tempt him with treats, but Warren Buffett always resisted. "He made out those checks over and over again, but he never had to sign a single one," his biographer reports.[421]

Chess legend Garry Kasparov emphasizes the importance of strict discipline. When he was ten years old, he was enrolled at the chess academy run by three-time world champion Mikhail Botvinnik, who became his role model, coach and harshest critic. "Botvinnik laid out the ideal tournament regime, establishing a strict timetable for meals, rest and brisk walks, a system I myself followed during my entire career. Botvinnik had no patience for people who complained they didn't have enough time. And forget about telling the great teacher you were tired that day!" Sleep and rest periods were scheduled as meticulously as every other aspect of the daily routine.[422] Kasparov was used to it from his own home, where his mother had enforced order and strict discipline.

"If discipline sounds dull, or even impossible in today's fast-paced world," he comments, "we should take a moment to consider what areas of our lives we can successfully program and target for efficiency. Having a good work ethic doesn't mean being a fanatic, it means being aware and then taking action."[423] Above all, Kasparov says, it is vital to review what you have already achieved in order to get closer to your goal. He quotes his idol Botvinnik, who once said: "The difference between man and animal is that man is capable of establishing priorities!"[424]

In particular, self-discipline is paramount to developing new constructive habits, or to wean yourself off old destructive ones. Habit is your worst enemy and your best friend. You can get into the habit of not meeting deadlines, missing appointments and falling short of your goals. But you can also get into the habit of doing things right. Getting used to a new habit, which helps you to achieve your goals, should take no more than a few weeks or months. But during that time, you will need self-discipline.

Many people seem to think that punctuality and discipline are antiquated virtues which have lost their importance in the modern world. But punctuality is just reliability in a different guise. It is vital for our relationships with others and thus for our success. Nobody likes working with people who promise more than they deliver, who are all talk and no action. Unreliable people are not trustworthy.

In fact, they cannot even trust themselves. How can I gain the confidence to achieve large goals if I keep failing to achieve minor ones? In order to gain self-confidence, you have to follow a plan through to the end. Finishing what you have set out to do will always make you feel good – not finishing it will make you feel bad.

Punctuality is also a sign of respect. I remember an argument I had with the chairman of the board of a company who didn't take punctuality very seriously and who claimed that punctual people made life difficult for themselves and everybody else. Because we were friends, I didn't take this personally, but I did ask him: "If you could choose, out of all the people in the world, who to have dinner with tonight – who would it be?" He replied that his dining partner of choice would be the then German President, Roman Herzog. Personally, I could have come up with many more interesting people I would rather have dined with, but that's neither here nor there. "So how late would you be if you were meeting Roman Herzog? Ten minutes, twenty minutes, or maybe even thirty?" He said: "Oh no, I would make sure to get there early." It was an honest answer, and I countered: "Well, I consider myself just as important as Roman Herzog, and if I'm meeting somebody, I extend the same courtesy and consideration to them as I would to Roman Herzog."

Without discipline, you will not achieve your goals, because without discipline, others will not trust you and will not consider you reliable. Discipline is particularly important for those with a rebellious nature, which – as we have seen in Chapter 6 – is true of many successful entrepreneurs. "If you can't follow your own orders, you have to take orders from others" – and because I have never liked taking orders, I consider self-discipline a fundamental prerequisite for success.

However, discipline is only a means to an end – it cannot replace enthusiasm, which is the real driving force of success. If you have to keep disciplining yourself to do something you don't enjoy, you are bound to fail sooner or later. That's why you need to find something which will keep you interested and enthusiastic over a long period of time.

Take a long hard look at your life and ask yourself whether you really feel enthusiastic about whatever it is you are doing. The most important goal anybody can set for themselves is to find the one thing they feel most enthusiastic about and then turn it into their day job. Most people have long since buried this childhood dream because they have been told to be 'realistic' too many times.

How to find that one thing which you feel most enthusiastic about? I recommend you carry out the following thought experiments:

1. What would you do if you only had six months to live, and if you had enough money so you didn't have to worry about 'earning a living?'
2. If you were to inherit $10 million tomorrow, which job would you do voluntarily, even though you didn't have to work for a living anymore?

3. Is there anything you enjoy doing so much that time flies when you're doing it? Have you ever seriously considered trying to turn your hobby into a bread-winning pursuit? That's exactly what Arnold Schwarzenegger, Heidi Klum, Madonna, Coco Chanel, Steve Jobs, Bill Gates, Michael Dell and many others featured in this book have done: they've made their fortunes by turning their hobbies into jobs.

If you have a job which you feel enthusiastic about, rather than just comfortable or content with, the necessary self-discipline will come easy. The next thing you will have to learn is to organize your life and your work efficiently. If you follow the rules laid out in the next chapter, which deals with 'efficiency', your life will automatically run far more efficiently than before.

CHAPTER 14

Efficiency

How can you significantly increase your income, whether you work for yourself or for somebody else? We can pretty much exclude two factors that determine your income – fortunately, they aren't key factors. If your goal is to earn twice as much as you are earning now, you can neither become twice as intelligent as you are now, nor work twice as much. While undeniably useful, intelligence is not essential for your career. In any case, you will just have to make do with the wits you were born with. As for trying to double your workload, there are natural limits to how much you can work in a day. If it's ten hours now, you may be able to add another three or four hours – at times, you may in fact have to do so. But increasing your workload is not the cleverest way to increase your income.

In principle, that only leaves two options:

1. Increase your knowledge.
2. Increase the efficiency with which you work.

Both strategies are likely to lead to success – but the most crucial, and most frequently underrated, factor that will increase your income is efficiency. Most people believe they work fairly efficiently – in reality, only very few people do. If you realize that you haven't been working very efficiently, that's good news rather than bad. It shows that you have enormous untapped resources at your disposal.

Efficiency means achieving the best results with the lowest possible expenditure of time and energy. All of us spend most of our time doing things which contribute in very different ways to the overall 'result.' You may have heard of the 80/20 principle, which the Italian economist Vilfredo Pareto formulated a hundred years ago. In confirmation of Pareto's theory, subsequent studies in different fields have shown that "the world routinely divides into a few very powerful influences and the mass of totally unimportant ones ... We find that the top 20% of people, natural forces, economic inputs, or any other causes we can measure typically lead to about 80% of results, outputs, or effects."[425]

Once you have determined which 20% of your activities lead to 80% of your results, you need to focus on this 20%. Being successful is not about working hard, about acting busy and fiddling about. Being successful is about working at the right things, that is at the things that will get you results. No client will pay you for spending long hours procrastinating in your office. Your clients will pay you for the results you deliver. In order to work efficiently, first of all you need to have a clear idea of the most important results you are aiming to achieve. Every once in a while, it's well worth taking some time to sit back and think about which 20% of your activities lead to 80% of your results. Many people find it hard to distinguish between what is important and what isn't. They fritter away their time and energy on secondary activities – on issues which need to be addressed as well, but which only have a minor impact on your results. Some people act very busy because they think their bosses or colleagues will be impressed by their commitment. Others waste far too much time on trivialities in order to avoid having to tackle the larger, more important – and more complicated – jobs.

Compare your own attitude to your work with that of one the most successful investors in the world, George Soros, who once told his friend Byron Wien: "The trouble with you, Byron, is that you go to work every day and you think that because you go to work every day, you should do something. I don't go to work every day. I only go to work on the days that make sense to go to work." But, he added: "And I really do something on that day."[426]

Keep account of everything you do in the course of a working day, and then focus on the really important things: on those 20% of things which lead to 80% of your results. What about the remaining 80%? In some cases, you will come to realize that it doesn't make a lot of difference whether those things get done at all. Other jobs do have to get done – but not necessarily by you.

Focus on your strengths, and start delegating everything else to your staff. Always ask yourself whether a given job can only be done by you, or whether somebody else might be just as capable (or almost as capable) of getting it done. If somebody who earns $75,000 does jobs that could be performed by his secretary, who only earns half as much, then he is wasting valuable resources.

Have you ever asked yourself how often you take on jobs your staff could handle? If you make $75,000 or $150,000 a year and still book your own flights, arrange your own appointments, make your own photocopies, or do your own grocery shopping, you are doing something wrong. You could spend that time doing other things, which would not only give you greater satisfaction, but would also contribute far more to your results.

Delegating work is the key to efficiency. Why do people find this so difficult? Many people say: "Explaining what needs to be done to somebody else takes far too long, it's quicker to do it myself." That may well be true in many cases, but it's short-sighted thinking. Initially, you will have to take the time to show somebody else what needs to be done, of course. But in the long run, it will save you time, which you can invest in your own professional development. And although it may be frustrating to have to explain things to others who don't immediately get them – imagine how much more frustrating it will be having to do them yourself for the rest of your life!

Perfectionists in particular are reluctant to delegate work. Many freelance professionals, lawyers or accountants for example, insist on handling even the smallest of tasks themselves. Although there is a positive side to perfectionism, as we have seen in Chapter 10 on 'Dissatisfaction as a Driving Force', it can also cause a lot of damage. If you spend 50% of your time trying for the last 5% of perfection, you are wasting time and energy. You have to learn to accept that certain things will not get done with 100% perfection, but with only 95%. Being satisfied with 95% may well be more efficient than insisting on 100%.

Also remember that most complex tasks can be divided into a number of smaller simple tasks. In many cases, your knowledge or your creativity is only required for 10% of a task, which you take on yourself. The remaining 90% consists of comparatively simple tasks, which you can delegate, once you have split the complex task into different steps. Always remember: you can't be in two places at once. The time you spend doing one thing is time you can't spend doing something else. That's why delegating work is such an essential skill.

However, it's a skill you need to acquire. Delegating doesn't mean passing the job on to an employee without explaining what needs to be done and by when. It certainly doesn't mean giving a job to somebody else without making sure the result passes muster. "Delegating without supervision is laissez-faire," as German mail-order king Werner Otto said.[427] Without supervision, you will not get the expected result, which will in turn confirm your belief that you need to do everything yourself if you want it done properly. You have to avoid both extremes: don't try to do everything yourself. And don't pass jobs on to others without adequate training and supervision.

Werner Otto would get angry whenever he saw anybody in a leading position wasting time on non-essentials. He expected them to see the "larger picture" instead. "All other tasks were supposed to be delegated to subordinate employees, because for Otto, being able to delegate was probably a key leadership skill ... He knew that the preoccupation with minor tasks hampers creativity, which is the essential driving force for any company."[428]

John D. Rockefeller believed in the same principle, laying out the rules for a new recruit to his team as follows: "Nobody does anything if he can get anybody else to do it ... As soon as you can, get someone you can rely on, train him in the work, sit down, cock up your heels, and think out some way for the Standard Oil to make some money."[429]

People who lack self-confidence tend to regard others as competitors, and in extreme cases, they will make sure that none of their staff acquire any skills, and make themselves indispensable by refusing to let others benefit from their experience. David Ogilvy emphasizes that good leadership means precisely the opposite: "If you hire people who are bigger than you are, Ogilvy & Mather will become a company of giants; if you hire people who are less than you are, we shall become a company of dwarfs."[430] He insisted on hiring only the very best – even if they were better than he was. "Pay them more than you pay yourself if necessary."[431]

Even those who give the impression of always wanting to be the center of attention will often know better than to take on everything themselves. CNN founder Ted Turner is a prime example. His biographer affirms: "Ted's talent for picking the right individual for the job has always been vastly underrated ... He knew instinctively, right from the beginning, that he couldn't do it all alone, even though he has often given the impression he would like to."[432]

Warren Buffett has mastered the art of delegating to perfection. After the Salomon Brothers debacle, he made Deryck Maughan the new CEO of the badly shaken company. Maughan asked him: "Do you have any views on who should form the management? Is there any direction you want to give me as a strategy?" Buffett gave him short shrift. "If you have to ask me questions like that, I picked the wrong guy," he curtly replied and walked away.[433]

Mary Buffett says about her former father-in-law: "If there is a single management skill that is uniquely Warren, it is his willingness to delegate authority way beyond the boundaries that most CEOs would be comfortable with ... Warren owns more than 88 diverse businesses, and he has turned over the management of these companies to 88 highly competent CEO managers."[434] When Buffett bought Forest River, he told the company's CEO, Peter Liegl, that he did not want to hear from him more than once a year. He explicitly asks the CEOs of his Berkshire companies never to write anything intended only for him. When one of his CEOs asked him about buying new company planes, Buffett said: "That is your decision. It's your company to run."[435]

So why is Buffett far more willing to delegate than most company owners? First of all, he realizes that he lacks the expert knowledge required to make a decision – although he might very well take a different view, since Buffett is actually extremely knowledgeable on a lot of industry-specific matters. Recognizing the limits of his knowledge is one of his great strengths. His own job, as he sees it, is motivating his executives rather than making decisions for them.

Buffett also believes that his executives would not appreciate having him breathe down their necks and question their judgement. As a matter of fact, studies have shown that the freedom of employees to make decisions and to manage their own workload independently is one of the most essential factors that contribute to job satisfaction. Employees who feel that their work is constantly being monitored realize that their bosses don't really trust them. Of course, this is a learning curve: if your natural tendency is to 'micromanage' your staff, you will find it hard to relinquish responsibility all of a sudden by allowing your employees to make decisions that you are used to making yourself. But this is exactly what you must force yourself to aim for.

Learning to delegate smaller tasks in order to focus on your core responsibilities is of vital importance. Once you have identified those factors which contribute most significantly to the overall result, focus your attention on those very factors and don't allow yourself to get distracted by anything else. When you are in the middle of an important job, having to talk to other people – colleagues who come into your office, or contacts who call you on the phone – becomes a major distraction which costs time and energy. It is your responsibility to make sure you focus on the job at hand without allowing yourself to get distracted. Don't blame distractions on those who distract you – it's you who is to blame for them.

Clients visiting my former company would often ask about the signs on every door, which, like traffic lights, showed either a red or a green figure. I had introduced these signs many years ago to provide employees with a way of signaling to their colleagues whether they are happy to be interrupted, or not. I have since learned that David Ogilvy used to have "a set of red and green lights outside his office door" to indicate whether he was willing to receive visitors.[436]

You have to plan your work and design your working environment in a way which will allow you to finish everything you start. Starting projects and not being able to finish them quickly will seriously decrease your efficiency. There are exceptions, of course – for example, you may sometimes come to realize that you should never have started a certain project in the first place. In cases like that, it's always best to acknowledge your mistake and to get the job over with as quickly as possible rather than wasting even more energy which might more efficiently be expended on other things.

Starting a project and not finishing it quickly also spoils the satisfaction we take from a job well done. At the end of the month, a carpenter who has made a number of tables and wardrobes will be happier than his colleague whose workshop is full of unfinished items. Successfully finishing a project you have started will always make you feel good about yourself. Starting many projects at once and not finishing any of them will always make you feel bad about yourself – not to mention the time and resources wasted.

Procrastination is a common complaint, and one that is more harmful than you might think. If you keep postponing something which needs to be done, you will create several serious problems for yourself. First of all, your subconscious will keep nagging you about the job you've left undone and you will have to waste a lot of energy on repressing those reminders. Secondly, sooner or later you will have to explain to your boss, your colleagues, or your clients why the job in question still hasn't been done. Thirdly, the job itself will often become much harder the longer you leave it undone. For example, it's far easier to write up the minutes right after a meeting, rather than a week later. Finally, you will feel increasingly uncomfortable the longer you postpone something.

You can never find the time to take care of things straight away? Try getting to the office a couple of hours early on occasion. You will be surprised how much you can get done without any colleagues to disturb you and without the distraction of phone calls or emails. And you will be able to surprise your boss or your clients, too, by finishing a project straight away, before the agreed deadline, if at all possible. I have made a habit of delivering everything earlier than promised.

Of course, this will only work if you plan realistically. Any planning based on the assumption that everything will work out according to plan is unrealistic. Expect the unexpected – if you don't, you know what they say about best-laid plans ...

Some people keep day planners or appointment books in which they will enter all their meetings and appointments as a matter of course – whilst forgetting to make a note of the appointments they have to keep with themselves. If I know I have to finish a draft before a certain date, I will always note it down in my day planner – in the same way in which I remind myself to keep appointments with clients or employees.

Time is our most valuable resource and has to be used wisely, as Warren Buffett knows. "He did only what made sense and what he wanted to do. He never let people waste his time. If he added something to his schedule, he discarded something else," his biographer Alice Schroeder reports, adding that he would keep phone calls "warmhearted and short. When he was ready to stop talking, the conversation simply died."[437]

Efficiency is also a question of doing things in the right order. Often, one step of a process needs to be completed before you can start on the next step. Unless you plan ahead, the entire process may become bottlenecked for days or even weeks because you have failed to anticipate the next step by completing all other steps which have to be completed first.

A lot of time-wasting and inefficiency is due to people 'forgetting' to do something. If a member of my staff tells me they 'forgot' to do something, that just doesn't cut it. Of course, I don't expect anybody to remember everything – nobody can, no matter how fantastic their memory. What I do expect them to do is write things down. That may sound simple – but it obviously isn't for many people, who would rather rely on their memory than on a 'to do' list. Others may write things down, but not straight away. After a phone call to a client, write down what needs to be done – do it straight away or you probably won't do it at all. We have all been in this situation: after a phone call, you make a mental note to yourself to write something down 'asap.' Before you get around to it, the phone rings again, or somebody comes into your office with another problem.

Because you haven't written down whatever it was that the first client asked you to do, you won't remember about it until days later. I'm no fan of the little yellow post-it notes stuck to people's screens or underneath all their other papers on their desks, either. It's far better to keep a proper 'to do' list, and to cross out each item as soon as you've completed it. You can get a real sense of achievement from crossing out one item after another!

Experience is not necessarily as valuable as some people claim. They may have gathered a lot of experience over the years – but whether or not they have learned anything from their experience is another matter entirely. Some people seem to be unable to draw the right conclusions from their experiences, which means that they make the same mistake – or similar mistakes – over and over again, which can cause a lot of trouble. The important point to remember is that you need to be capable of abstraction and of generalizations in order to avoid repeating similar mistakes.

A child who touches a hot stove may conclude that it's a mistake to touch a hot stove – and not do it again. The next day, the child touches a hot iron – and learns not to touch hot irons ever again. Two weeks later, the child touches a hot toaster and learns another lesson. A more intelligent child will generalize after the first incident, and know better than to touch anything hot from then on.

In other words: after you've made a mistake, don't just think about how to avoid making the same mistake again. Think about what general lessons you can learn from that mistake, in order to avoid making similar mistakes in the future. Efficiency means being able to abstract from an individual mistake to see the larger picture and not to waste any more time and energy by making similar mistakes. Don't just ask yourself: "What can I do to make sure the same mistake won't happen again?" Instead, you need to ask yourself: "What can I do to make sure similar mistakes won't happen again either?"

George Soros thinks his success is largely due to the fact that he is better than others at learning from mistakes. Soros freely admits that he is no more infallible than anybody else. "But where I do think I excel is in recognizing my mistakes ... And that is the secret to my success."[438]

And don't forget that your successes have as much to teach you as your mistakes. Any manager of a soccer team worth his salt learns from victory as well as from defeat. Many people are happy to have succeeded, without trying to isolate the reasons for their success. But unless you do just that, you will not be able to repeat that success.

Time spent analyzing your successes, your mistakes, your inefficiencies and any other factors which prevent you from achieving your goals even faster, is time well spent.

The key to increasing efficiency is knowing which of your activities are crucial for your results. Focus on those activities, and try to delegate any routine tasks that require less knowledge and creativity. Above all, you need to learn to divide your projects and processes into those tasks which require knowledge, experience or creativity, and others which don't. The latter can be delegated to less experienced and less competent members of your team. Always ask yourself: "Am I really the only person who can do this, or would somebody else be able to do it just as well, or almost as well?"

You will never achieve higher goals unless you learn to delegate, and to stop thinking "I might as well do that myself." Get into the habit of asking yourself every day which of your activities really contribute to your progress towards your chosen goal – and then get started on those first. Of course, you will only be able to do that if your day is not clogged up with one 'urgent' job after another, most of which would never have become urgent if only you had done them straight away, rather than wasting your time with procrastination.

CHAPTER 15

Speed Is of the Essence

Once you've improved your efficiency, your speed will also improve considerably – a crucial prerequisite for achieving more ambitious goals. Computers, the internet and modern telecommunications as a whole have all contributed to an acceleration of working processes. Speed is more important today than ever before. Large companies don't necessarily beat smaller competitors – in fact, the latter often have a competitive advantage because in the contemporary business world, being faster than everybody else is everything.

The more a company grows, the slower it tends to become. Increasingly inflexible, hampered by bureaucracy and administrative procedures, large companies may even come to resemble government agencies or state-run enterprises. Instead of focusing exclusively on their clients' or customers' needs, they develop cumbersome bureaucratic apparatuses devoted to administrative tasks. Many employees at managerial and executive level spend as much time on 'company politics' – in other words, on securing their own positions and trying to trip up rivals – as on developing new product lines or looking after their clients.

Like aircraft carriers, large companies find it difficult to change course. Reading the fascinating life story of Jack Welch, you will find that he spent his 20 years at the helm of General Electric, a global corporation with over 301,000 employees, fighting the bloated bureaucracy within the company.

When he took over as CEO in 1980, Welch recalls, GE was "a formal and massive bureaucracy, with too many layers of management." It took in excess of 25,000 managers to run the company "in a hierarchy with as many as a dozen levels between the factory floor and my office. More than 130 executives held the rank of vice president or above, with all kinds of titles and support staffs behind each one."[439] A simple boiler in one of their plants was supervised by four different organizational layers, and "almost every request for a significant capital expenditure" landed on Welch's desk. "In some cases, 16 other people had already signed it, and my signature was the last one required. What value was I adding?"[440] The company headquarters was ruled by bureaucrats "pleasant on the surface, with distrust and savagery roiling beneath it. The phrase seems to sum up how bureaucrats typically behave, smiling in front of you but always looking for a 'gotcha' behind your back."[441]

Welch, whom some consider the 'best manager in the world,' succeeded because he started a 'revolution.' In the early days, he says, "I was throwing hand grenades, trying to blow up traditions and rituals that I felt held us back."[442] Welch devised a system of dividing managers into three categories: A, B and C. Every year, he got rid of 10% of the worst-performing managers in the C category. After a year or two, leading executives started sabotaging his system by classifying employees who had already left the company as belonging to the C category. However, Welch stuck to his guns because he was convinced that his was the only way for GE to regain flexibility.

His main focus was on cutting bureaucratic structures and gaining speed. Although he was known for his quick decision-making, in his autobiography he reflects: "Yet 40 years later, when I retired, one of my great regrets was that I didn't act fast enough on many occasions." He couldn't remember many occasions when he had thought: "I wish I'd taken six more months to study something before making a decision." Rarely, if ever, had he regretted taking action – what he did regret was not having acted faster in certain situations.[443]

In some ways, smaller companies have it easier. If they are good, they can change tack from one moment to the next, like speedboats, allowing them to adapt to changes in the market. Any mistake they make becomes noticeable straight away, and either they realize that they've veered off course and rectify their mistake, or they sink without a trace. Larger companies have more leeway and can survive mistakes, even huge mistakes, because customers trust established brands, believing they can't go wrong if they stick with big names. That's why large enterprises are often able to stay afloat for a long time before they finally fail.

Staying within the metaphor, if an aircraft carrier sustains extensive damage to its hull, it won't sink immediately, whereas a speedboat will. That's why small companies can't afford to make even minor mistakes, whereas it takes a lot to bring down a corporate behemoth.

Larry Ellison's life story is an excellent case study in the importance of speed in today's business world. For the first 31 years of his life, Ellison was just an ordinary guy who had never achieved anything of note. And yet he is now one of the world's ten richest people: in 2019, he had a personal fortune of $66 billion. But let's start at the beginning, and find out how a small new company was able to beat a giant like IBM, with an illustrious company history dating back all the way to 1924.

Ellison was born in 1944 in Manhattan. His mother was only 19, his father long gone. She gave Larry up for adoption. He didn't do very well in school, refusing to learn anything he couldn't see the point of. In college, he paid his way by working as a programmer. He would study by day and spend his nights working on IBM computers for various companies.

Ellison lived in a one-bedroom apartment with his wife. They owned little more than the bed they slept in. In the counselling sessions they started attending in an attempt to save their failing marriage, Ellison's wife accused him of being a loser who'd never get anywhere. He told her: "If you stay with me, I will become a millionaire and you can have anything you want."[444] At that moment, his wife said, he made "a commitment to himself that he was not going to be a failure. That was the turning point of his life."[445] After seven years of marriage, she left him anyway. There didn't seem to be any indication whatsoever that Ellison would ever turn his life around.

In 1974, he started working for a computer company called Ampex, where he met Bob Miner and Ed Oates, who would later become co-founders of Oracle. He left after a while to take another job with Precision Instrument Company, a company specializing in hardware. They didn't know much about developing software so they were forced to outsource all their programming work. That's when Larry Ellison came up with an idea that would change his life. He called his former co-workers Miner and Oates and suggested founding a new company to apply for the contract. He himself would stay on at Precision Instrument Company as a liaison for the time being, while Miner and Oates would develop the software with another employee.

What motivated Ellison to take this step was the fact that he had realized that he wasn't made to climb the corporate ladder. A career in an established company would have involved kowtowing to people in more senior positions, something he had hated even as a schoolboy. "If people asked me to do things that didn't make sense, I just couldn't start my own school, but I could start my own company."[446]

On August 1, 1977 Ellison and his two former co-workers founded the company that was later to become Oracle, which employed about 136,000 people in more than 175 countries in 2019. He retained 60% of the company ownership – after all, it had been his idea – and gave 20% each to the two others. In many ways, the company structure wasn't unlike Microsoft and Apple in their early years. All three companies were founded by a visionary with a technical background, together with a gifted programmer. They were Bill Gates, Steve Jobs and Larry Ellison respectively, with Paul Allen, Steve Wozniak and Bob Miner fitting the bill as their gifted programmer sidekicks.

Oracle's phenomenal success is impossible to understand without taking stock of the problems companies were faced with at the time. Many companies had started introducing computer technology into their operations, but the available database systems, which were structured hierarchically, proved unsuitable to their requirements. Researchers had been working for some time on a new kind of database system, which they called "relational." In 1970, a member of IBM's research and development division had published a groundbreaking article, *A Relational Model of Data for Large Share Data Banks*. In the mid-1970s, programmers in the IBM Research Lab in San Jose started working on the practical application of these ideas.

Ed Oates had read this article and was fascinated by the conclusions it came to. "We all knew that relational was the trick. We all knew especially that network and hierarchical databases were not. Those were old technology."[447] Ellison, Oates and Miner saw an opportunity and grabbed it: they were determined to use the ideas the IBM researchers were working on and to come up with a solution before they did.

Although the Oracle founders started work on the project long after IBM, they succeeded in releasing their software five years earlier. The IT giant was simply too slow. Like GE, it had accumulated too many organizational layers over the decades of its existence. According to a former IBM programmer, the company itself commissioned a study into the reasons for its slowness. "What they found is that it would take at least nine months to ship an empty box."[448]

The other problem was that IBM had created a commercially success-ful hierarchic database system called IMS. Why should they take a risk by competing with their own product and launching a new system which would consign the old one to the dustbins of computing history? IMS had many defenders within the company, who fought tooth and nail against developing a new system.

Although IBM had originally come up with the idea, Larry Ellison was the one who took it and ran with it. A few years later, IBM would play midwife for another company, which would go on to become the largest computer company in the world. That company was Microsoft, of course. In 1980, IBM, which had been producing large mainframe computers, decided to get into the personal computing market. The company's previous attempt to launch a 'microcomputer' (the 5100 series) had failed miserably in the late 1970s.

IBM decided to buy the software they needed rather than waste time developing their own (they obviously realized how slow they were). In particular, they needed to buy an operating system to make their computers functional. Negotiations with a company called Digital Research came to nothing.

IBM approached Bill Gates as well, but his company Microsoft wasn't able to develop a new operating system from scratch within 12 months. Attempting to come up with a solution, Gates negotiated the purchase of an operating system from another company – Seattle Computer Products – and in November 1980, signed an agreement with IBM to develop the software and disk operating system (DOS) for the personal computer the company was planning to launch. He ended up paying $50,000 to Seattle Computer Products for the licensing rights to their operating system 86-DOS – probably the best deal of the 20th century.

IBM had originally suggested to buy all licenses from Microsoft for a flat rate, which was the deal Microsoft had made with Seattle Computer Products. But Bill Gates was smarter than that, insisting on a percentage of every operating system IBM sold. In 1981, IBM launched its first personal computer, which became a raving success and laid the foundations for Microsoft's empire. By late 1982, the company had 200 employees and software sales of $32 million.

According to Larry Ellison, IBM's decision to use MS-DOS as the operating system for their personal computers was "the single worst mistake in the history of enterprise on Earth ... a hundred-billion-dollar mistake."[449] Publishing the article on relational database systems, and not developing their own product more quickly, was another mistake which cost the company dearly, while making Larry Ellison one of the richest men in the world.

Not recognizing the potential and the ideas of employees, who then decide to set up their own company, is a common mistake large companies make. Again, IBM is a prime example. In 1972, five former employees of the company's German subsidiary founded their own company, which they called SAP. Today, SAP is a public limited company, one of the largest software companies in the world with around 98,000 employees and sales of €25 billion and operational profits of €5.7 billion in 2018.

It all started with some of IBM's most talented employees feeling increasingly frustrated because they were able to read the market better than the corporation did. One of them was Dr. Claus Wellenreuther, who had started working as a systems consultant for IBM in 1966 straight out of university. His degree in business made him rather an outsider among all the physics, mathematics and engineering graduates. He specialized in developing software for the accounting department. "Bookkeeping and Wellenreuther," SAP co-founder Dietmar Hopp reflects, "were used as synonyms."[450]

Up to this point, IBM had focused almost exclusively on selling hardware; for a long time, the company failed to realize the importance of software. In 1971, IBM finally decided to centralize Wellenreuther's hobbyhorse, the development of accounting software. "I expected to be appointed as project manager," Wellenreuther affirms, "because I had developed and implemented financial accounting systems all the time."[451] He was informed, however, that he wasn't qualified for a job at managerial level. Wellenreuther saw that he had got stuck in a rut and that there was no future for him at IBM. He took his remaining time off of two months and used it to do some serious thinking. The result was that he quit his job to set up his own business, rather blandly described as "systems analysis and program development" in his letterhead.

Another IBM employee, Dietmar Hopp, did some thinking as well. His field of expertise was dialog programming – the process which enables computers to execute programming prompts immediately, rather than with a time delay, as was originally the case.

Previously, customers and consultants had developed their own software applications with support from IBM, which basically meant inventing the wheel over and over again – and charging their customers for it. "What we do at each IBM client is always the same," Hopp realized. "Therefore, it can be standardized."[452] Hopp decided to develop a standard software which could then be used in many different companies. His idea was the basis for the new company he started with Wellenreuther, Hasso Plattner and two other former IBM employees. They knew that speed was of the essence. If their enterprise was a success, other companies – perhaps even IBM – would copy their idea. Having an ingenious idea for a standard software and the knowledge required to develop it wasn't enough: they also needed a good marketing strategy.

Pitching their idea to IT specialists in large companies may have seemed the obvious approach, but they soon realized it was pointless. Not only were the IT specialists reluctant to risk making themselves and their staff redundant, they also feared that the new software would reveal errors and deficiencies in their own systems, which nobody in the company had ever noticed because nobody else knew anything about computers.

So SAP went straight to the top instead, approaching CEOs and CFOs. That was their first brilliant marketing idea. Even more importantly, from the very beginning they sought the cooperation of large auditing companies and hardware manufacturers. After all, CEOs and CFOs were far more likely to be swayed by an endorsement from independent auditors and consultants whom they trusted, rather than by some inexperienced newcomers trying to flog their own product.

This saved SAP the trouble of having to promote their software and allowed them to concentrate on developing and optimizing it. "We regard the ability to innovate as a synonym for efficiency," Hopp says, citing constant anxiety "whether competitors are better and could overtake us" as a major driving force.[453] Certainly, SAP did not want to go the way of their rival Nixdorf, a company which ultimately failed because it focused entirely on marketing at the expense of product development.

SAP was more consistent and faster than the competition precisely because the company invested its resources exclusively into developing standard software. "Its competitors, on the other hand, spent years undecided between developing standard software and customized proprietary software, or overspent on special fields."[454] SAP quickly succeeded in winning almost all leading German companies as customers, and within a few years, the company had practically monopolized the German market. SAP is now Europe's largest software company – there are only three larger companies on the market, and they are all in the U.S. None of this would have been possible if it hadn't been for IBM's failure to predict future developments and to give talented employees who did predict them correctly the opportunity and the leeway to grow within the company.

IBM isn't the only corporation guilty of this kind of short-sighted thinking. Something quite similar happened with Xerox, whose name had become synonymous with the copy machines the company owed its success to. Xerox ran a highly secretive research center in Palo Alto, which was reverentially known to the IT community as "Xerox PARC." Apple founder Steve Jobs couldn't wait to see with his own eyes what was being developed in this top-secret location. Putting his considerable powers of persuasion to good use, he was finally granted access to the inner sanctum.

Jobs could hardly contain his excitement about what he saw there. He was "pacing around the room, jumping up and down and acting up the whole time," PARC scientist Larry Tessler remembers.[455] He had good reason to be excited, because what Tessler showed them was nothing less than the future of personal computing. "What Apple saw that day," Jobs' biographer explains, "was a display on which the user made selections, not by typing out cryptic commands, but by moving a pointer to designate the desired object. And individual windows for different documents. And onscreen menus."[456] And there was something else which was new and special – a gadget called a mouse. Today, we can hardly imagine using a computer without one anymore, but at the time it was a complete novelty.

Demonstrating his inventions to Jobs and his Apple team, Tessler was overjoyed at their excitement and the intelligent questions they kept pestering him with. You can well imagine how he must have felt, this employee of a large corporation who was fully aware that his team had created something special and significant, but who knew as well that his company would never give him the recognition he deserved. By the end of the demo, he said later, he had already made the decision to leave Xerox and start working for Apple, where he was made a vice president and chief scientist.[457]

All these stories – IBM and Oracle, IBM and SAP, Xerox and Apple – have similar outcomes: a large company employs brilliant people with great ideas, but fails to recognize their potential and to turn those ideas into commercially viable products. In defense of the two large companies in question, it has to be said that their decisions were motivated in part by the fear of damaging their image by launching products before they had been fully tested and developed.

Larry Ellison, Bill Gates and Steve Jobs were strangers to that fear. Their motto was: it's better to be fast than perfect. Or, to be more precise: they too wanted to be perfect – but they didn't want to wait until their product was perfect before launching it. If it wasn't perfect already, it could always be perfected by taking on board feedback from users – which would allow them to release new versions and updates every so often and to cash in on the licensing fees. Since all other software manufacturers did exactly the same, users were left with no choice, disgruntled though they may have been.

Ellison, Jobs and Gates realized that being fast can often be more important than being perfect. This is especially true at the initial stage, when it's all about grabbing as large a share of the market as possible as quickly as possible. Attacked by his competitors for being too quick to launch products prematurely, Ellison replies: "How much does it cost Pepsi to get one half of 1% of the market from Coke once the market has been established? It's very expensive ... If we don't run as hard as we can as fast as we can, and then do it again twice as fast, it'll be cost-prohibitive for us to increase market share."[458]

Bill Gates followed a similar strategy of always "anticipating the market and being the first out with a new product."[459] However, this would frequently get Microsoft into considerable trouble. "Too often Gates set unrealistic goals for product development. Deadlines were missed, products weren't always well-designed, and contracts had to be revised due to unforeseen obstacles or delays."[460]

It was a price Gates was willing to pay. His close associate Steve Wood says: "Bill's approach, and you can still see it now in things like Windows, was always to go for creating the standard, to get the market share. He just hated to turn down business. If it meant we had to drop our price to get the business, he was typically much more willing to argue that we do that ..."[461]

Bill Gates had such confidence in his problem-solving abilities that he would take on any challenge, no matter how impossible. Wood attests to the prevailing can-do attitude at Microsoft: "Okay, so no one has done this for a personal computer before, so what? We can do it. No big deal." Nobody ever thought to ask whether it might not be doable. "We overcommitted ourselves."[462]

This often meant that the products didn't work very well at first, but Gates wasn't too bothered about that. The former head of Microsoft's consumer products division once said in an interview: "With few exceptions, they've never shipped a good product in its first version. But they never give up and eventually get it right. Bill is too willing to compromise just to get going in a business."[463]

Gates didn't want to be overtaken by the competition from Asia. "I went into Japan only two years after I started Microsoft knowing that in terms of working with hardware companies, that was a great place to be. A lot of great research goes on there. And also, it was the most likely source of competition other than the U.S. itself."[464]

Any would-be successful entrepreneur is faced with a conflict between two mutually exclusive goals: being fast and being perfect. 'Perfect hesitation' may well lead to losing out, as it did for IBM or Xerox. Conversely, caring only about speed at the expense of quality may destroy your reputation.

The success story of the Walmart corporation demonstrates the importance of being faster than the competition. Today, Walmart is the world's largest private employer and the company with the highest turnover in the world, with around 2.3 million employees. In 2018, Walmart's operating income was more than $20 billion. Three members of the Walton family – Jim Walton, Alice Walton and S. Robson Walton – are listed among the wealthiest people in the world. Their estimated combined worth totaled $155 billion in 2018. Their father, Sam Walton, opened the original Walmart in Rogers, Arkansas, on July 2, 1962. His story is an object lesson in the importance of speed.

Walton opened his very first shop in 1945. He had bought a franchise in a small town for $25,000. Of that, he was able to put up $5,000 himself and the remainder was a loan from his father-in-law. In his first year, sales reached $105,000 – almost 50% more than the $72,000 his predecessor had made. In the next two years, that number rose to $140,000 and $172,000, respectively. The shop's owner was so impressed with Walton's success that he refused to extend the contract when it expired – he wanted his own son to take over the profitable franchise.

Walton recalls: "It was the low point of my business life. I felt sick to my stomach. I couldn't believe it was happening to me."[465] Being forced to give up the successful business he had built was a traumatic experience, but it would prove to be the making of him. Walton moved to Bentonville, another small town of 3,000 inhabitants, and opened a new shop, which would become one of the first in the United States to be based on the self-service model.

Walton, who was always eager to try out new ideas, had read a magazine article on the two shops which had pioneered self-service in the U.S. He was so intrigued by the concept he decided to put it into practice himself. Walton didn't care about being the first, all he wanted was to be the fastest.

"Most everything I've done I've copied from somebody else,"[466] he readily confesses in his autobiography. Many people are too proud to copy ideas somebody else has come up with before them. They think an achievement is worth nothing unless it's based on your own idea. Walton never shared those scruples.

He was happy to walk into his competitors' shops or company headquarters and ask them anything he felt he needed to know. He told his staff to follow his lead and to focus only on what the competitors were doing better, while ignoring their mistakes. "Check everyone who is our competition," he would say. "And don't look for the bad. Look for the good."[467]

Soon after that, the first discount stores opened in the U.S., offering products at prices which were far lower than those of their competitors. Walton copied that idea, too, realizing much sooner than most that discount stores were the way of the future. "We really had only two choices left: stay in the variety store business, which I knew was going to be hit hard by the discounting wave of the future; or open a discount store. Of course I wasn't about to sit there and become a target."[468]

His staff were extremely skeptical at first, as was his brother Bud. "They thought Walmart was just another one of Sam Walton's crazy ideas. It was totally unproven at the time, but it was really what we'd been doing all along; experimenting, trying to do something different, educating ourselves as to what was going in the retail industry and trying to stay ahead of those trends."[469] Walton's first Walmart proved a success, but his competitors were fast catching on to the idea. "We figured we'd better roll the stores out just as quickly as we could."[470]

And so they did. Walton bought a small plane and would often spend the whole week flying all over the country and scouting out potential locations for new stores. Once he had identified a suitable property from the air, he would land, find the owner and make him an offer to buy the land for a new Walmart. He initially focused on small towns, which many of his competitors wouldn't even bother with.

The number of Walmart stores increased from 32 in 1970 to 51 in 1972, 78 in 1974, 125 in 1976, 195 in 1978, and 276 in 1980. In 2019, Walmart has 4,770 stores in the United States and 11,766 stores worldwide.

Sam Walton owes his phenomenal success to the speed with which he outpaced his competitors. In the early 1970s, he had formed a research group with some other discount chains. The other members couldn't believe how quickly he would open one store after another. "We would be putting in 50 stores a year, when most of our group would be trying to start these three, four, five, or six a year. It always confounded them. They would always ask, 'How do you do it? There's no way you can be doing that.'"[471]

Of course, Walmart's rapid growth came at a price. Finding enough qualified employees to man the shops proved extremely difficult and Walton was forced to hire people without any retail experience. Ferold Arend, a leading Walmart manager, recalls: "In my opinion, most of them weren't anywhere near ready to run stores, but Sam proved me wrong there. He finally convinced me. If you take someone who lacks the experience and the know-how but has the real desire and the willingness to work his tail off to get the job done, he'll make up for what he lacks."[472]

Walton couldn't understand why his competitors did nothing to stop Walmart's expansion. "It's amazing that our competitors didn't catch on to us quicker and try harder to stop us. Whenever we put a Walmart store in a town, customers would just flock to us from the variety stores."[473] Most of them, he realized, simply weren't prepared to reduce the high profit margins they were used to – and those that did enter the discount market did so half-heartedly. "What happened was that they didn't really commit to discounting. They held on to their old variety store concepts too long. They were so accustomed to getting their 45% markup, they never let go."[474]

The power of dissatisfaction, which we have discussed in Chapter 10, was an important driving force for Walton's success. "As good as business was, I never could leave well enough alone, and, in fact, I think my constant fiddling and meddling with the status quo may have been one of my highest contributions to the later success of Walmart."[475] He also stresses the importance of aiming higher than his competitors. "I've always held the bar pretty high for myself: I've set extremely high personal goals."[476]

What Sam Walton did for the retail market in the United States, the Albrecht brothers, Karl and Theodor, did in Germany. When Theo Albrecht died in March 2010, he was the third-richest man in Germany and ranked 31st on the *Forbes* list of billionaires, with an estimated net worth of $16.7 billion. Four years later, his brother Karl also died, leaving behind a fortune worth $29 billion.

The brothers' parents had run a small grocery shop, no more than 12 square feet in size, since 1913. When the brothers returned from captivity after World War Two, they started opening one shop after another all over Germany, much as Sam Walton would do in the United States two decades later.

Their successful concept was born out of sheer desperation. After the war, they didn't have enough capital to stock a shop with the usual range of products. So they started out with a limited range, which they were planning to extend as soon as they had the means to do so. Karl Albrecht later said: "We were planning to stock our branches with a wide range of food items, just like any other grocery store. We never did that, though, because we realized that we could make good money even with our limited range of products and that our overheads were very low compared to the other companies, which was largely due to our limited range of products."[477] They deliberately only stocked one brand of each item. "We only had shoe polish from Erdal, Blendax toothpaste, and only Sigella floor polish in tubs, always only the brand which sold best," said Karl Albrecht as he outlined his business policy in the early 1950s.

They also knew that they had to offer their consumers something else to make up for their limited product range. From 1950 onwards, they consistently focused on value for money rather than a wide choice of products. "Customers come to us for our low prices, and their allure is so strong that they are quite willing to queue up," Albrecht said.[478] At the time, their shops stocked no more than 250 to 280 products. Everything was arranged in plain sight on the counters and shelves, there were no frills or decorative touches of any kind.

Unlike other retailers, the Albrecht brothers would pass on any savings they were able to make to consumers. "There is always a strong temptation to keep charging customers the same, even though an item has become cheaper for us to buy. But that would end in tears sooner or later, because the aim is to make customers believe that they can't shop for less anywhere else.

Once you've achieved that much – and I'm convinced that we have done so – then the customer is willing to accept anything."

By 1960, the two brothers had 300 shops and an annual turnover of 90 million deutsche marks. They renamed their company Aldi, short for Albrechts Discount, and divided it between themselves. Theo Albrecht got Aldi North, which comprised the northern part of Germany, while Karl took Aldi South.

Their competitors soon recognized the enormous potential of the discount market. Other retail chains started copying the Aldi concept, some of them very successfully. However, Aldi remained the market leader in the discount segment because both brothers were fast and agile enough to stay way ahead of the competition. Once again, speed proved to be of the essence, particularly in the beginning. As soon as other players in a given market start realizing how well a novel concept is working, and how much profit it is generating for those who have taken the risk to pioneer it, they will copy it. Being the first to enter a new market gives you a competitive edge – but it's up to you to use that advantage to dominate the market on a permanent basis, as Sam Walton and the Aldi brothers did, making it hard for competitors to challenge your position.

Even with an enormous financial outlay, Walmart failed to conquer the German discount market, which is dominated by the likes of Aldi and Lidl. In 1997, Walmart bought up 21 Wertkauf-SB stores in Germany for 1.5 billion deutsche marks. A year later the company spent another 71.3 billion deutsche marks on taking over 74 Interspar stores. However, after racking up huge losses to the tune of €3 billion, the global corporation finally left the German market to the competition in 2006.

If you are planning to start your own business, there's no need to be overly scared of large and powerful established companies. As long as your idea is good and you succeed in positioning yourself correctly, a small, new, 'hungry' company will often be faster than its competitors who may well be encumbered with bureaucratic procedures. That doesn't mean that you can afford to underestimate the competition, let alone the value of experience, long-standing tradition and brand recognition. What it does mean is that you need to be aware of your competitive edge – and use it to your advantage.

Even if you are an employee in somebody else's company, speed is essential for your career. Surprise your clients and your superiors by completing projects long before they are due. Once you have improved your efficiency by following the advice in Chapter 14, increasing the speed with which you finish your work should be no trouble at all.

And the next time your manager needs somebody to take on an important project, who do you think he or she will opt for: a colleague who keeps coming up with new excuses about how busy he is and who might not even finish the job by the agreed due date? Or someone who may not have been with the company for quite as long, but who has organized his or her work so efficiently that your manager can be sure any project will be completed long before it is due? Make sure that person is you!

CHAPTER 16

Money Matters

This book analyzes the success stories of people whose success also manifests itself not least in the huge fortunes they have been able to amass – tens or hundreds of million dollars, in some cases even billions. How much does money matter as a motivating force? There are two schools of thought on this. The first one claims that money alone is not sufficient as a motivating force. The most successful people, according to this way of thinking, are those who do whatever it is they do for its own sake. They love what they do, and money is an incidental by-product rather than an end in itself – wealth comes to them more or less automatically, precisely because they love their work and excel at it. The second hypothesis assumes that the ambition to become a millionaire, a multi-millionaire, or even a billionaire, is an essential motivating force for high achievers, and that anybody who wishes to be truly successful needs to aim for quantifiable goals.

So how much does money matter? In Europe, and to a lesser extent in the U.S., admitting that you are primarily motivated by money is socially unacceptable. Dismissing money as insignificant, or at best as a secondary consideration, is de rigueur. People who openly admit that they are driven by the ambition to increase their wealth are considered crass, greedy and of somewhat dubious character, their lives devoted to the pursuit of filthy lucre rather than lofty ideals.

Don't believe a billionaire who claims not to care about money. The richest man in history, the legendary oil baron John D. Rockefeller himself, who was constantly under pressure because of his wealth and his success, was fond of affecting disinterest in money matters. "Throughout his life," his biographer reports, he "reacted in a vitriolic manner to accusations that he had lusted after money as a child and yearned to be fabulously rich ...

he contested insinuations that he was motivated by greed instead of a humble desire to serve God or humanity. He preferred to portray his fortune as a pleasant accident, the unsought by-product of hard work."[479]

However, Rockefeller's biographer Ron Chernow doesn't set much store in these claims. Chernow blames Rockefeller's obsession with wealth on his father. "The old man had a passion for money that amounted almost to a craze," he quotes a family friend. "I never met a man who had such a love of money."[480] Rockefeller himself was full of admiration for his father's habit of "never carrying less than $1,000, and he kept it in his pocket. He was able to take care of himself, and was not afraid to carry his money."[481] Even as a young boy, he is said to have dreamt of great riches. He couldn't have known that his wealth would one day exceed his wildest dreams, but even the $100,000 he aimed for back then – several million in today's currency – constituted a considerable sum. "Someday, sometime, when I am a man, I want to be worth a hundred thousand dollars. And I'm going to be, too – someday," he told a childhood friend. There are many such stories from various sources.[482]

Making money hand over fist may not have been the top priority for every billionaire. However, it seems more than likely that, in public, many of them prefer to cite 'loftier' motivations, which are considered more socially acceptable. No millionaire or billionaire has ever been known to turn down the opportunity to make money – if they had, they wouldn't be millionaires or billionaires.

On the other hand, people who have had no success in life will often express a dislike for money which verges on disgust. A few years ago, at a class reunion, I got talking to a former classmate, a self-confessed anarchist when we were at school. I asked him how he was doing and whether his attitude had changed, to which he replied: "I'm still fighting for the cause." I asked what cause he was talking about, and he said: "The abolition of money." I ventured an ironic remark: "It looks as if you've at least managed to achieve that for yourself." He had no choice but to laugh – I had guessed right. Shortly after that encounter, I ran into an acquaintance – a very intelligent and courageous journalist whose opinions I rate very highly. He told me he was disgusted by money. I asked him how much money he had, and even though he gets paid fairly well, he still doesn't have any money. No wonder, I told him – if money disgusted him so much, it was probably avoiding him to the same extent he was avoiding it.

People who have not succeeded in making any money tend to look for reasons and excuses why not. The simplest one they can come up with is: "The rich are morally corrupt; they have come by their money through ruthlessness and dubious means." According to an opinion poll in which respondents were asked why they think some people are richer than others, 52% of Germans said that rich people had made their fortunes by dishonest means.[483]

Implicitly, what they mean to say is: "The reason I don't have any money is because I am such a good and moral person." A lot of people who have not succeeded in making money live and breathe by this lie, which is of course nonsense. In every social class, there are those who have high moral standards, and those who don't. I really don't believe the percentage of people with moral integrity is higher in the lower strata of society than among the rich and famous.

In spite of all their attempts to justify their lack of financial means, most people would rather be rich than poor. However, their attitude is not conducive to improving their financial situation. And even those who do make a lot of money frequently feel forced to stress that money isn't really all that important to them.

We've all come across sentiments along the lines of "I'd rather be poor and healthy than sick and wealthy." Nobody with even a modicum of sense is going to argue with that. But personally, I'd rather be healthy and wealthy than poor and sick. "Money can't buy you love" is another popular rejoinder, and equally hard to argue with. But does that make money any less important?

What drives people to make a lot of money? Why do people want to become millionaires? What does money mean to them?

Depending on the individual, the answers to these questions fall into three categories:

1. Money as a means to win approval and recognition.
2. Money as a means to prove your success or your intelligence.
3. Money as a symbol of freedom and an opportunity to fulfill your dreams.

Looking at the life stories of very successful people, you find that for most of them, one of these motivations predominates, although in some cases, they work in conjunction with each other.

Let's start with the first one: for men like Oracle founder Larry Ellison, recognition and the approval of others was certainly a powerful motivation.

Ellison was the owner of the tenth-largest yacht in the world, a boat called *Rising Sun*, which he bought for some $200 million. He was well-known as a playboy and for him the status and recognition bestowed by his wealth is certainly an all-important factor.

The same is true of Warren Buffett and George Soros, although neither is the least bit interested in luxury goods. Buffett still lives in the same house he bought years and years ago and has never even bought himself an expensive car, let alone a yacht. He definitely doesn't fit the playboy image. His wife once said that all he needed to be happy was a light bulb and a book. Even as a boy, Buffett wanted to make money, a lot of money. For him, it's all about results and returns – he regards the profits from his investments as a kind of objective yardstick which proves his superior intelligence. For this reason alone, he would never cheat, use shortcuts or profit by unfair means precisely because he prides himself on his superior investment strategies.

Being right is probably almost as important to him as being rich. That's why he has invested a lot of time and energy into disproving Eugene Fama's efficient-market hypothesis, according to which men like Buffett are nothing but freaks of nature, akin to lucky gamblers or multiple lottery winners. The market, proponents of this theory claim, cannot be outwitted. For Buffett, the insult must have been almost unbearable.

Making money is an end in itself for Buffett. Everything else is secondary, except for his ethical and moral principles. These he sees as a vital asset, an essential prerequisite for his success because they gain him the trust of others. Buffett is definitely not motivated by a desire for conspicuous consumption and creature comforts. He is famously reluctant to spend any of his money and countless stories attest to his thriftiness and ascetic tastes. After they had moved house in the late 1950s, his wife bought chrome-and-leather furniture and huge paintings. "The $15,000 decorating bill totaled almost half of what the house itself had cost, which 'just about killed Warren,' according to Bob Billig, a golfing pal. He didn't notice colors or respond to visual aesthetics and so was indifferent to the result, seeing only the outrageous bill."[484] He would protest to his wife that he didn't see the point of spending hundreds of thousands of dollars on a new pair of shoes, or on having her hair done. Of course, neither the shoes nor the hairdresser came to that much – but Buffett always calculated the returns he would have gotten if he had invested and reinvested the money over decades, rather than 'wasting' it so foolishly. When his daughter asked him for a loan to buy a new kitchen (she already knew he would never give her the money), he advised her to borrow money from the bank like everybody else.

Once he had become one of the richest men in the world, Buffett decided to give away most of his money. But unlike other billionaires, he had no intention of establishing a Buffett Foundation, a Buffett University or Buffett Library as a memorial to himself. He had come to the conclusion that his friend Bill Gates, with whom he took turns at the top of the list of the richest men in the world, knew more about charity than he did. And Buffett applied the same maxim to donating money which had served him so well in earning it: find the most competent person for the job, then delegate it.

Buffett's fellow investor George Soros, was "no hedonist" either, his biographer says, and "money could bring him only so much."[485] He had never planned to become an investor; as a young man he dreamt of making his living as an intellectual, presenting "the world with some major insight, 'like Freud or Einstein.'"[486]

But Soros soon realized that his true talents lay elsewhere. At first, he tried his hand as a writer of philosophical treatises and books on economic theories, which were neither very well received, nor as brilliantly argued as he may have thought. Today, Soros likes to refer to himself as a "failed philosopher." What he did have a remarkable gift for, however, was predicting the markets and making enormous amounts of money from those predictions. Like Buffett, he regards the fortune he has amassed as evidence of his intelligence and his ability to understand political and economic contexts better than most.

According to his biographer, Soros entered the world of high finance out of frustration at not being able to conquer the world of ideas. "The decision was, in one sense, easy. He had to make a living anyway. Why not try to show all those economists that he understood the workings of the world better than they did by making as much money as possible? Soros believed that money would give him a platform from which he could expound his views."[487]

Soros likes to joke that he is "the world's highest-paid critic." He claims: "My function in the financial markets is a critic, and my critical judgments are expressed by my decisions to buy and sell."[488]

Both Soros and Buffett lean to the political left (Soros even more so than Buffett), which has a lot to do with their craving for intellectual recognition.

Academics and intellectuals tend to regard money with suspicion.[489] Only by professing left-wing views and reservations about capitalism can a man like Soros win a certain amount of respect in those circles. However, it would be wrong to say that money meant nothing to him, or even that he was indifferent to its allure. According to his biographer, he had a sign on the wall in his office which succinctly expressed his credo: "I WAS BORN POOR BUT I WILL NOT DIE POOR."[490]

The third reason people are interested in making money is the freedom it brings. Money, many rich people know, is the currency of true independence. In her autobiography, fashion designer Coco Chanel reflects on the promise money has always held for her. The two aunts who raised her after her mother's death kept drumming into her: "You won't have any money ... you'll be very lucky if a farmer wants you." This raised her hackles, making her all the more determined to grow rich and successful. "Very young, I had realized that without money you are nothing, that with money you can do anything. Or else, you had to depend on your husband. Without money, I would be forced to sit on my behind and wait for a gentleman to come and find me."[491]

Even as a 12-year-old, Chanel knew full well that "money is the key to freedom."[492] She claims that money meant "nothing more than the symbol of independence ... I've never wanted anything, just affection, and I had to buy my freedom and pay for it whatever the cost."[493]

For her, too, making a lot of money was an objective measure of her success – it proved that her unconventional creations and designs hit a nerve. "Money that is earned is merely material proof that we were right: if a business or a dress is not profitable, it's because they're no good. Wealth is not accumulation; it's the exact opposite; it serves to free us."[494] Less successful designers and artists like to pretend it's the other way around: that commercial success is the hallmark of artistic compromise, of 'selling out.' Of course, this is just another way of rationalizing and justifying failure.

The fact that the wealthy associate money, above all, with "freedom and independence" was also one of the key findings of my dissertation, *The Wealth Elite*: my 45 super-rich interviewees associated very different advantages in their lives with 'money,' that is, with a large fortune. In order to better understand the motives of the interviewees, each was presented with six aspects that can be associated with money. They were asked, based on the importance of these factors to them, to rate each aspect on a scale from zero (totally unimportant) to ten (very important).

The wide variety of responses reflects the broad spectrum of motivations. Being able to afford the finer things in life (namely expensive cars, houses, or holidays) was of major importance to 13 of the interviewees, whereas ten asserted that this plays no role whatsoever for them. For the remaining interviewees, this aspect was neither very important nor totally unimportant. Security was rated important by roughly half of the interviewees, but there were also nine who said that this was of no importance to them whatsoever.

There was only one motivation about which almost all of the interviewees agreed. They associate wealth with freedom and independence. The notion of being financially free united almost all of the interviewees. No other motivation was so frequently rated so highly. Only five of the interviewees rated this aspect with a grade that was not in the highest category of between seven and ten. Of the interviewees, a total of 23 went as far as to rate this aspect with the highest possible score of ten.

For whatever reasons, money is an important motivator for many high achievers. Others couldn't care less about it. McDonald's founder Ray Kroc belonged to the second group. "Although he became one of the country's wealthiest men, with an estimated worth of $600 million when he died in 1984, he never talked of accumulating wealth. He was not driven by acquiring money. He never analyzed a business by its profit-and-loss statement, and he never took the time to understand his own company's business sheet."[495] This attitude brought McDonald's close to the brink of bankruptcy. "What converted McDonald's into a money machine had nothing to do with Ray Kroc or the McDonald brothers or even the popularity of McDonald's hamburgers, French fries, and milkshakes. Rather, McDonald's made its money on real estate and on a little-known formula developed by a financial genius named Harry Sonneborn."[496] Kroc himself had to concede: "His idea is what really made McDonald's rich."[497]

Even in an eminently successful company such as McDonald's, the founder or company director may not be driven by the desire to make money. However, there has to be another person high up in the company hierarchy – though usually less exposed to the public eye – for whom money is an important consideration.

Whereas investors tend to pursue money in the abstract, for its own sake, most entrepreneurs are far more likely to be driven by their enthusiasm for a certain business idea, by passion for their work and a constant desire to grow, to learn, to develop and expand, to try out new things, to excel themselves and triumph over others.

Advertising made David Ogilvy famous – and fabulously wealthy, allowing him to buy a château in France. He was passionate about wanting to change the way things were done in the advertising world. However, the fact that he was on a mission to replace pure entertainment with fact-based information doesn't mean that money wasn't important to him. On the contrary, he was "obsessed with money," his biographer says.[498] "Although he entered advertising to make money, Ogilvy had become interested in the business itself."[499]

Ogilvy was a voracious reader of books on successful businesspeople. He was very interested in finding out how they had made their money and what they did with it. His biographer reports: "Whether due to childhood poverty or other reasons, money was never far from the surface with Ogilvy. And he could be startlingly direct."[500] He would probe successful professionals he had only just met: "How much do you make? How much are you worth? – Do you make a good buck?"[501]

There is no conflict of interest between wanting to make money and feeling passionate about a certain job or issue. "Many of the greatest creations of man have been inspired by the desire to make money," Ogilvy claimed. "If Oxford undergraduates were paid for their work, I would have performed miracles of scholarship. It wasn't until I tasted lucre on Madison Avenue that I began to work in earnest."[502]

If you are unhappy with your own financial situation, I would strongly advise you to review your attitude towards money. Subconscious negative feelings about money may very well be the reason you don't have any, or not enough of it. If you envy others who have more money than you, you definitely need to review your attitude. Whenever I meet somebody who is significantly better off than I am, I feel admiration for them – as long as they made their money with honest work. I see that person as a role model, somebody I can learn from – envy doesn't come into it.

If you want to build a fortune, you should take guidance and inspiration from the success stories of the men and women featured in this book.

The one thing you should never do is choose a field or a job merely because it's well-paid, or because you think it will look good on your CV.

Warren Buffett is very adamant on this point. "I think you are out of your mind if you keep taking jobs that you don't like just because you think that it will look good on your resumé. Isn't that a bit like saving up sex for your old age?"[503]

Speaking personally, all my life I have always worked in jobs I enjoyed doing – whether it was as a historian, a senior editor for a publishing house, a journalist, a real estate expert, a PR consultant, or an author. You won't achieve success in life unless you do something you love and which suits your talents.

CHAPTER 17

Tension and Relaxation

The speed, intensity and the sheer amount of time that successful people commit to their work is nothing short of amazing. In her biography of Bill Gates, Jeanne M. Lesinski writes: "No one at Microsoft worked harder than Bill Gates. He was so preoccupied with his work that he often forgot to tend to his appearance or eat meals. Sometimes, when his secretary came to work in the morning, she found her boss asleep on the floor of his office."[504]

Prince Alwaleed, too, handles an incredible workload every single day. According to his personal physician: "With him there's action, it's not standing still, it's just on your toes. You can't just sit and relax like on my vacation, where I can sit for two, three hours doing nothing, but with him, we do this, we do that, we go there ... it's action with him."[505]

Alwaleed, his physician reports, regularly allows himself no more than four or five hours of sleep. He is always on the move – once he had business meetings in ten different African countries in the space of five days with a full schedule of activities from morning to night. "Sometimes he overdoes it, like on his trips, when he goes from six o'clock in the morning to eleven o'clock, midnight, then he comes back to the hotel and stays in the lobby till four o'clock in the morning. He wants to read the papers, he wants to see the magazines, to eat something, he wants people to be around him."[506] Every night after midnight, Alwaleed peruses the latest editions of *The New York Times, The Wall Street Journal, The Washington Post* and *The International Herald Tribune* and magazines such as *Newsweek, Times, Business Week* and *The Economist* as well as other publications and books on finance.

John D. Rockefeller was another workaholic. "He fretted endlessly about his company and, below the surface, was constantly on edge," his biographer says. Rockefeller himself, not a man prone to dwelling on his weaknesses, once admitted that "for years on end I never had a solid night's sleep, worrying about how it was to come out ... I tossed about in bed night after night worrying over the outcome ... All the fortune that I have made has not served to compensate for the anxiety of that period."[507]

His way of life was bound to take its toll. By the time he reached 50, Rockefeller was suffering from constant fatigue and depression. "For several decades," his biographer writes, "he had expended superhuman energy in the creation of Standard Oil, mastering myriad details; all the while, pressure had built steadily beneath the surface repose. One could now see in his face the subdued melancholy of a man who had sacrificed too much for work."[508]

Eventually his unspecified illness – which nowadays would most likely be classed as 'burn-out syndrome' – got so bad he was unable to make it to his office for several months. He then decided to take Saturdays off and to take longer vacations – all to no avail. Finally he followed his doctor's advice and took an eight-month vacation. His staff were under strict orders only to contact him in emergencies. Rockefeller started cycling a lot and working alongside his field-hands. In July 1891, he wrote in a letter: "I am happy to state that my health is constantly improving. I can hardly tell you how different the world begins to look to me. Yesterday was the best day I have seen for several months."[509]

Over the next few years, he rarely went to his office, and at the age of 56, he retired completely from the business in order to focus on his charity work. He started paying attention to his lifestyle, devising a regime that was to help him live to a hundred. "Extremely finicky about diet, rest, and exercise, he reduced everything to a routine and repeated the same daily schedule, forcing other people to fall in step with his timetable. In a letter to his son, Rockefeller credited his longevity to his willingness to reject social demands."[510] He almost made it, missing his goal by little more than two years – Rockefeller died seven weeks short of his 98th birthday.

Top athletes devote themselves to their sport with a similar intensity. World-famous goalkeeper Oliver Kahn says about his life as a professional soccer player: "I had become a machine, an engine which was constantly rotating at the red end of the scale."[511] Success was like a drug to him. "Like a 'real' addict, you isolate yourself from your surroundings. And everything starts turning faster and faster, you become caught up in the rat race."[512]

This sort of commitment comes at a price. Kahn remembers the time just after he had been voted the number one goalkeeper in the world in 1999. With that, he had achieved the big goal he had set himself early on. But it was the start of a terrible time for him. "I felt empty, exhausted, completely burnt out, horribly tired inside. All of a sudden, I couldn't feel anything anymore. Even walking up the steps to the bedroom, I was already completely shattered." In the morning, he hardly had enough energy to get dressed and the joy had gone out of everything.[513]

Kahn found himself incapable of winding down. He talks about lying in bed hours before a game, drenched in sweat and utterly without control over his thoughts. "Thoughts keep racing through my head. Like a thunderstorm. It's like lightning and thunder in my head."[514] He felt nothing anymore – except for tension and fear which tormented him. But he still tried to cope: "If that's the price for chasing after success, then I'll have to pay it. Hopefully nobody will notice what's going on inside me when I join the team."[515]

Kahn was experiencing the classic symptoms of burn-out syndrome: "Exhaustion and fatigue have become my normal state of being, headaches, fear, tension, irritability and feelings of guilt are my constant companions. Feelings of frustration when success fails to materialize. In the 'final phase', you become haunted by despair and the feeling that everything is pointless and the smallest effort leaves me exhausted."[516]

Kahn got through his burn-out experience and continued to achieve phenomenal success. He was voted best goalkeeper in Germany and best goalkeeper in Europe three more times each and best goalkeeper in the world twice. These successes would have been unattainable if he hadn't learned to maintain a balance between tension and relaxation. He also had to learn to redefine the concept of discipline: "It's essential to learn from experience at what point discipline becomes a compulsion and can then become counterproductive, destructive even." Discipline is a necessary requirement. But Kahn now had a better idea of what discipline really meant. "It's the discipline of 'not too much.'"[517]

Realizing how important it is to internalize Kahn's "discipline of 'not too much'" can often be a painful process for top athletes, executives, entrepreneurs and other high achievers. In his autobiography, the former tennis star Boris Becker describes the daily routine of a world-class athlete: "The endless training, the weeks of preparation for a Grand Slam – it was like being in prison.

Killing time, coping with monotony, a thousand forehands, a thousand backhands, until you didn't think any more but turn into a machine."[518] In the two weeks between October 19 and November 2, when Becker was only 19 years old, he won three tournaments on three different continents. His body, the doctors said, was in a state of complete and utter exhaustion. "The defense mechanisms of my immune system are drastically reduced, as a result of which I'm suffering from bronchitis, a complete lack of energy, and a slightly raised temperature ... The slightest draught could give me a cold."[519]

The hard training, the tournaments, the many hours and days he spent fulfilling his contractual obligations to his sponsors – all of that might have been just about bearable if it hadn't been for the extreme pressure he was under. As a top athlete, you have to be "acutely aware of your limits, physical and mental, in order to go beyond them. That is why any kind of help that's legal is quite welcome – that's how it was for me, anyway."[520]

Becker talks about his addiction to sleeping pills because he could find no other way to relax. "I used this stuff for several years. Eventually I started waking up in the middle of the night because the effect began to wear off after three or four hours, so then I doubled the dose."[521] Without sleeping pills, he wasn't even able to shut his eyes anymore. "Obviously I had to cut down the dosage before matches – at least I had to try. The result would be that I couldn't sleep at all."[522] Sometimes he would wake up in the morning and have no idea where he was.

Like world-class athletes, top executives are a high-risk group for addiction to prescription drugs, alcohol, antidepressants, or illegal substances. Like athletes, they are subject to enormous pressure, which sooner or later they may find themselves unable to cope with. Burn-out syndrome is a condition which affects mainly very ambitious and goal-oriented people. Sleeplessness, susceptibility to colds and other minor illnesses, extreme irritability and even fits of depression and psychosomatic illnesses are all symptoms which indicate that the balance between tension and relaxation has been upset.

If that really was the price of success, being successful would not be desirable. A life which is unbearable without antidepressants or other drugs is about as far from real success as it gets.

However, you don't have to pay that price. In fact, you will not be successful in the long run unless you learn how to cope with stress. A fit and healthy body might be able to sustain that kind of abuse for a while, but not forever. If you wish to remain successful for decades to come, you have to find ways to relax.

Many high achievers do not realize they have substance abuse issues until it is too late. What makes addiction so dangerous is that those who suffer from it can't or won't admit to it – or only after causing and experiencing a lot of pain and misery. Many successful people have suffered from addiction because they can no longer cope with the enormous pressure they are under – Elvis Presley, Britney Spears and Whitney Houston, to name but a few.

Finding the right balance between tension and relaxation is one of the keys to success. I am not talking about any trendy notions about 'work-life balance' here. That expression is problematic in itself because it implies that life is what happens away from the workplace. Successful people love their work. Work is their hobby and their hobby is working. For people like them, working hard and over many hours is not the problem. Stress is usually the result, not of too much work, but of work that isn't satisfying.

You probably know the feeling: everything is going well, you are enjoying your work and achieving great results, one success after another. You are in harmony with yourself and the people around you. On days like this, you can easily work for 14 or even 16 hours without feeling tired. Another day, nothing works the way you want it to. You get mad at your staff and at yourself, everything that can go wrong does. After only three or four hours of this, you are already exhausted. Obviously what causes stress and exhaustion is not the quantity but the quality of the work.

Ad man David Ogilvy, who had a reputation as a workaholic and expected the same of his staff, writes: "I subscribe to the Scottish proverb: hard work never killed a man. Men die of boredom, psychological conflict and disease. They do not die of hard work. The harder people work, the happier they are."[523]

However, things don't always work out as smoothly and harmoniously as you would like them to. Top executives are problem solvers above everything else. Any major problems which others have been unable to solve end up on their desks. That's what they are getting paid large salaries for. And while it is true that stress is not a question of the quantity of work, there are limits to the amount of work a single person can handle. Intensity and duration are in inverse proportion to each other. It's like running: some people are long-distance runners, others are sprinters. Sprinters run far more intensely, but they can only keep their performance up for 9 to 15 seconds, rather than for minutes or even hours. The more intensively you work, the more frequently you will need relaxation phases in which you focus all your attention on relaxing, much in the same way in which you focus on working.

Unless you manage to integrate regular 'relaxation oases' into your daily, weekly and yearly routines, you will not be successful in the long run, because you will not be able to cope with the intensity your work requires.

Everybody has to find his or her own solution. You might opt for autogenic training like me. Or lock yourself away somewhere in a quiet room for half an hour to practice yoga or similar relaxation exercises. Can't you spare the time to do that? Well, in that case make sure you can spare the time to visit doctors and hospitals later on in life.

Virgin founder Richard Branson says: "My brain is working all the time when I am awake, churning out ideas. Because Virgin is a worldwide company, I find I need to be awake much of the time, so it's fortunate that one of the things I am very good at is catnapping, catching an hour or two of sleep at a time." Branson even stresses that of all the skills he has acquired over the years, he considers this one "vital." "Churchill and Maggie Thatcher were masters of the catnap and I use their example in my own life."[524]

As Winston Churchill put it: "You must sleep some time between lunch and dinner and no halfway measures. Take off your clothes and get into bed. That's what I always do. Don't think you will be doing less work because you sleep during the day. That's a foolish notion held by people who have no imagination." Regular naps, he said, increased his productivity so much he could do two days' worth of work in one. "When the war started, I had to sleep during the day because that was the only way I could cope with my responsibilities."[525] Chess world champion Garry Kasparov also extolled the benefits of regular naps.

Bill Gates is known for his ability to sleep anywhere and anytime. In college, "Gates never slept on sheets. He would collapse on his unmade bed, pull an electric blanket over his head and fall asleep instantly and soundly, regardless of the hour or activity in his room." In later life, he retained the ability to fall "asleep instantaneously. When he flies, he often puts a blanket over his head and sleeps for the entire flight," his biographers write.[526]

Research carried out by the American space agency NASA confirms that even a 40-minute nap increases performance by 34% and concentration by 100%.

Scientists at Harvard University discovered that test subjects whose performance decreased by 50% over the course of the day were able to bring it back up to 100% by napping for an hour.[527]

Even during the week, you have to take time to relax and forget about work. This is something many people find hard to do. Instead, they take their problems home with them. Of course, it may sometimes be necessary to do so – the point here is not to overdo it. If you work until late into the night, the likelihood is high that you will lie awake thinking about any problems you have encountered during the day. That's why it is important to create a buffer zone between work and going to bed – exercising works for me.

High achievers often find it hard to switch off and do nothing without feeling guilty about it. They take work-related problems with them wherever they go, even on vacation. A friend of mine, who is chairman of the board in a company, once told me about how his wife had packed her suitcase after three days of vacation. She said there was no point in her staying, because all she did was watch him on the phone to his office for several hours a day. They came to an agreement that he would spend no more than an hour every day answering emails and making phone calls.

I think even an hour is too much. On vacation, you have to let go of your everyday work. If your company stops functioning because you are on vacation for two weeks without phoning in every few minutes, you have chosen the wrong people to work for you. Nor is it very flattering for your staff, if you do not trust them to handle problems by themselves for two weeks. How are they supposed to gain the confidence to think and act independently? After working intensely and hard for a whole year, you need the time to think about other things, to read books, to exercise and to pursue activities that have nothing to do with work.

Any cell phone will stop working if its battery is not charged on a regular basis. The same goes for the human mind and body – you need to recharge yours every day, every week, every year. A leading sports psychologist once explained to me how a lot of top athletes learn to switch off by finding another physical activity they enjoy – such as fishing, archery or golf. He talked about parallel worlds in which you have to immerse yourself in order to refuel.

Top executives and entrepreneurs would do well to adopt the diet and lifestyle of world-class athletes, because both groups are subject to similar physical and mental strain. If you abuse your body by eating unhealthily, smoking and not allowing it to relax and refuel, you cannot expect it to achieve top performance over several decades.

This also means that you have to permit yourself to be ill every once in a while. Many top executives consider themselves so indispensable that they simply cannot afford to stay in bed for a week if they are ill. I once knew a leading executive who died of a myocardial inflammation after having ignored a minor infection.

To my mind, not allowing your body the time it needs to get over an illness is a sign of weakness and lack of discipline. Do you really think you will achieve less in life if you spend a few days – or even the occasional fortnight – at home in order to recover from an infection? By giving your body enough time to get over a minor illness, you will avoid more serious long-term health problems.

It is important to develop a mental attitude that will allow you to gain distance from work-related problems. I have seen people leave a company because they couldn't cope with the stress anymore. I have told them: "If you find a new job with another company where you have to take on responsibility, most likely nothing will change for you. You will still be the same person with the same mental attitude. Changing your circumstances usually does less for you than changing your attitude."

The question is how close you allow your problems to get to you. Thinking about problems is good, but worrying about them isn't. Easier said than done, I know. The more ambitious you are, the harder it is to switch off completely and let go at all times. But you have to be aware that, unless you learn to do exactly that, you will not be able to achieve top performance. This book is about setting your goals high. But to do so, you have to find the right balance between tension and relaxation. Otherwise, aiming for high goals will crush you.

The people who are most successful in life are the ones who know how to let go and to make themselves dispensable. No matter whether you are aiming to get promoted to a leading managerial position, or whether you run your own company: you will not succeed by letting yourself get sucked into the rat race, or by believing you have to do everything yourself.

Werner Otto always used to say that the most important task any manager had to solve was building a good team in his department. No company could grow without a "first-class foundation," he firmly believed. "Build up a good team. In our company you will only get to the top by standing on the shoulders of capable co-workers," the founder of the largest mail-order company in the world claimed.[528]

The company director, Otto said, must constantly "work at freeing himself from work ... Only when you have freed yourself will you have time to tackle new tasks creatively, tasks which are essential to the growth of the company."[529] As soon as Otto had built up a management team which "functioned fairly well," he moved his own office off the company's premises in order to cut his communication lines with the managers in charge of the various departments, with whom he had been in close contact until then. They kept trying to circumvent the new company management and get him to make decisions. "Putting a distance between myself and Otto Mail-Order had freed me from the day-to-day business so that I could dedicate myself to the large problems and finding solutions which would advance the company."[530]

Once you have gone self-employed and formed your own company, you may call yourself an entrepreneur. But are you really doing the work of an entrepreneur? An entrepreneur's job is to develop a strategy for the company, and to build company value. Any entrepreneur worth his salt must aim to make himself dispensable in the long run.

But in many small and medium enterprises, the situation is quite different: the company founder is doing the work his managers and employees should be doing. Instead of working for the company or on the company's development, as he should be doing, he works mainly within the company. In fact, many people who call themselves entrepreneurs approach their work as though they were freelance professionals such as doctors or lawyers who handle most of the workload themselves.

If you do decide to start a company, in the beginning you will have to do much or even most of the work yourself. However, make sure you are aware of the danger of getting used to that state of affairs and losing sight of your real goal, which is gradually to make yourself dispensable.

If you do everything yourself because you are unable to delegate tasks and to build a competent management team and well-functioning systems and processes, you will not build company value. What is the value of a company that is worthless without you running it? Not much. As soon as you try to sell your company, any prospective buyer will want to know whether you have installed well-functioning processes and a capable management team, or whether the company's success depends on you alone. After I sold my company to my best employee in 2016, the business carried on as before, even without me. With the strong foundations I had laid, the company could continue to flourish without me.

So, what should you do after finishing this book? I would recommend you take a two-week vacation, during which you do not phone your office even once and do not answer a single email. Instead, you should reread this book and start thinking about your goals and putting them down on paper.

This book has provided you with the equipment you need in order to put ideas into practice, which you thought were too big and too unrealistic even to dream of turning them into reality. Now it's time for you to pluck up the courage to go your own way, to be different from others! Don't be afraid to think independently and to swim against the tide! Learn to combine stamina and experimentation. And remember always to remain honest and trustworthy – without the trust of others, you will never be able to achieve your goals. Above all: stop waiting for the 'right moment' to arrive. The right moment to start making your dreams come true is – today.

ENDNOTES

1 Schultz/Yang, 1.

2 Vise, 11.

3 Walton, 15.

4 Branson, Screw It, 196.

5 Walton, 47.

6 Kasparov, 23-24.

7 Matthews, 76.

8 Matthews, 76.

9 Quoted in Matthews, 76.

10 Matthews, 77.

11 Schroeder, 99.

12 Schroeder, 226.

13 Quoted in Leamer, 39.

14 Quoted in Andrews, 23.

15 Quoted in Andrews, 24.

16 Quoted in Hujer, 46.

17 Hujer, 201.

18 Quoted in Leamer, 174.

19 Quoted in Leamer, 175.

20 Quoted in Andrews, 18-19.

21 Quoted in Hujer, 52.

22 Quoted in Andrews, 18.

23 Quoted in Hujer, 89.

24 Quoted in Leamer, 153.

25 Andrews, 57.

26 Quoted in Leamer, 128.

27 Quoted in Leamer, 128.

28 Hujer, 158.

29 Quoted in Hujer, 174.

30 Quoted in Hujer, 286.

31 Schwarzenegger, 137-38, 298-99, 142.

32 Quoted in Love, 23.

33 Love, 23.

34 Love, 39-40.

35 Quoted in Love, 40.

36 Quoted in Love, 45.

37 Love, 45-47.

38 Quoted in Friedmann, 79.

39 Quoted in Peters, 29.

40 Quoted in Friedmann, 64-65.

41 Quoted in Friedmann, 90.

42 Quoted in Chernow, 67.

43 Quoted in Chernow, 68.

44 Quoted in Chernow, 2231.

45 Chernow, 26.

46 Covey, 59.

47 Sturm, 119.

48 Sturm, 119.

49 Ogilvy, *Confessions*, 82.

50 Bettger, 103.

51 Bettger, 104.

52 Quoted in Covey, 62.

53 Covey, 31.

54 Glatzer et al., 65.

55 Chernow, 130.

56 Quoted in Chernow, 132.

57 Chernow, 134.

58 Chernow, 554.

59 Chernow, 556.

60 Jungbluth, Ikea, 26.

61 Quoted in Jungbluth, Ikea, 75.

62 Jungbluth, Ikea, 75.

63 Jungbluth, Ikea, 92.

64 Bloomberg, 1.

65 Schroeder, 582.

66 Schroeder, 583.

67 Quoted in Schroeder, 808.

68 Quoted in Schroeder, 604.

69 Schroeder, 467.

70 Quoted in Schroeder, 472.

71 Platthaus, 31.

72 Platthaus, 38.

73 Platthaus, 193.

74 Schultz/Yang, 15.

75 Schultz/Yang, 25.

76 Schultz/Yang, 26.

77 Schultz/Yang, 39.

78 Quoted in Schultz/Yang, 42.

79 Schultz/Yang, 44.

80 Schultz/Yang, 52.

81 Quoted in Schultz/Yang, 62.

82 Quoted in Schultz/Yang, 73.

83 Schultz/Yang, 73-74.

84 Quoted in Schultz/Yang, 93.

85 Schultz/Yang, 93-94.

86 Quoted in Schroeder, 623.

87 Quoted in Wallace/Erickson, 30.

88 Wallace/Erickson, 34.

89 Quoted in Wallace/Erickson, 61.

90 Quoted in Wallace/Erickson, 273.

91 Quoted in Schroeder, 64.

92 Hill, 22.

93 Becker, 27.

94 Becker, 125.

95 Becker, 6.

96 Becker, 6.

97 Becker, 8.

98 Becker, 9.

99 Becker, 13-14.

100 Becker, 238.

101 Kahn, 55.

102 Kahn, 43.

103 Kahn, 101.

104 Kahn, 160.

105 Kahn, 166-167.

106 Kahn, 169.

107 Kahn, 319.

108 Kahn, 256.

109 Hujer, 125.

110 Schroeder, 635.

111 Schroeder, 636.

112 Quoted in Jungbluth, Ikea, 91.

113 Uhse, 73.

114 Uhse, 74.

115 Uhse, 96.

116 Uhse, 97.

117 Uhse, 102.

118 Uhse, 112.

119 Uhse, 118.

120 Uhse, 122.

121 Uhse, 128.

122 Uhse, 136.

123 Uhse, 140.

124 Uhse, 160.

125 Uhse, 161.

126 Charles-Roux, 168.

127 Chanel, 145.

128 Chanel, 148.

129 Charles-Roux, XVI.

130 Chanel, 146.

131 Quoted in O'Brien, 49.

132 Quoted in O'Brien, 69.

133 O'Brien, 200

134 O'Brien, 35.

135 Quoted in O'Brien, 46.

136 Quoted in O'Brien, 64.

137 Quoted in O'Brien, 73.

138 Quoted in O'Brien, 86.

139 Quoted in O'Brien, 74.

140 Quoted in O'Brien, 79.

141 O'Brien, 204.

142 Quoted in O'Brien, 83-84.

143 Quoted in O'Brien, 99.

144 Hujer, 301.

145 Quoted in Khan, 139.

146 The following originally appeared in my autobiography, *Wenn du nicht mehr brennst, starte neu! München* 2017.

147 Quoted in Schroeder, 719.

148 Schultz/Yang, 31.

149 Welch, Jack, 98.

150 Welch, Jack, 110.

151 Welch, Jack, 120.

152 Welch, Jack, 121.

153 Welch, Jack, 122.

154 Welch, Jack, 130-131.

155 Welch, Jack, 131.

156 Welch, Jack, 138.

157 Welch, *Answers*, 58.

158 Welch, *Answers*, 58.

159 Welch, *Answers*, 84.

160 Welch, *Answers*, 85.

161 Welch, *Answers*, 86.

162 Welch, *Answers*, 99.

163 Welch, *Answers*, 99.

164 Welch, *Answers*, 128.

165 Hujer, 23.

166 Carnegie, *Friends*, 126.

167 Carnegie, *Friends*, 139.

168 Wallace/Erickson, 50.

169 Wallace/Erickson, 277.

170 Wallace/Erickson, 101.

171 Wallace/Erickson, 149.

172 Wallace/Erickson, 266.

173 Wallace/Erickson, 280.

174 Wallace/Erickson, 266.

175 Wallace/Erickson, 282-283.

176 Quoted in Wallace/Erickson, 293.

177 Wallace/Erickson, 161-162.

178 Quoted in Wallace/Erickson, 266.

179 Quoted in Wallace/Erickson, 298.

180 Wolff, 35.

181 Wolff, 18.

182 Young/Simon, 77.

183 Young/Simon, 184.

184 Young/Simon, 185.

185 Young/Simon, 235-236.

186 Quoted in Roman, 86-87.

187 Roman, 171.

188 Roman, 52.

189 Quoted in Slater, 94.

190 Slater, 114.

191 Love, 89.

192 Love, 110.

193 Love, 89.

194 Love, 90.

195 Love, 90.

196 Quoted in Love, 102.

197 Snow, 299

198 Jungbluth, Oetkers, 69.

199 See Zitelmann, *The Wealth Elite*, Chapter 10.

200 Becker, 28.

201 Becker, 28.

202 Becker, 29.

203 Kahn, 22-23.

204 Khan, 26.

205 Khan, 30

206 Khan, 33.

207 Quoted in Young/Simon, 10.

208 Young/Simon, 12.

209 Quoted in Young/Simon, 21.

210 Quoted in Young/Simon, 22.

211 Wilson, 23.

212 Quoted in Wilson, 23.

213 Quoted in Wilson, 24.

214 Wallace/Erickson, 38.

215 Wallace/Erickson, 38.

216 Wallace/Erickson, 89-90.

217 Quoted in Bibb, 18.

218 Quoted in Bibb, 29-30.

219 Quoted in Bibb, 31-32.

220 Quoted in Schroeder, 86.

221 Schroeder, 87.

222 Quoted in Schroeder, 87-88.

223 Quoted in Schroeder, 88.

224 Chanel, 21.

225 Chanel, 21.

226 Chanel, 30.

227 Chanel, 73.

228 Chanel, 131.

229 Quoted in Roman, 23.

230 Quoted in Roman, 29.

231 Kasparov, 64.

232 Branson, *Screw It*, 70-71.

233 Branson, *Screw It*, 71.

234 Branson, *Screw It*, 71.

235 Quoted in Young/Simon, 22-23.

236 Quoted in Young/Simon, 23.

237 Young/Simon, 51.

238 Quoted in Young/Simon, 42.

239 Young/Simon, 42.

240 Quoted in Young/Simon, 76-77.

241 Young/Simon, 77.

242 Quoted in Young/Simon, 119.

243 Bettger, 66.

244 Bettger, 49.

245 Wilson, 89-90.

246 Quoted in Buffett/Clark, *Tao*, 138.

247 Schroeder, 208.

248 Leamer, 22.

249 Lommel, 119.

250 Lommel, 91.

251 Lindemann, 16.

252 Lindemann, 18.

253 Quoted in Mensen, 45.

254 Murphy, 132.

255 Mensen, 20.

256 Tracy, *Goals*, 12.

257 For more details, please see the books by Locke and Latham referenced in the bibliography.

258 The findings of this research are summarized in Chapter 3.2.5 of my book *The Wealth Elite*.

259 Kasparov, 9.

260 Kasparov, 9.

261 Kasparov, 11.

262 Kasparov, 72-73.

263 Quoted in Gerber, 6.

264 Quoted in Gerber, 107.

265 Quoted in Gerber, 108.

266 Quoted in Gerber, 109.

267 Schultz/Yang, 141.

268 Schultz/Yang, 141.

269 Quoted in Schultz/Yang, 142.

270 Schultz/Yang, 143.

271 Schultz/Yang, 145.

272 Schultz/Yang, 142-143.

273 Schultz/Yang, 21.

274 Schultz/Yang, 21.

275 Bloomberg, 32.

276 Bloomberg, 33.

277 Bloomberg, 33.

278 Bloomberg, 34.

279 Bloomberg, 46.

280 Bloomberg, 53.

281 Bloomberg, 43.

282 Bloomberg, 45-46.

283 Bloomberg, 52.

284 Bloomberg, 78.

285 Jack Ma, quoted in Clark, 73.

286 Jack Ma, quoted in Lee/Song, 29.

287 Jack Ma, quoted in Clark, 110.

288 Jack Ma, quoted in Clark, 93.

289 Jack Ma, quoted in Clark, 111.

290 Jack Ma, quoted in Clark, 121.

291 Jack Ma, quoted in Clark, 123.

292 Jack Ma, quoted in Lee/Song, 19.

293 Jack Ma, quoted in Lee/Song, 83.

294 Vise, 59.

295 Quoted in Vise, 84-85.

296 Quoted in Kahn, 275.

297 Kahn, 134.

298 Kahn, 213.

299 Kahn, 263.

300 Quoted in Love, 120-121.

301 Quoted in Love, 106.

302 Quoted in Love, 7.

303 Love, 120-121.

304 Quoted in Wallace/Erickson, 128-129.

305 Quoted in Wallace/Erickson, 298-299.

306 Kasparov, 185.

307 Kasparov, 184.

308 Kasparov, 52.

309 Welch, Jack, 27.

310 Welch, Jack, 28.

311 Welch, Jack, 29.

312 Welch, Jack, 30.

313 Branson, *Screw It*, 2.

314 Quoted in Roman, 232.

315 Roman, 7.

316 Quoted in Roman, 220.

317 Quoted in Love, 115.

318 Quoted in Love, 141.

319 Quoted in Love, 141.

320 Quoted in Love, 120.

321 Quoted in Love, 144.

322 Quoted in Love, 102.

323 Becker, 128.

324 Becker, 128.

325 Becker, 128.

326 Quoted in Schmoock, 73.

327 Quoted in Schmoock, 73.

328 Quoted in Schmoock, 76.

329 Quoted in Schmoock, 76.

330 Quoted in Schmoock, 219.

331 Quoted in Schmoock, 226.

332 Quoted in Schmoock, 227.

333 Quoted in Schmoock, 229.

334 Quoted in Schmoock, 46.

335 Quoted in Schmoock, 78.

336 Bibb, 408.

337 Quoted in Bibb, 19.

338 Quoted in Bibb, 43.

339 Bibb, 154.

340 Quoted in Bibb, 23.

341 Quoted in Bibb, 153.

342 Quoted in Bibb, 166.

343 Quoted in Bibb, 171.

344 Quoted in Bibb, 172.

345 Lauder, Estée. *Estée: A Success Story*, quoted in Meiners, 141.

346 Quoted in Israel, 29.

347 Israel, 50.

348 Quoted in Israel, 53.

349 Quoted in Israel, 67.

350 Quoted in Israel, 62.

351 Quoted in Israel, 70.

352 Quoted in Israel, 97.

353 Lommel, 16.

354 Quoted in O'Brien, 185.

355 Doubek, 269.

356 Doubek, 278.

357 Quoted in Snow, 49.

358 Snow, 194.

359 Snow, 261.

360 Mezrich, 65.

361 Quoted in Mezrich, 105.

362 Zuckerberg interviewed in *Vanity Fair*, October 29, 2008.

363 Welch, Jack, 193.

364 Welch, Jack, 193.

365 Welch, Jack, 196.

366 Fürweger, 16.

367 Fürweger, 57.

368 Fürweger, 58.

369 Exler, 10.

370 Quoted in Jungbluth, Oetkers, 50.

371 Quoted in Jungbluth, Oetkers, 62.

372 Quoted in Jungbluth, Oetkers, 55.

373 Quoted in Jungbluth, Oetkers, 56.

374 Quoted in Jungbluth, Oetkers, 67.

375 Jungbluth, Oetkers, 67.

376 Quoted in Jungbluth, Oetkers, 62.

377 Quoted in Jungbluth, Oetkers, 61.

378 Branson, *Screw It*, 15.

379 Branson, *Screw It*, 12.

380 Branson, *Virginity*, 80.

381 Branson, *Virginity*, 81.

382 Branson, *Virginity*, 84.

383 Branson, *Virginity*, 113-114.

384 Branson, *Virginity*, 154.

385 Branson, *Virginity*, 154.

386 Branson, *Virginity*, 164.

387 Branson, *Screw It*, 39.

388 Branson, *Screw It*, 53.

389 Branson, *Screw It*, 163.

390 Branson, *Screw It*, 163.

391 Branson, *Virginity*, 465.

392 Branson, *Virginity*, 468.

393 Branson, *Screw It*, 58.

394 Branson, *Screw It*, 1.

395 Branson, *Virginity*, 238.

396 Ries, xi.

397 Ries, xvi.

398 Lommel, 50.

399 Lommel, 120-121.

400 Schwarzenegger, *Total Recall*, 342.

401 Lommel, 126.

402 Lommel, 13.

403 Lommel, 108.

404 Quoted in Leamer, 242.

405 Matthews, 67.

406 Schroeder, 238.

407 Klum, 7.

408 Klum, 46-47.

409 Klum, 14.

410 Klum, 22-23.

411 Klum, 28.

412 Klum, 189.

413 Ogilvy, *Confessions*, 36.

414 Ogilvy, *Confessions*, 42.

415 O'Brien, 96.

416 Uhse 288.

417 Kahn, 223.

418 Kahn, 225.

419 Kahn, 202.

420 Kahn, 203.

421 Schroeder, 286.

422 Kasparov, 81.

423 Kasparov, 83.

424 Quoted in Kasparov, 21.

425 Koch, 11.

426 Slater, 65.

427 Schmoock, 143.

428 Schmoock, 143.

429 Quoted in Chernow, 178.

430 Ogilvy, *Autobiography*, 130.

431 Quoted in Roman, 106.

432 Bibb, 74.

433 Schroeder, 596.

434 Buffett/Clark, *Tao*, 19-21.

435 Buffett/Clark, *Tao*, 22.

436 Roman, 84.

437 Schroeder, 730.

438 Quoted in Slater, 68.

439 Welch, Jack, 92.

440 Welch, Jack, 97.

441 Welch, Jack, 96.

442 Welch, Jack, 97.

443 Welch, Jack, 398.

444 Quoted in Wilson, 38.

445 Quoted in Wilson, 38.

446 Quoted in Wilson, 58.

447 Quoted in Wilson, 64.

448 Quoted in Wilson, 68.

449 Quoted in Wilson, 69-70.

450 Quoted in Meissner, 10.

451 Quoted in Meissner, 10.

452 Quoted in Meissner, 16.

453 Quoted in Meissner, 72.

454 Meissner, 30.

455 Quoted in Young/Simon, 60.

456 Young/Simon, 61.

457 Young/Simon, 61.

458 Quoted in Wilson, 90.

459 Wallace/Erickson, 109.

460 Wallace/Erickson, 120.

461 Quoted in Wallace/Erickson, 120.

462 Quoted in Wallace/Erickson, 136.

463 Quoted in Wallace/Erickson, 237.

464 Quoted in Wallace/Erickson, 122.

465 Walton, 38-39.

466 Walton, 47.

467 Walton, 81.

468 Walton, 55.

469 Walton, 60.

470 Walton, 59.

471 Walton, 153.

472 Walton, 154.

473 Walton, 151.

474 Walton, 160.

475 Walton, 34.

476 Walton, 15.

477 Quoted in Brandes, 19.

478 Quoted in Brandes, 20.

479 Chernow, 33.

480 Quoted in Chernow, 24.

481 Quoted in Chernow, 24.

482 Chernow, 33.

483 Glatzer et al., 65.

484 Schroeder, 217.

485 Slater, 12.

486 Slater, 38.

487 Slater, 9.

488 Quoted in Slater, 10.

489 See Zitelmann, *The Power of Capitalism*, Chapter 10.

490 Quoted in Slater, 2.

491 Chanel, 39.

492 Chanel, 39.

493 Chanel, 39.

494 Chanel, 119.

495 Love, 151.

496 Love, 152.

497 Love, 153.

498 Roman, 16.

499 Roman, 57.

500 Roman, 57.

501 Roman, 57.

502 Quoted in Roman, 110-111.

503 Quoted in Buffett/Clark, *Tao*, 66.

504 Lesinski, 34.

505 Kahn, 191.

506 Kahn, 192.

507 Quoted in Chernow, 122.

508 Chernow, 319.

509 Chernow, 323.

510 Chernow, 405.

511 Kahn, 322.

512 Kahn, 326.

513 Kahn, 321.

514 Kahn, 328.

515 Kahn, 329.

516 Kahn, 327.

517 Kahn, 219.

518 Becker, 64.

519 Becker, 230-231.

520 Becker, 73.

521 Becker, 74.

522 Becker, 75.

523 Ogilvy, *Autobiography*, 130.

524 Branson, *Screw It*, 88-89.

525 Quoted in Schwartz/Loehr, 61.

526 Wallace/Erickson, 55.

527 Schwartz/Loehr, 61.

528 Quoted in Schmoock, 227.

529 Quoted in Schmoock, 220.

530 Quoted in Schmoock, 221.

BIBLIOGRAPHY

Aldenrath, Peter, *Die Coca-Cola Story*, Nuremburg, 1999.

Andrews, Nigel, *True Myths. The Life and Times of Arnold Schwarzenegger.* New York/London, 1995.

Avantario, Vito, *Die Agnellis. Die heimlichen Herrscher Italiens,* Frankfurt/New York, 2002.

Becker, Boris, *The Player. The Autobiography,* London, 2004.

Behar, Howard/Goldstein, Janet, *It's Not About the Coffee, Lessons on Putting People First from a Life at Starbucks,* New York, 2007.

Bettger, Frank, *How I Raised Myself From Failure to Success in Selling,* New York, 1949.

Bibb, Porter, Ted Turner. *It Ain't As Easy As It Looks,* Boulder, 1993.

Bloomberg, Michael, *Bloomberg by Bloomberg,* New York, 1997.

Brandes, Dieter, *Konsequent einfach. Die Aldi-Erfolgsstory,* Munich, 1999.

Branson, Richard, *Screw It, Let's Do It. Lessons in Life and Business. Expanded,* London, 2007.

Branson, Richard, *Losing My Virginity. The Autobiography.* London, 1998.

Branson, Richard, *Business Stripped Bare. Adventures of a Global Entrepreneur,* London, 2008.

Buffett, Mary, Clark, David, *The Tao of Warren Buffett: Warren Buffett's Words of Wisdom: Quotations and Interpretations to Help Guide You to Billionaire Wealth and Enlightened Business Management,* New York, 2006.

Carnegie, Dale, *How to Win Friends and Influence People,* London, 1936.

Charles-Roux, Edmonde, *Chanel. Her Life, Her World, the Woman Behind the Legend,* New York, 1975.

Chernow, Ron, *Titan. The Life of John D. Rockefeller, Sr.,* New York, 1998.

Clark, Duncan, *Alibaba. The House that Jack Ma Built*, New York, 2016.

Collins, Jim, *Good to Great. Why Some Companies Make the Leap and Others Don't*, New York, 2001.

Colvin, Geoff, *Talent is Overrated. What Really Separates World-Class Performers from Everybody Else*, London/Boston, 2008.

Covey, Stephen M.R., with Rebecca R. Merrill, *The Speed of Trust. The One Thing That Changes Everything*, New York, 2006.

Csikszentmihalyi, Mihaly, *Flow. The Psychology of Optimal Experience*, New York, 1990.

Doubek, Katja, *Blue Jeans. Levi Strauss und die Geschichte einer Legende*, Munich/Zurich, 2003.

Exler, Andrea, *Coca-Cola. Vom selbstgebrauten Aufputschmittel zur amerikanischen Ikone*, Hamburg, 2006.

Fürweger, Wolfgang, *Die Red-Bull-Story. Der unglaubliche Erfolg des Dietrich Mateschitz*, Vienna, 2008.

Gerber, Robin, *Barbie and Ruth. The Story of the World's Most Famous Doll and the Woman Who Created Her*, New York, 2009.

Glatzer, Wolfgang et al., *Reichtum im Urteil der Bevölkerung. Legitimationsprobleme und Spannungspotentiale in Deutschland*, Opladen & Farmington, 2009.

Hill, Napoleon, *Think and Grow Rich. Revised and Expanded by Arthur R. Pell*, London, 2003.

Hujer, Marc, *Arnold Schwarzenegger. Die Biographie*, Munich, 2009.

Israel, Lee, *Estée Lauder. Beyond the Magic. An Unauthorized Biography*, New York, 1985.

Jungbluth, Rüdiger, *Die 11 Geheimnisse des Ikea-Erfolgs*, Frankfurt, 2008.

Jungbluth, Rüdiger, *Die Oetkers. Geschäfte und Geheimnisse der bekanntesten Wirtschaftsdynastie Deutschlands*, Frankfurt/New York, 2004.

Kahn, Oliver, *Ich. Erfolg kommt von innen*, Munich, 2008.

Kasparov, Garry, *How Life Imitates Chess*, London, 2007.

Khan, Riz, *Alwaleed. Businessman, Billionaire, Prince*, London, 2006.

Klum, Heidi, with Alexandra Postman. *Heidi Klum's Body of Knowledge. 8 Rules of Model Behavior*, New York, 2004.

Koch, Richard, *Living the 80/20 Way. Work Less, Worry Less, Succeed More, Enjoy More*, London, 2004.

Lanfranconi, Claudia/Meiners, Antonia, *Kluge Geschäftsfrauen.
Maria Bogner, Aenne Burda, Coco Chanel, u.v.a.*, Munich, 2010.

Leamer, Laurence, *Fantastic. The Life of Arnold Schwarzenegger*,
New York, 2005.

Lee, Suk; Song, Bob, *Never Give Up. Jack Ma In His Own Words*,
Chicago, 2016.

Lesinski, Jeanne M., *Bill Gates*, Minneapolis, 2007.

Lindemann, Dr. Hannes, *Autogenes Training. Der bewährte Weg zur
Entspannung*, Munich, 2004.

Locke, Edwin A.; Latham, Gary P. (editors), *A Theory of Goal Setting &
Task Performance*, Englewood Cliffs, New Jersey, 1990.

Locke, Edwin A.; Latham, Gary P. (editors), *New Developments in Goal
Setting and Task Performance*, New York/London, 2013.

Lommel, Cookie, *Schwarzenegger. A Man with a Plan*, Munich/Zurich, 2004.

Love, John F., *McDonald's. Behind the Arches. Revised Edition*,
New York, 1995.

Matthews, Jeff, *Warren Buffett. Pilgrimage to Warren Buffett's Omaha.
A Hedge Fund Manager's Dispatches from Inside the Berkshire Hathaway
Annual Meeting*, New York, 2009.

Meissner, Gerd, *SAP. Inside the Secret Software Power*, New York, 2000.

Mensen, Herbert, *Das Autogene Training. Entspannung, Gesundheit,
Stressbewältigung*, Munich, 1999.

Mezrich, Ben, *The Accidental Billionaires. The Founding of Facebook,
a Tale of Sex, Money, Genius and Betrayal*, New York, 2009.

Morand, Paul. *The Allure of Chanel*, London, 2008.

Murphy, Joseph, *The Power of Your Subconscious Mind*,
Englewood Cliffs, 1963.

O'Brien, Lucy, *Madonna. Like an Icon. The Definitive Biography*,
London, 2007.

Ogilvy, David, *Confessions of an Advertising Man*, London, 1963.

Ogilvy, David, *An Autobiography*, New York, 1997.

Otto, Werner, *Die Otto Gruppe. Der Weg zum Großunternehmen*,
Düsseldorf/Vienna, 1983.

Peters, Rolf-Herbert, *Die Puma-Story*, Munich, 2007.

Platthaus, Andreas, *Von Mann & Maus, Die Welt des Walt Disney*,
    Berlin, 2001.

Rogak, Lisa/Gates, *Bill, Impatient Optimist: Bill Gates in His Own Words*,
    London, 2012.

Ries, Al/Ries, Laura, *The Fall of Advertising & the Rise of PR*,
    Frankfurt, 2003.

Roman, Kenneth, *The King of Madison Avenue. David Ogilvy And
    the Making of Modern Advertising*, New York, 2009.

Schmoock, Matthias, *Werner Otto. Der Jahrhundert-Mann*, Frankfurt, 2009.

Schroeder, Alice, *The Snowball. Warren Buffett and the Business Of Life*,
    London, 2008.

Schultz, Howard/Yang, Dori Jones, *Pour Your Heart Into It. How Starbucks
    Built a Company One Cup at a Time*, New York, 2007.

Schultz, Johannes H/Luthe, Wolfgang, *Autogenic training: a
    psychophysiologic approach in psychotherapy*, New York, 1959.

Schwarzenegger, Arnold (with Peter Petre), *Total Recall. My Unbelievably
    True Life Story*, Simon & Schuster, New York, 2012.

Schwartz, Tony/Loehr, Jim, *The Power of Full Engagement: Managing
    Energy, Not Time, Is the Key to High Performance and Personal Renewal*,
    New York, 2003.

Slater, Robert, Soros. *The World's Most Influential Investor*, New York, 2009.

Snow, Richard, *I Invented the Modern Age. The Rise of Henry Ford*,
    New York, 2013.

Sturm, Karin, *Michael Schumacher, Ein Leben für die Formel 1*,
    Munich, 2010.

Timmdorf, Jonas (editor), *Die Aldi-Brüder. Warum Karl und Theo Albrecht
    mit ihrem Discounter die reichsten Deutschen sind*, Mauritius, 2009.

Tracy, Brian, *Goals! How to Get Everything You Want – Faster Than You
    Ever Thought Possible*, San Francisco, 2003.

Tracy, Brian, *Time Power. A Proven System for Getting More Done in Less
    Time Than You Ever Thought Possible*, New York, 2007.

Uhse, Beate, *"Ich will Freiheit für die Liebe." Die Autobiographie*,
    Munich, 2001.

Vise, David A./Malseed, Mark, *The Google Story*, New York, 2005.

Wallace, James/Erickson, Jim, *Hard Drive. Bill Gates and the Making of the Microsoft Empire*, Chichester, 1992.

Walton, Sam, *Made in America. My Story*, New York, 1993.

Welch, Jack/Byrne, John A., *Jack. Straight from the Gut*, London, 2001.

Welch, Jack/Welch, Suzy, *Winning: The Answers. Confronting 74 Of the Toughest Questions in Business Today*, London, 2006.

Wilson, Mike, The Difference between God and Larry Ellison. *Inside Oracle Corporation*, New York, 2002.

Wolff, Michael, *The Man Who Owns the News. Inside the Secret World of Rupert Murdoch*, London, 2008.

Young, Jeffrey S./Simon, William, L., *iCon Steve Jobs. The Greatest Second Act in the History of Business*, Frankfurt, 2006.

Zitelmann, Rainer, *The Wealth Elite. A Groundbreaking Study of the Psychology of the Super Rich*, London, 2018.

Zitelmann, Rainer, *The Power of Capitalism. A Journey Through Recent History Across Five Continents*, London, 2018.

Zuckerman, Gregory, *The Greatest Trade Ever. How John Paulson Bet Against the Markets and Made $20 Billion*, London/New York, 2009.

INDEX OF PERSONS

INDEX OF COMPANIES

"Rainer Zitelmann's study of the psychology of the super-rich is an ambitious project. Few could be better qualified for it than Dr. Zitelmann – an historian, sociologist, journalist, businessman and investor. There has been no comparable study and it is a compelling read for all who need to understand the characteristics and motivations of rich entrepreneurs."
Michael Maslinski, *Financial Times*

RAINER ZITELMANN

The

Power

of

Capitalism

**A JOURNEY THROUGH RECENT HISTORY
ACROSS FIVE CONTINENTS**

"This wide-ranging tome, which covers economic systems across China, Africa,
Germany, the U.S. and the U.K. exploring the power of capitalism, may not persuade
staunch anti-capitalists of the author's alternative viewpoint. However, it certainly
offers a robust challenge to anti-capitalist views and provides a series of well-
defined and researched arguments in favour of a capitalist society."
Jess Clark, *City A.M.*